Fascinating Torah Prophecies
Currently Unfolding

ראי רחל ראי הם שבו לגבולם

Fascinating Torah Prophecies

Currently Unfolding

by

Rabbi Nisan Aryeh Novick

Netzach Yisrael Publications, Inc.

Fascinating Torah Prophecies Currently Unfolding

ISBN: 1-889251-26 (paperback)
       1-889251-37 (hard cover)

Published by:
Netzach Yisrael Publications, Inc.
274 Crafton Avenue,
Staten Island, NY 10314
(718) 494-7620

Distributed by:
Judaica Press
123 Ditmas Avenue
Brooklyn, NY 11218
(718) 972-6200

Designed and produced by:
Bottom Line Design/NY

Printed in the United States of America

To order additional copies of this book, please call (800) 972-6201.

To arrange for lectures by Rabbi Novick or to communicate with him, please write or call:

Netzach Yisrael Publications, Inc.
274 Crafton Avenue
Staten Island, NY 10314
(718) 494-7620

To discuss ideas or submit manuscripts for publication, please write to the above address for a speedy response.

אהרן הלוי סולוביציק
ישיבה ד'בריסק, שקאגו

בע"ה

יום ד' לפרשת ויקרא כ"ט לחדש אדר התשנ"ו

ברצוני להביע את הסכמתי על הספר היפה והנחמד שנכתב על ידי הרב ניסן אריה נוביק שליט"א. ועברתי על כמה פרקים וראיתי אותם כולו יפה ונחמד ובהיר.

ויש בזה הספר מרגליות ופנינים שכליות עד מאוד וראוי לכל בן תורה לעבור על הספר, וגם לרב ולמחנך, כדי להשפיע על תלמידיו.

ויהי רצון שיהיו המרגליות עולות על שולחנות של כל בני תורה. ודבר בעתו מה טוב.

בכבוד רב, ידידו,

אהרן הלוי סולוביציק

Translation of Haskamah

The fourth day of the week of Parshas Vayikra, 29 Adar 5756

I am taking this opportunity to render my endorsement to the wonderful and precious book written by Rabbi Nisan Aryeh Novick — may he live a good and long life. I have reviewed several chapters and I see that they are thoroughly wonderful and [the Torah concepts] explained lucidly.

Contained within this book are gems and pearls of sound reason and it is therefore desirable for every Torah person, Rabbi, and teacher to review [the material in] the book in order to inspire others.

May it be His Will that these gems be appreciated by all Torah people. How important it is for subject matter to be presented in a timely fashion.

With great respect and in friendship,

Ahron HaLevi Soloveichik

Comments from Reviewers

After reading the entire English *sefer*, **Rav Chaim Malowitsky** transmitted its content in Hebrew to the *Roshai HaYeshiva* of Yeshiva Shaar HaShamayim — the Yeshiva that was organized by the Gaon **Reb Chaim Yehuda Leib Auerbach** *zal* and then, after his death, directed by his son, the giant of our generation, the Gaon **Reb Shlomo Zalman** *zal.* (This was in addition to his regular responsibilities to Yeshiva Kol Torah).

The Gaon **Reb Yaakov Meir Schechter,** the Gaon **Reb Yechiel Eisenbach,** the Gaon **Reb Moshe Luria,** and the Gaon **Reb Daniel Frisch** — all revered and leading members of the Yeshiva – expressed pleasure with the author's style of writing and with his treatment of the subject matter. They also stated that Jews must familiarize themselves with the various passages from Written and Oral-Torah – certainly those discussed in the *sefer*. More importantly, and as Rabbi Novick emphasizes throughout his *sefer,* Jews must be constantly aware that all events in the world were already envisioned by Hashem and that everything occurs according to Hashem's plan. As such, they continued, it is vital for the *sefer* to be introduced to as wide an audience as possible in order for Jews to familiarize themselves with the passages that promote this outlook.

Strongly endorsing this *sefer* for these reasons, they further wanted it to be known that Jews should not become depressed about current events in Israel, that Jews not lose hope in the future nor that their hope for Moshiach wane in any way whatsoever. We must keep the hope of Moshiach alive, they continued, and anticipate his arrival with great excitement. Indeed, we look forward to the day when people will develop themselves into a perfect society and when Jews will develop an absolutely comprehensive Torah community – and we pray to see this great day very soon.

After reviewing several chapters, **HaRav Noach Weinberg,** the very articulate and world renowned Rosh HaYeshiva of Aish HaTorah, expressed delight with the passages that were quoted from Torah and *Chazal*. "Important and timely issues and concepts are being discussed and explained," he declared, "and the *sefer* should, therefore, be widely distributed."

ודבר אחד מדבריך אחור לא ישוב ריקם
(מסכת סופרים פרק י"ג, הלכה י"א)

**_From all that Hashem has declared,
every single iota will be fulfilled._**
(Talmud Sofrim Chapter 13, Halachah 11)

"If you attempt to translate each word with a single word while retaining the original sequence of words (i.e. translate literally), you will work very hard and your translation will be unreliable and very inaccurate... Whosoever wishes to convey from one language to another must first understand the text [in the original language] and then afterwards he can express and explain it ... in a lucid fashion [in the second language]. But he cannot possibly accomplish this unless he alters the sequence [of words], or unless he utilizes many words in place of the original or few instead of many, or unless he adds or deletes words until the new text is properly ordered and explained in a clear fashion [in the second language]...."

(Rambam, Letter to Rebbi Shmuel ben Rebbi Yehuda ibn-Tibon)

Table of Contents

Israel: Reenter the Jews

Buy, Hold or Sell: The Facts Behind the Headlines

Prospects For the Immediate Future

PREFACE

How I Got Here:
Influences on the Person

many people think they understand a concept or passage in TaNaCh or Talmud, but as Reb Chaim Brisker zal, used to say: "If you cannot articulate a Torah concept or explain a topic so that it is understood by others, then you yourself do not really understand it". In this regard, there are many people who helped me formulate and clarify my thinking and learning — my students, some who have been with me for fifteen years. They have challenged me to refine my insights, they have shared their own insights with me, and they have motivated me to learn even more. Special thanks are also extended to Ethel Gottlieb, Reb Yitzchok Saftlas and Reb Yaakov Gerber for their marvelous professional skills in the areas of editing and graphics; I never realized the extent of the 'behind the scenes' efforts that are necessary in order to translate thoughts into a clear and pleasingly readable format.

In addition, I have had many Rabbeim who taught me well and who have made indelible impressions upon me. They were educated in Europe (Brisk, Kletz, Mir, and Slabodka) and in America (Lubavitch, Ner Yisrael, Stolin, Telz, and Yeshiva University). Each was critical and indispensable for my development at the very time each was my *Rebbi*. But I would like to take this opportunity to recognize two exceptional giants who taught me how to really learn during my adult years — whether it was a passage in *TaNaCh*, a piece of G'mora, or an especially difficult metaphysical passage *(Agadeta)*. I am **daily** appreciative of having been a student of the Gaon Reb Yosef Dov HaLevi Soloveitchik *zal* and, *sheyibadel l'chayim tovim v'aruchim,* the Gaon Reb Ahron HaLevi Soloveichik. I am also indebted to two special *Rabbe'im* who very caringly nurtured me during my teenage years — the Gaon Reb Pinchas Mordechai Teitz *zal* and the Gaon Reb Berel Peker *zal.*

There is so much to be thankful for and Divine Providence *(Hashgachah P'ratis)* is so obvious when we observe the various events in our lives. As for me, I also had the good fortune to be raised by two very special parents. Mother, Rae Novick, was an exceptional person who was one of the few girls to have been afforded a formal Jewish education in her youth, while still in Russia. No doubt her parents, whom I'm named for, were visionaries to have seen the need to provide for their daughter in this manner — decades before it became accepted and even fashionable. And, no doubt, their parents before them, and so on. My brother Joseph and I benefited beyond words from our unique mother. Were it not for the loss of her entire savings when banks failed during the Depression, she would have attended college to become a teacher. But Hashem had other plans for her; instead, she spent all her time teaching us everything. From Mother we learned how to play ball, how to sew and knit, and how to wash dishes and floors. Most of all, she taught us to love Torah. When we were toddlers, she told us stories of the *G'dolim,* our giant Torah leaders; when we were a little older, she read with us; when we were of school age, she learned with us.

Father, Irving Novick grew up during the difficult Depression years when his plans for a profession in accounting remained unactualized because of the basic need to survive. I remember once accompanying him to a *Siyum,* where the participants were celebrating the completion of the study of a tractate of Oral-Torah. After the program, one of the Rabbis asked Father to drive him home.

Father responded by asking: "Which car would you like to ride in?" (You must remember that this incident occurred in the early 1950's when most people didn't even own *one* car.)

And sure enough, the Rabbi asked Father: "You mean you have more than one car?"

And without blinking an eye, Father responded, "Certainly. I have two cars..."

"Oh, no," I'm thinking. "Father doesn't even possess a driver's license. Father was never dishonest; why is he lying now? He was always truthful. Why is he saying these untruths about owning two cars?"

Without blinking an eye, Father continued: "Certainly. I have two cars — one goes to the Yeshiva of Hudson County and the other goes to Rav Teitz's Yeshiva."

That's the way they saw their purpose in life — working so hard so we could go to yeshiva — and, remember, this was during a time when American Jews ridiculed those individuals who learned in yeshiva. Father was strong; as a matter of fact, Father was probably one of the strongest people in the world. When he decided on an approach, he insulated himself from comments, criticism, or ridicule. Anyone who didn't live in America during the 40's or 50's cannot appreciate the superhuman strength that was required in order to be observant. One cannot possibly fathom the determination that was necessary or the commitment that was required in order for parents to fight the currents and send children to yeshiva. And work hard they did. Their efforts on our behalf do not go unnoticed!

My father-in-law, Jerry Savitsky, also grew up during those terrible years that were threatening the continuity of Judaism.[1] Indeed, he was one of the few exceptions who remained *Shomer Shabbos* like his parents before him and their parents and so on. He worked very hard for shul, yeshiva, and community and he worked very hard so that my wife and brothers-in-law could learn in yeshiva. Vacations didn't exist for our parents because **tuition was the number one priority.** There were many fascinating aspects to him that deeply affected us, but I want to mention one insight that he would repeatedly share. He would always tell us, in his own inimical style, that the State of Israel could not physically survive in this violent world as an island in an ocean of extreme hostility and anti-Semitism. He knew that on the level of probability and based upon the world's hatred — there was no way for Israel to survive, unless Hashem would protect the little sheep from the wolves of the world.

My mother-in-law, Hilda Savitsky, may Hashem grant her 120 years, has been a source of boundless support and love for the entire family. The best way to demonstrate the strength of these feelings is to note that she is constantly on the phone — because every one of her children and grandchildren respect her and love her and want to speak to her when they're unable to

---

1. Even *Look Magazine* was predicting the death of Judaism with its famous cover story entitled "The Vanishing American Jew" — the climate was that precarious during the post-war years. (Ironically, Judaism survives while *Look Magazine* has vanished.)

visit or invite her for Shabbos; even from Israel they call regularly. May she be afforded the years to enjoy continued *nachas* from grandchildren and great grandchildren.

My wife Alice and I both realize that we owe everything to our nuclear family for everything that they've done for us throughout the years — including all the anxieties they helped ease and the disasters that were averted because of their presence and support — and with the help of Hashem. These are not mere words. We are indeed fortunate to have such a loving family who are real role-models in a world fraught with false values.

Our parents looked forward to the occasions when my wife or I would speak or give *shiurim* (lectures) to the public — sometimes traveling great distances to attend. They took pride in us. And so it is with deep gratitude, respect, and love that I dedicate this *sefer* in honor of our mother Hilda Savitsky — that she continue her work for Russian Jews, for New York Jews, and for the Jews of Israel and may she merit to enjoy the 'interest on all her investments'. In addition, may the learning that will be engendered because of this *sefer* serve as a merit and as an elevation for the souls of our parents: Rachel, daughter of Nisan and Libah; Reb Aharon Yitzchak, son of Yisrael and Chayah Yehudis; and Reb Yoel, son of Avraham and Rivka — may their memories be a blessing. We owe everything to our parents for molding us and we are forever indebted to them for all their focused efforts on our behalf. We are what we are only because of them. In recognition of their efforts, I am privileged to name this *sefer*

ראי רחל ראי הם שבו לגבולם[2]

❖ because the word **"ראי"** contains the first letter of the names of each of our deceased parents

❖ because the **"ה"** in the fourth word is the beginning of the name of our mother Hilda Savitsky — may Hashem grant her 120 years;

❖ because, indeed, Hashem is exclaiming:

> *"Look, Rachel, Look!! Your children — [after thousands of years] — Your children are finally returning to their borders!"*

Indeed, we are very thankful to Hashem for all our blessings and, above all, we thank Hashem for granting us four beautiful children and their magnificent spouses — all who continue in the paths of our parents before us and their parents before them — to the time of Sinai. They not only live Torah lives, but they do it with serious commitment and with a gusto

---

2. Adapted from Yirmiyahu 31:14-16

that demonstrates their love for Torah and their concern for other Jews; though still relatively young, they are already teaching in their respective communities.

We have spent many hours of quality-time together during which we've done everything; we've talked, played, traveled, and repaired what had to be repaired. But more than that, we have learned together in a formal fashion for many years during which, especially as adults, they really challenged me to formulate and refine my Torah explanations. Now that the children are married and no longer living at home, we're only able to 'talk in Torah learning' irregularly. I certainly miss each and every one of those earlier contacts of bonding but I do thank Hashem for granting us those moments of the past and, together with my wife, look forward with great excitement to the future — personally, nationally, and internationally:

- ❖ We pray to Hashem that: Kaylee, Azriel, Leora Aliza, Meir Eliezer, and Yael Ahuva; Nechama, Yehuda, and Elisheva Tamar; Tova and Noam; and Rivka and Moshe — we pray so hard that they will be role-models of Torah living in their respective communities world-wide and may they merit the honor of building families who will also live the lives of genuine Torah Jews.

- ❖ More importantly, we sincerely pray that *all* Hashem's children conduct themselves as is expected. We pray to Hashem to create the special world where Jews will comport themselves as Jews should; when the *Bais HaMikdash* will be rebuilt; when all people in the world will conduct themselves in a civilized fashion; and when Moshiach will lead us in singing and dancing in all the peaceful streets of Yehuda, Shomron, and Yerushalayim. May this happen **Today!!**

CHAPTER
I

The Introduction
to All Introductions:
What is Torah?

obody, for 3300 years — not even any of the other religions of the world — nobody ever rejected the Torah's divinity (see Chapter 20). The entire world, even pagan historians — everyone always knew that the Torah was Divine. But what does it mean that the Torah is Divine, that Hashem gave us the Torah?

There are Five Books of Moses, otherwise referred to as *Chumash,* that were given to us by Hashem through Moses, on Mount Sinai. These five Books consist of: B'reishis (Genesis), Sh'mos (Exodus), Vayikra (Leviticus), Bamidbar (Numbers), and D'varim (Deuteronomy). These Books were later supplemented by the writings of various prophets that give us general guidance as to how we should lead our lives, the values we should be developing, and what we should expect in the future — as individuals, as members of a community, and as a nation.

Chumash contains 613 *mitzvot* or precepts while the Books of the Prophets and Their Writings were specifically designed to remind us of our overall responsibilities. These Writings of the Prophets also provide us with practical guidance through the application of Torah principles from

Chumash — sometimes through the narration of an incident. *Torah*, as a word, means *instruction* for living. Torah is not a history book — although some historical details are mentioned, discussed, and/or analyzed. Torah is not a book of medicine — although health concepts are taught. Torah is not a story book,[1] although there are some stories included and it is through the various stories that guidance is provided us. The Torah contains many stories because Hashem does not teach us in abstractions. Hashem teaches us proper behavior on a concrete level — through events that are very rich in content, through incidents that are vivid and colorful, through stories that will always be fresh in our mind. Hence, we will be constantly alert to Hashem's teachings. But more importantly, because Torah is generally not written in abstractions, the specifics of the teachings will always be easily remembered and recalled. So, the story serves as the vehicle for the absorption of difficult concepts and the incorporation of legal details into our daily activities.

Even though there were thousands of prophets, only the messages and teachings of a limited number of additional books were included in *TaNaCh*[2] because only these specific teachings and messages would be relevant for us, several thousands of years later.[3] You see, those thousands of other prophets did have very specific messages — but only for the generation when they lived — but not for us, today. The Books of Prophets and Their Writings remind us of our responsibilities that have already been addressed in the Torah.[4] The prophets counsel us to recognize our failings and character defects and then to change our ways. The prophets also encourage us during the period of our lengthy exile, in the oppressive Diaspora. That is why in the Messianic Period, when Jews will be conducting their lives as expected of Jews, there will be virtually no need to remind Jews how to conduct themselves in a responsible manner — as individuals, as communities, and as a nation. For this reason during the Messianic period, when people will be conducting their lives on a higher level, the instruction from the Prophets and Writings will no longer be as pertinent. Then people will no longer need to be reminded about their responsibilities[5], nor will their spirits need to be uplifted.

It is important to note that these messages were obviously written in the language of their day. So, for instance, when trying to bolster spirits so that

---

1. Zohar Bamidbar 152a

2. An abbreviation for *Torah, N'vi'im,* and *K'suvim* referring respectively to Torah (the Five Books of Moses), The Prophets, and [their] Writings

3. Talmud M'gilah 14b

4. It is important to note that there are virtually no innovations or new concepts in The Prophets or Writings. See Talmud Ta'anis 9a

5. Jerusalem Talmud M'gilah 1:9; see also Talmud N'darim 22b

the Jews do not lose hope[6] but instead develop vibrant lives and communities — the prophet says that when you see Jews being transported to Israel like clouds, despite all the vast discrimination and violent oppression that we would be suffering throughout the world — when you see this mass migration through the air, you will then know that we are approaching the Messianic Age and you should create and build with renewed vigor. While the prophets could not use the specific word 'airplane' (which had not yet been invented and which could never have been understood until this century anyway),[7] the prophets could certainly talk about masses of Jews being transported from their homes in Diaspora to Israel through air travel (during the period before Moshiach). Packaged in this manner, the message could be understood in a somewhat limited fashion by all generations — but especially understood by ours. Similarly, the Jewish nation is described by the prophets as being attacked, not by people or armies but by iron rods[8] — again, because missiles and scuds are words that were only recently invented. That's why sometimes we have difficulty understanding — because the language and the symbolism are from days-gone-by, while the message is eternal and is being studied now, thousands of years later.

These additional books were collected by the last generation of prophets, by an assembly of 120 prophets which included such giants as Mordechai (of Purim fame), Ezra, and Daniel. These prophets are referred to as the *An'shay K'nesses HaG'dolah,* the Men of the Great Assembly who gathered together to collate the various books and then close *TaNaCh* as a completed unit. The Five Books, the Books of the Prophets, and Their Writings — this whole body of Literature is referred to as the *Torah She'bichtav,* the Written-Torah, the Torah that was written at Hashem's direct request.

But there is much more to the Torah which was not recorded — a whole body of knowledge that was not recorded until world events became so unbearable and oppressive for Jews. *Torah She'bichtav,* the Written-Torah, is only an introduction, an overview, and a summary. Another huge section of Torah knowledge was transmitted orally from the days of Sinai until environmental circumstances were such that Jews were unable to study intensively with their teachers in a relaxed fashion, for the usual twenty year period of time. This body of Torah information came to be written down because the cruel nations who governed the Jews were prohibiting Jews from

---

6.   Zohar B'reishis 212a states: 'A function of all prophets is to fill the depressed Jewish spirit with optimism.'

7.   *"Dibrah Torah bil'shon b'nay adam"* (Talmud B'rachos 31b) — The Bible only utilizes the language that people used at the time when the Bible was written.

8.   T'hilim 2:9 and 107:16

studying Torah or were creating conditions where great Torah Study Centers were being closed down one after another. Additionally, Jews were constantly fleeing their murderers; others were being forcibly uprooted and exiled. There was no longer any way that Jews could study in a serene setting for a prolonged period of time.[9] This body of Torah knowledge had to be written down if this sea of knowledge was to survive. This body of Literature is known as *Torah She'b'al Peh* — the Torah that had to be memorized because it had been transmitted orally from teacher to student — the body of Torah knowledge that was transmitted orally for 1400 years, from the time of the giving of the Torah at Sinai in the year 2448 (1312 BCE). What is the nature of this Oral-Torah and what is contained therein? An example or two should help illustrate its nature while simultaneously shedding light on why *Torah She'b'al Peh* is so vital and critical for Judaism.

There is a *mitzvah* in the Torah for men to don *T'filin*. What's fascinating is that no one ever wears *T'filin* at night. Although the Written-Torah does not provide us with the details of their appearance or how they are to be worn, every single pair of *T'filin* is exactly the same — and so it has been since the Torah was given to us by Hashem. They are only made from hides of kosher animals, they are always shaped like cubes and never any other form or shape. *T'filin* are painted black and they always contain the same four paragraphs from the Torah. There are always two units — one that is placed on the forearm and one behind the hairline on the head. The hand-*T'filin* has one compartment while there are four compartments for the headpiece. This is extremely fascinating because nowhere in the Written-Torah are any of these details discussed, yet every single pair of *T'filin* in the world — even those that have recently been discovered in archaeological ruins from thousands of years ago — every single pair of *T'filin* is exactly the same. No one ever saw purple *T'filin*, never any other paragraphs, nor does anybody ever wear them on Shabbos or Holidays and it is always placed on the muscle of the forearm. How do Jews know all these details — especially in view of the Written-Torah's terseness on this issue?

When giving us the Written-Torah, Hashem introduced a new Hebrew word, *T'filin*. This new term had to have been defined and explained simultaneously with the giving of the Written-Torah some 3300 years ago. To enable us to fulfill this *mitzvah* properly, when Hashem instructed us to don *T'filin*, Hashem had to define this new Hebrew word in addition to explaining all the pertinent details, namely: their shape and color, the rationale, etc.

Similarly, while the Torah mentions *sh'chitah,* the Written-Torah does not provide us with any specific details. Is slaughtering a procedure done on a

---

9. See also Talmud Sanhedrin 88b

limb? Can the action be done slowly, with pausing? What renders the knife unacceptable? How deep must the incision be? How high or low on the neck? What about the vertebra, the trachea, the esophagus? As Hashem states[10] *"You must slaughter animals as I have commanded you"*. Where are all these details that *"I have commanded you"*? In this instance, as well as with *T'filin* and every other concept or *mitzvah*, in the Orally-transmitted Torah Hashem provided us with *all* the necessary details including definitions of terms. Every Jew slaughters an animal in the exact same fashion as every other *shochet*— past, present, or future. The Written-Torah does not provide us with the details; Hashem provided us with the necessary details in the Oral-Torah. The Written and Oral-Torah are an indivisible unity. One without the other is meaningless. Each is only a part of an integral unit. They are each individual halves of a sacred whole.

Hashem also gave us this body of knowledge, the Oral-Torah; these details were studied orally until the Roman persecutions became so violent and oppressive, and Jews were not able to devote enough years to study because the Roman persecutions were causing the Jews to flee to far-away places where few teachers existed. In some areas and at some times, public Torah study was forbidden under pain of death (i.e. Torah study was a crime, a capital offense). So, to allow Jews to study independently, the process began whereby this body of Oral knowledge came to be transcribed — in several stages.

The first step is referred to as the age of the *Tanna'im* and includes such works as the Mishnah, Tosefta, B'rysa, M'chilta, Sifra, Sifri, Zohar, and Midrash. They were each written independently by different Rabbis and much of the information is exactly the same. The second and third stages spanned several hundred years, ending around the year 600 CE, and is known as the period of the *Amora'im* and *Sabora'im*. These works include the *G'mora* which was recorded in Israel as well as the one that was transcribed independently in Babylon. The main parts of these works include the details that emanated from Sinai, but that were not included in the earlier transcriptions of the *Tanna'im*.[11] Completed during these three stages, these recordings which consist of Mishnah and *G'mora* are called Talmud. Talmud plus all these monumental transcriptions of *Chazal*[12] are referred to as Torah *She'b'al Peh*— the massive body of knowledge that accompanied the Written-Torah which Hashem gave us at Sinai — the Torah that was originally transmitted orally,

---

10. D'varim 12:21

11. Talmud Avos D'Rebbi Nasan 7:1

12. *Chazal* is an abbreviation for <u>Cha</u>chamim <u>z</u>ichronam <u>l</u>ivracha — [the Oral-Torah as transmitted by] the sages of blessed memory. Throughout this book, *Chazal* is used interchangeably with Oral-Torah.

the Sea of Knowledge that contains the definitions of terms, the details, and specifics of all that is alluded in the Written-Torah.

It is important to note that when a specific teacher (*Tanna* or *Amora*) is credited with a statement — whenever the Oral-Torah quotes a certain principle, concept, or legal detail — this does not mean that the statement originated with that Rabbi. Rather, at the time when the Oral-Torah was being written down, this particular Rabbi was alive and was publicizing a concept that had been taught to him by his teacher (going back to Sinai). To reiterate, **the quoted teacher did not innovate the statement;** he is merely reporting Torah explanations that were transmitted to us at Sinai from Hashem. This principle becomes all the more obvious when we compare various transcriptions from this period: one Rabbi may be quoted in one source, while another source will quote another Rabbi, and a third source quotes a third teacher — where all three Rabbis are simultaneously teaching exactly the same concept or principle, all in different locations of the world. For example, the earlier referenced principle that *TaNaCh* includes only the writings of prophets that have relevancy for our day and that the teachings are not limited to the era of that prophet — this principle can be found in Talmud M'gilah 14a and B'rachos 34b as well as in the Midrash (Shir HaShirim Rabah 4:22) and in P'sikta that was transcribed by Rav Kahana (Chapter 13). This principle is also implied in Talmud N'darim 22b. Many teachings were recorded in several different works — oftentimes, the same principle or statement being ascribed to different teachers.

One more example in so far as the recitation of Sh'ma is concerned: the definition of morning, '*boker*' extends for the first ¼ of the day — this *halachah* is stated in Talmud B'rachos 3b and 9b; Jerusalem Talmud B'rachos 1:1; M'chilta *Parshas Bo* 13; and Bamidbar Rabah 15.

Unfortunately, not everything was written down, but the major parts were indeed transcribed and as a result have survived for posterity. Some details did escape this monumental undertaking and, even to this day, later generations sometimes have to struggle to fill in the missing blanks.[13] Judaism survived because, as a result of these transcriptions, generations of Jews would have notes to study from; now Jews could easily review what they were taught by their teachers. But even so, the Talmud still requires so much intensive study that it has remained essentially a 'closed book' for all those Jews who never had a formal Talmud teacher. Fortunately, in the last few years, several fine English translations have appeared and are making Talmud study somewhat accessible for those who did not spend their early adult years in

---

13. See Y'rushalmi Peah 6:2

intensive study, for those who are non-Hebrew speaking, and for people who do not have a command of Aramaic — the languages of the Talmud. But even in written form — no matter the language — the study of Written and Oral-Torah requires extensive effort under the guidance of an exceptionally gifted teacher.

CHAPTER
II

How They All Got There:
Influences on Israel's Independence

t is really interesting as to how this *sefer* came to be written. I was also hoping that you would be interested in hearing how the *sefer* evolved and, more importantly, I do hope that you will enjoy learning from this *sefer* as much as I enjoyed preparing it for you.

One day, I was learning the *parshah* (Biblical portion for the week) and as a practice, each year I supplement the usual commentaries with 'something'. One year it was Reb Shimshon Raphael Hirsch, another year it was the Ramban, and so on. Last year, I tried to learn a little Zohar; I gave up — Oh, how difficult it is to understand! This year, I was utilizing Midrash Rabah and I'll never forget *parshas* Vayishlach[1] and the kidnap, rape, and torture of Dinah by Sh'chem whose terrorist activities were supported by the entire male population of his community. Dinah was being held hostage for a very unusual ransom and there was just no way to free her. Together with all his townspeople, Sh'chem was planning to infiltrate this very special family in

---

1. Especially B'reishis 34

order to eventually gain control of **all their assets.**[2] Marrying Yaakov's children was a subterfuge and he states this to his followers:

> *"Let us marry their children and let them develop the country ... because all their wealth will be ours ..."*

The ransom was the **entire family and their vast financial estate.** After kidnapping, raping, and torturing Dinah, Sh'chem asks Dinah's family for permission to marry her. How smart do you have to be to figure out that there's no basis for a real marriage — for a marriage rooted in mutual respect and mature love?! But, apparently in an earnest fashion, Shimon and Levi begin negotiating with the terrorist.[3]

> *'[Your demand to marry our sister and for all your townspeople to marry all our sisters] we will meet these demands if you will allow yourselves to be circumcised.'*

Sh'chem and his cohorts agree to be circumcised, and while they're recuperating from the operation and in a weakened condition, Shimon and Levi invade the city in order to rescue Dinah. In the course of the rescue operation, they also kill each and every one of the people who were involved in this terrible rape-kidnap hostage-taking episode — the entire adult male population who wholeheartedly supported their leader, with no dissenters and no one criticizing such criminally violent behavior.

You would think that, after seeing his freed daughter, Yaakov would be overjoyed. His daughter is alive! Dinah is freed of those monsters. The rescuers are also unharmed. What a miracle! Instead, Yaakov expresses anger[4]

"עכרתם אתי להבאישני בישב הארץ ... ואני מתי מספר ...
והכוני ונשמדתי אני וביתי"

How could any father be less than excited to see his kidnapped daughter returned home? Who wouldn't thank Hashem for the return of a captured child?! Yet, Yaakov criticizes Shimon and Levi.

Oral-Torah explains[5] that Yaakov was afraid that the actions of the two brothers might precipitate an attack by the neighboring Canaanites against this family that was first beginning to bud into a nation. Yaakov tells his sons that what they did was the same as 'stirring up' a calm barrel of water, with the sediments and pollutants now rising and clouding up[6] the clear liquid — thus making it undrinkable and unusable — because the Canaanite nations

---

2. Ibid., verses 21 and 23
3. Through Sh'chem's chief negotiator, his father
4. Ibid., verse 30
5. B'reishis Rabah 80:12
6. That's what the term *'achartem'* means.

have a tradition that **the Israelites only become invincible once they number 600,000.** He continues:[7]

ויאמר יעקב אל שמעון ואל לוי "עכרתם אתי" צלולה היתה החבית ועכרתוה. מסורת היא בידי הכנענים שהן עתידין ליפול ביד בני אלא שאמר לו הקב"ה "עד אשר תפרה ונחלת את הארץ" בששים רבוא.

> *'If the neighboring Canaanites feel personally threatened by your actions, they may attack us now and since we're fewer than 600,000 and thus very vulnerable, they'll wipe us all out. Our family may thus never attain nationhood because of the aggression you just committed. Certainly we had to rescue Dinah but it should have been accomplished in a manner that wouldn't panic the Canaanites into attacking us while we're still a small family. Your actions may cost us our promise of nationhood because **the Canaanites know that we are only invincible when we reach 600,000.** As long as we're still a small family, we are unfortunately very vulnerable — and the Canaanites know this. If you wouldn't have acted so aggressively, we could have quietly grown to 600,000 and then, when numbering 600,000 — at that point, with Hashem's assistance we would become invincible and be able to weather any attack. Were they to attack us at that time when we'd be so numerous, they would lose. Now you have "clouded up the waters"; now you may have caused them to attack us earlier and should we be attacked now, we may have no chance at surviving such an attack.'*

Chazal certainly help us with the imagery of the "clouding and stirring up of sediments in the water"— the implication being that Jews can become useless and worthless. After all, Yaakov's family would be without value if they were all dead; there would then be no Torah nation.

But what made an even greater impression on me is the statement that when the Jews first achieve a population of 600,000 they become invincible.[8] You know why it made such an impression? Because, even though I usually do not remember trivia, I do remember some interesting statistics. I recalled that the Jewish population in Israel was approximately 56,000 around the time of World War I and that just prior to World War II the Jewish population had already mushroomed to 400,000. I said to myself — I know it already; I don't even have to check. So I researched the matter to discover the Jewish

---

7. Yalkut Shimoni 33:135

8. Not invincible forever, but invincible for an initial period of time — the length of which is dependent upon our actions and our values.

population of Israel before the first Arab war. I think you, too, can already guess correctly. It is totally mind boggling. In the 1946 census conducted under British auspices, **the number of Jews in Israel finally excceded 600,000** which is the exact same number that Yaakov referred to when he reprimanded his sons. 600,000 makes us invincible. Wow! I mean, like ... I was speechless. I was extremely excited. Needless to say, that was my daughter Rivka's 'bedtime story' that Friday night. For the next month, I began to talk about this *Chazal* to everyone that I saw. What amazed me even more was that I discovered that few were really learning Midrash on a regular basis — including me (until then). So I was happy to share this *Chazal* with many people, and my friends were amazed and very happy to be introduced to this concept of **the invincibility of the 600,000.**

Of course, we are invincible — but **only with Hashem's help!** And so it was: the Jewish population of 604,000 was invincible in the face of the millions of attacking Arabs who were determined to murder every single Jew in the Land in order to make the Land *Judenrein.* "Please, Hashem, not again." With Hashem's help, the 604,000 unprepared Jews survived the massive Arab invasion. Not only were they able to weather the vicious Arab onslaught, but the 604,000 **weaponless** Jews were **miraculously victorious** against the millions of well-armed Arabs. Incredible miracle? Certainly! But this is the precise principle of **the invincibility of the 600,000.**

The concept we just discussed deals with invincibility; essentially, we are rendered invincible when the total number of Jews in the Land reaches 600,000. I'll also never forget how, two weeks later, I came across another equally incredible *Chazal,* another Torah concept that expands upon this Divinely-granted invincibility. Now I discovered an additional *Chazal*[9] that indicates that the Land of Israel will be returned to us when ... I think you may have already guessed it!

מה יציאתם ממצרים בששים רבוא וכניסתן לארץ בששים רבוא
כן לימות המשיח בששים רבוא

'Just as the Exodus from Egypt and entry into the Land occurred with 600,000 so will the EXACT same thing happen again. Right before the Era of Moshiach, we'll INHERIT the Land and become INDEPENDENT when we number 600,000.'

Oral-Torah points out that **the Land will be returned to us when the total Jewish population in the Land reaches 600,000.** In another place[10] the year 5708 (1947/8) is specified as the time when the Land will be redeemed.

---

9. Zohar, Introduction; Talmud Shabbos 88b with Maharsha; see also Yalkut Shimoni on Hoshea, Chapter 2, paragraph 918
10. Tikunay Zohar on Yeshayahu 60:23

The Oral-Torah, so far, stresses two principles regarding the Jews of Israel. With Hashem's help:

1) We are **invincible** when our population reaches **600,000**.

2) We will regain our **independence** when there are **600,000** of us in the Land.

And so it was!! This is just beyond belief. I never experienced anything as earth shattering as this before. Certainly, I had learned prophecies from *TaNaCh* and Oral-Torah before, but somehow this was different. To this day I am unable to verbalize my emotions and am somewhat breathless as I write these words several months later.

Perhaps my heart beats with excitement because I found a third *Chazal* that is associated with these two. This makes an electrifying package of three different types of prophecies about the 600,000 Jews in today's Land of Israel. Besides our **invincibility at 600,000** and besides our becoming **independent at 600,000** — in addition to these two discoveries, I came across another astonishing passage.

We know that during the Exodus, there were 600,000 Israelites who left Egypt — at least, that is what most people think. But, all in all, including women and the elderly and all those below the age of 20, there were really about 2½ million souls who left Egypt. Indeed, a careful reading of the text indicates that there were **600,000 males above the age of 20** who left Egypt and it is *this fact* that is of interest to me now: the 600,000 adult males. Do you think this has any significance?

You are probably saying to yourself right now: 'He wrote this *sefer* and if he's asking the question, then he must know something. What could it be? What could be associated with **600,000 Jewish male adults?'** What could be more earth shattering than the two previously cited Torah statements?

Well, I discovered another remarkable fact. While it was easy to discover, because of the British census, that there was a *total* Jewish population of 600,000 in the Land in 1946, would there also be information about the *male* Jewish population above the age of 20. *"A yid git an aytzah"* — there's always a solution. It struck me that there had to be a source that could provide this information pretty accurately. After all, the Torah describes the Jewish male adults as *"yotzay tzava"* — as the **soldiers**. But of course, the Israeli military needs to know the ages and whereabouts of all the draft-eligible males in the country who are **above the age of 20**. Are you ready for this?! I discovered that the **adult male population** of present-day Israel **exceeded 600,000** for the first time in the year 5725 (1965). In that census, the adult male population was registered as 631,330.

Chazal[11] continue by emphasizing one more point: the position of **Jerusalem and Israel** in this scenario.

הכי אמינא לך דלא ליעול אנא לעילא עד דייעלין בך אוכלוסך לתתא

> *"[Hashem will only end His self-imposed Galus when He will accompany the Jews in their world-wide exile][12] and Hashem will only enter Celestial Yerushalayim when there are 600,000 adult Jewish males below [in physical Israel]."*

When there are more than 600,000 Jewish men above the age of 20 — **Hashem reigns in the Celestial Yerushalayim.** Celestial Jerusalem is the mirror image of our Jerusalem: Hashem reigns supreme because we reign with 600,000. **When there are 600,000 Jewish male adults in Israel,** Oral-Torah tells us, **Hashem's presence will be felt through all the various special occurrences in the Land.** Well, as difficult as it may seem to penetrate to the depths of this passage which describes a seemingly complicated matter, we will review one event. The Israeli census of 5725 (1965) indicated that there were 631,330 adult Jewish males and what followed was precisely as predicted.

In 1967, shortly after we achieved this milestone of 600,000 male adults, **Jordan entered the Six Day War** at a time when the war was just closing down. The entire Arab military machine was already totally decimated. Hashem and the Jews are about to be victorious again. The war was virtually over. But out of nowhere, Jordan decides to invade Israel. Jordan wasn't stupid. Jordan entered the war because Jordan's King Hussein received a phone call in the midst of the war.

> *"MISTER KING OF JORDAN", the voice on the phone said. "MISTER KING OF JORDAN, I KNOW THE ARABS HAVE BEEN DEFEATED ALREADY AND I KNOW THAT YOU DIDN'T ENTER THE WAR WITH THEM BECAUSE YOU'RE AFRAID OF THE ISRAELI MIGHT. BUT YOU MUST ENTER THE WAR **NOW!***
>
> *IT DOESN'T MAKE SENSE TO YOU? YOU'RE CORRECT. IT CERTAINLY DOESN'T MAKE SENSE FOR YOU TO ENTER A WAR ON THE SIDE OF THE LOSERS. BUT YOU **MUST** INVADE ISRAEL **NOW!!** THERE ARE NOW 600,000 MALE ADULTS IN ISRAEL. MY CHILDREN AND I HAVE BIG PLANS FOR JERUSALEM. WE HAVE A LOT OF CONSTRUCTION AHEAD OF US. MY CHILDREN NEED JERUSALEM NOW. ALL THESE*

---

11. Zohar, ibid.

12. In order to protect them from annihilation

YEARS THEY'VE WAITED AND CRIED AND PRAYED AND FASTED AND SAID TIKUN CHATZOS[13] AND NOW MY CHILDREN ARE RETURNING TO THEIR BORDERS. YOU MUST ENTER THE WAR NOW. YOU'RE ALREADY VERY LATE AND THE WAR IS ALMOST OVER."

"YOUR HIGHNESS, THERE ISN'T MUCH TIME LEFT. MY CHILDREN ARE WAITING EXCITEDLY FOR BOTH OF US. I DID PROMISE THEM AND THERE ARE NOW 600,000 JEWISH MEN IN THE LAND. WE HAVE TO GO RIGHT NOW; IT'S TIME TO RESTORE JERUSALEM TO THE JEWS. MY CHILDREN ARE WAITING. THEY WILL BE DISAPPOINTED NO MORE."

"YOUR HIGHNESS, WE HAVE TO GO RIGHT NOW!"

After there were 600,000 adult Jewish males living in the Land, Mid-East events demonstrated Hashem's return to reign supreme in Celestial Jerusalem. It was so obvious: after we achieved a Jewish population of 600,000 male adults, we regained control over physical-Jerusalem under such unusual circumstances. We felt Hashem's presence. We were able to see Hashem as the Architect of History. The Oral-Torah[14] actually specifies the year 5727 as the time when Hashem would intervene on behalf of the Jews in a most glorious fashion. Indeed, Hashem reigns supreme in Celestial Jerusalem when there are 600,000 adult males in the Land.

Jerusalem-on-earth, is now controlled by Jews; Mid-East events indicate that Hashem reigns supreme in Celestial Jerusalem, its mirror image. All this has occurred because there are now 600,000 adult males in the Land.

---

13. This is a midnight service, bemoaning the loss of Jerusalem and Israel and the Holy Temple, wherein we pray for their complete restoration.

14. Zohar I, 117

CHAPTER
III

A Travelers Guide to History: *Codes - Torah Alludes to Every Event*

 odes are very intriguing and fascinating and lately Codes have become very popular because they are so breathtakingly prophetic. The Zohar states very clearly that Divine Names, for example, run through every single word in the Torah. Essentially, Codes are a method of reading words whereby an equal number of letters are skipped between the letters in a series of words. Spies often utilize this method of encoding a secret message within the larger and more obvious message. For example, in the phrase *'READ THIS PLEASE'*, if we read only every third letter beginning with the first letter, 'R', then we would have the combination *'RDILS'* (from *'**R**EA**D** TH**I**S P**L**EA**S**E'*); of course, *'RDILS'* is a nonsense word with absolutely no meaning. Once in a while by coincidence, we are able to find a word. For example, using the same three words, we do find the word 'RAT' if we join every second letter and stop after the 5th letter (from *'**R**E**A**D **T**HIS PLEASE'*). So, based upon several variables,[1] there is an

---

1. One of the variables is dependent upon the frequency that letters appear in written sentences. For example, the letter 'Z' is found less frequently than the letter 'A' but more frequently than the letter 'Q'.

element of probability that once in a while we will find a word encoded within a sentence if we read every fifth or seventeenth or ..th letter.

If you can picture the letters in a passage as forming a complete column in a Torah scroll, we will focus into one little section of that column. This is very much similar to viewing a section of a large map.

A visual presentation is utilized because it makes it easier for the reader to see the relationship between letters and the equidistant spacing between each and every letter from the encoded word.

To help the reader visualize the Codes, a specific number of letters of the text have been printed on each line so as to correlate with the number of intervals for that particular Code. In this way, the reader will experience and enjoy the dramatic effects of this unbelievable phenomenon. Thus, the reader will easily see the equidistant-Code standing out clearly and not have to count letters. In this manner of presenting the text, the reader will usually find the Coded information printed out vertically — one letter from the Codes below the previous one. Finally, to make the Codes readable, generally only the first 24 letters of a line are usually printed. This means that if a Code appears after every 50th letter, only the first 24 letters are **shown** on the printed page while the next 25 letters are **counted** — but **not printed**. The second line would then begin with the 50th letter and then continue for 48 more letters (although, again, only the first 24 are printed). The third line, similarly, begins with the 100th letter in the sequence and runs for 49 letters — again, with only 24 on the printed page. Aesthetically speaking, only a maximum of 24 spaced Hebrew letters can fit on the printed page without those letters having to be so drastically reduced in size so as to be rendered illegible. This is very much like a sectional map in that only a certain amount is magnified even though much more land exists outside the perimeter of the enlarged section.

Codes are commonly utilized in Oral-Torah. *Chazal* state often in a rhetorical fashion: ‫מן התורה מנין...‬ Here, essentially a Code of one space interval is utilized and a proper noun, an event, or a concept is revealed. Many times the Talmud states ‫...אל תקרי אלא...‬ with a skipping of every vowel. The consonants of the actual word remain, each vowel is skipped, and a new word is formed through Codes. In other words, utilizing the English language as the basis for comparison, by skipping every vowel, the equidistant spacing is two letters because every other letter is read. That is to say, ‫...אל תקרי אלא...‬ is a method of reading an encoded message where the equal distance between successive letters is two spaces.

Zohar often utilizes larger intervals between letters in revealing an important Code and, as indicated in their writings, Codes were also utilized by Torah giants such as Rabbeinu Bachya, Ramban, and the Vilna Gaon. In our generation, the Nitra Rav, Rabbi Michael Ber Weissmandl, reminded us of these methods — today, with a few hours of training on the computer, even a bright youngster can find the future predicted, (after the fact).[2]

There's another statement in Oral-Torah which is even more specific:[3]

אורייתא כולא שמא קדישא היא דלית לך מלה באורייתא דלא כלל בשמא קדישא

> *"The entire Torah is replete with Divine Names. Divine Names run through every single word in the Torah."*

For example, in the passage...

‫ויּקרא אל משה וידבר י-ה-ו-ה אליו מאהל מועד...‬

in this sentence, starting with the first ‫י‬, when every 8th letter is combined, the name of Hashem is spelled. This is but one example of how Divine Names span EVERY SINGLE WORD in the Torah and that the removal of even one 'plain' letter will obliterate *many* Divine Names. One letter's removal disturbs the delicate presence of many Divine Names that span that specific word (of which that letter is a part) — Divine Names that are found in Codes and that spanned that very letter prior to that letter's deletion. Now, with the removal of even one 'plain' letter, many Codes are expunged — including many Divine Names.[4] In our example, when combining every 8th letter, the Name of Hashem is spelled. However, if the ‫י‬ from ‫אליו‬ is deleted from the sixth word, then the combination of every 8th letter spells ‫יהול‬ and a Divine Name is obliterated.

---

2. Zohar l, 118a. See, below, Chapters 7 and 18 for a fuller discussion.
3. Zohar ll, 87a
4. See Ramban's introduction to his commentary on *Torah* where he states that this Zohar provides another reason for a Torah's becoming unfit for use if even one letter is missing.

Hashem also states:[5]

יגישו ויגידו לנו את אשר תקרינה ... הבאות השמיענו, הגידו האתיות
לאחור... ונראה יחדו

*"To know what will occur ... to have future events disclosed,
[sometimes] letters from words have to be read backwards ...
Let us take a look together."*

Do you think that the Hebrew word תורה can be found as one of the conventional words in B'reishis, the first Book in the Torah? Well, it does not exist.

What do you think the chances are that in the Book of B'reishis we will find the word תורה written, but not as a series of successive letters, not in the conventional manner of reading whereby one letter follows another in a successive fashion in order to combine and form a word (the way you're reading this selection)? What are the chances that we will be able to find that word תורה if we read every other letter or if we read every 12th letter or 34th letter starting with the first ת in the Book of B'reishis? Well, this is exactly what exists.

Encoded into the first few sentences in the first Book, B'reishis, and beginning with the first ת, we find the word תורה at equidistant letter intervals of 50 spaces (i.e. 49 letters intervene between each targeted letter when every 50th letter is combined and read). In fact, the actual Torah was given on the 50th day, after 49 days had elapsed from the Exodus from Egypt. Additionally, the actual Torah was given after the Jews had elevated themselves to the 49th level of perfection. The 50th level is the highest attainable level; Torah guides people to the highest level of functioning.

Some people might claim that perhaps this Code is a coincidence. So, what are the chances, then, of also finding the word תורה encoded as a

---

5.   Yeshayahu 41:22-23

word if we read every 50th letter starting with the first ת in the second Book, Sh'mos?

What are the chances of finding the word תורה encoded as a word if we read every 50th letter in the fourth and fifth Books, Bamidbar and D'varim? On both occasions, the Codes appear backwards and in Bamidbar the Code begins with the third ה.

In the Book of D'varim there are two very slight but quite interesting differences. In D'varim, the equidistant spacing is every 49th letter in addition to the presence of the word תורה in its conventional representation. In D'varim, the ה, the last letter of the encoded word תורה— that same letter is also part of the conventional word התורה.

After seeing just these four examples, you do have to admit — even if you don't have a scientific background in probability and statistics — that it is virtually impossible for the first two and the last two Books of the Torah to contain the identical Code while utilizing the same equidistant letter interval of 50 spaces — in each case right in the first few verses of each of the Books. The odds of something like this happening randomly or by coincidence — this can't be unless, of course, Hashem wrote the Torah on several levels at the same time

❖ on the conventional level that we utilize when we learn or read
  and

❖ on the level of reading words by joining letters together where the letters are at equidistant spacing, when we don't read the letters in the usual fashion of successive letters.[6] We refer to this system of reading by the term *Codes*.

Hashem wrote the Torah with the Coded words or messages purposely inserted because **encoded words have meaning, also**.

There are several references, in both Written and Oral-Torah, that Hashem encoded many such messages throughout the Torah. *Chazal* do state:[7]

אסתכל באורייתא וברא עלמא

'Hashem created the world to function in accordance with all that is contained within the Torah'. Hashem had to, therefore, have the Torah contain all the events that would occur at some future time in order to have the world function in that precise manner — exactly as the Torah predicts. Events can be read in the Torah in the conventional form of reading one letter directly after another. Words can also be read at a predetermined equidistant letter spacing sequence of, perhaps, every 50th letter. This is what Torah Codes are all about. Indeed, Hashem created a **world** system (including a **word** system in Torah) so that all prophecies are alluded to and that all prophecies will be fulfilled in a precise fashion. Indeed, מי איכא מידי דלא רמיזי באורייתא.[8] But more than all the above, in our introductory paragraph to this chapter, we only spoke about finding 'any old word' encoded in a Torah passage. What is the

---

6. Other levels of reading and study also include using numerical equivalents for the literary letters or words, since the Hebrew characters serve simultaneously as letters and as numbers; we refer to this system of reading by the term *g'matriya*. Two other levels of reading and comprehension are *'remez' and 'sode'*. See also Zohar lll: (Bamidbar) 202a and (Vayikra) 53b and 101b

7. Zohar II,161a; see also B'reishis Rabah 1:1; Tanchuma 1:1; and Raya M'hemna, B'reishis 23a.

8. Talmud Ta'anis 9a

possibility of finding my family-name (i.e. *Novick)* written out in this sentence that you are presently reading. It's impossible — the letters *'v'* and *'k'* are not even present in the last sentence, let alone with the remaining letters in their proper order and with equidistant spacing between them. It is really not easy to find special words encoded in every passage. But what if the Torah contains the coded-message with

- ❖ all the letters present,
- ❖ all the letters in their proper order,
- ❖ all the letters at equidistant letter spacing between each letter,
- ❖ and the Coded word is located where the subject matter of the Torah text is relevant to the encoded message.

For example, we would not expect our names to be encoded where the Torah discusses false prophets. What names do you think would be encoded in the chapter of false prophets?[9] We would certainly expect some of the infamous false prophets to have their names encoded there — like Shabtai Tzvi or the founder of Islam or other similar movements who distorted reality.

---

9. D'varim 13

Similarly, if we are looking for a reference to the PLO; we would not expect to find a coded message about Arabs in the Torah section dealing with Kosher birds or in the passage dealing with Yom Kippur or in the portion about interest-free loans or issues of ecology. How about finding references to Arafat in the sections dealing with negotiations with the non-Jewish inhabitants of the Land or in the section dealing with the prohibition of giving away the Land to non-Jews ?[10]

Similarly, we would expect to find references to the Nazis in the sections that deal with Jews being murdered by their host countries during our exile in the Diaspora.[11] You will also note that the name נצים is also spelled **backwards** because they appear at the **back-end** of the *Galus.*

These are probably the most important factors:

❖ Not only are all the letters present,

❖ Not only are they in their proper order to spell *Nazim,*

❖ Not only are the letters at equidistant interval spacing.

❖ The most important factor is that *Nazim* and all other Codes are not found in just any passage. What is truly amazing is that the terms are found in their **proper contexts**.

How about trying to find the names of *every one* of our great Torah leaders and their birthdates and the names of their publishings. Well, the name of every single *Gadol* appears encoded together with important biographical information. For example, Rambam is found encoded in the passage which discusses *Mishneh Torah,* which is also the name of one of his *halachah* masterpieces. But this phenomenon is not limited only to Jewish personages. **All important events** are in Torah. For example: what passage would contain reference to electricity or to Thomas Edison and the discovery of the light bulb?! We find these references in the section discussing the creation of light on the first day of Creation. Where could we find a reference to AIDS or diabetes?

---

10. Ibid. 7
11. Ibid. 28

Those who are interested in the statistics which show that **it is mathematically impossible for these Codes to occur accidentally, without Divine design or intent** are directed to two journal articles which discuss the incredible and sensational presence of these Codes.[12] In these two research articles, one can find the scientific data which demonstrate conclusively that the occurrences of Codes are way beyond the realm of mere coincidence. As a matter of fact, two of the renowned mathematicians who generated the statistics in this area — two of the mathematicians who were atheists are now 100% orthodox after they realized that **Codes prove that ONLY Hashem could have written the Torah**. The more one delves into Codes, the more one becomes convinced of their validity and reliability and their being inserted in Torah by Hashem and with a purpose. The Talmud states this very clearly[13] מי איכא מידי דלא רמיזי באורייתא —"Every event [past and future] is alluded to in the Torah."

One final passage — במה אדע כי אירשנה, Avraham asks Hashem to disclose the time when Jews would inherit the Land.[14] 'What special events will herald this era? What **milestone** will indicate that the time has arrived for my descendants to take possession of the Land?'

Hashem responds by stating:[15] 'The Jews will be split apart: they will suffer terrible massacres and the remnants will only survive as a weak bird.'

Hashem continues: 'Smelling the blood of the Jews who are lying dead, birds of prey will come to swoop down and lick up the remains.'

Hashem continues: 'But, Avraham, you and your merits will prevent a total destruction. You and your merits will prevent the other nations from killing off the fledgling survivors of this holocaust.'

'Avraham, You asked for an indicator that signals the imminent return of Jews to Israel. The Holocaust is the indicator; *this* is the catastrophic tragedy which will be the *signal* that the Jews are about to inherit the Land.'

Avraham is overcome with a horrific fright with this foreknowledge of a cataclysmic disaster — the likes of which are singular and unparalleled in the annals of world history.[16]

In this very short and frightening passage — the Codes include 14 references to Hitler, Nazis, and Holocaust. The appearance of fourteen references is a highly significant phenomenon, a combination of Codes that no human

---

12. Witzum, D., Rips, E., and Rosenberg, Y. *Journal of the Royal Statistical Society,* (1988), 151 part I, pp. 177-8 and Witzum et al. *Statistical Science,* (1994), 9, 3, pp. 429-33
13. Talmud Ta'anis 9a
14. B'reishis 15:8
15. See Reb Shimshon Rafael Hirsch, ibid., verses 7-21
16. See Pirkei D'Rebbi Eliezer 28, B'reishis Rabah 44:15, and Talmud Sotah 10b.

being could have envisioned 3300 years ago — let alone, insert in the Torah. Only Hashem could have inserted such magnificent and awesome Codes into Torah. It was this foreknowledge of the Holocaust which created such panic and terror for Avraham — notwithstanding the fact that the Jews would inherit the Land after this unspeakable massacre.

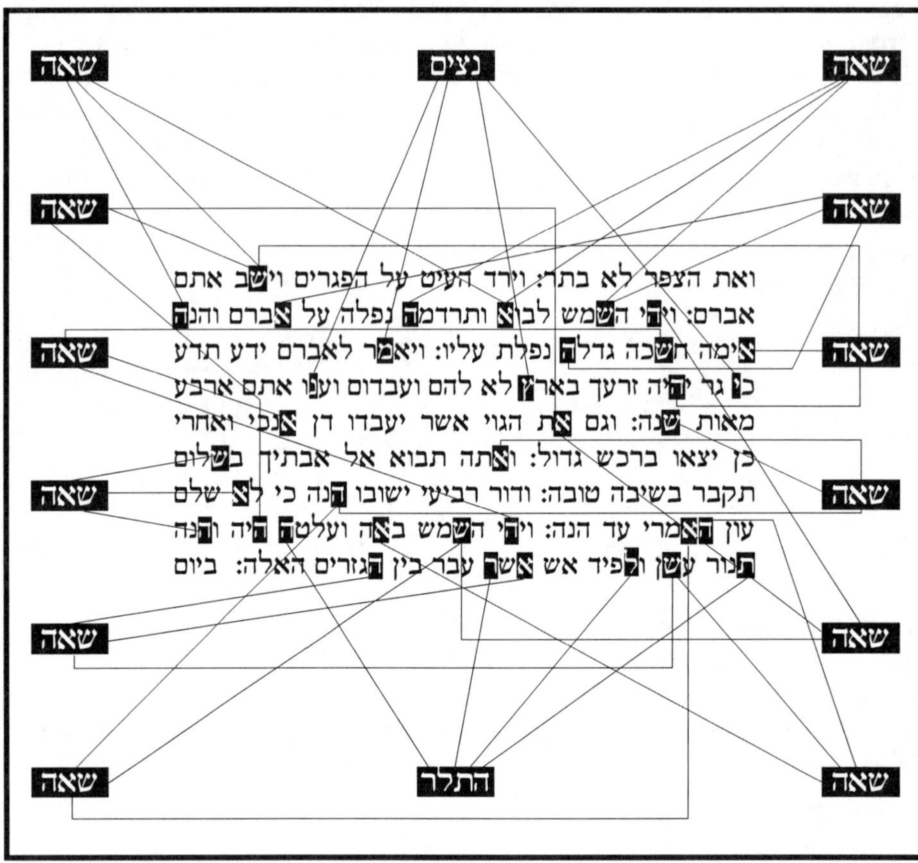

Hashem continues: 'After this terrible Holocaust, Avraham, your surviving offspring will emerge with the ability to take possession of the **entire** Land of Canaan (i.e. the territory of the ten Canaanite nations).'

The panic intensified when Hashem revealed that, in their attempts to escape this monstrous Holocaust, the fleeing Jews will encounter other peoples who will attempt to massacre these very survivors. From this second wave of attacks, the identity of a predator is encoded twice — in the verse about birds of prey attacking the survivors. It is important to note that a Code that is found more than once in a passage always emphasizes the gravity of a situation.

The Hebrew equivalent for the PLO is ארגון שחרור פלשתנאי which is אש"פ in its abbreviated form. The PLO is identified as a dangerous bird of prey with a history of attacking and murdering innocent Jews.

'Avraham, you, with your merits, will prevent a second massacre — the looming, sinister massacre of the survivors of the Holocaust (who fled to Israel). Avraham, you, with your merits, will prevent a second holocaust which will be planned and which will be labeled a *jihad*. Avraham, you will be able to prevent this second Holocaust. Avraham, your descendants will be able to chase away these predators.'

Hashem then reassures Avraham that the Jews are really entitled to all the territory that is between the Egyptian and Euphrates Rivers and that the Jews will possess the LAND IN ITS ENTIRETY. It is interesting to note that, here, Hashem posits the Jewish title to **all** the Land. After the Jews return to reclaim their land in its entirety, right in the midst of this latter sentence, there is an encoded reference to Rabin.

> *After the Jews return to reclaim the Land — "after sunset [on a particular day] ... a torch of fire passed between the cut-up pieces [of Jews] ..."*

In this passage which publicizes the Jewish legal rights to **all** of Canaan/Palestine/Israel — right here in the very section dealing with the **territorial integrity of the ENTIRE Land of Israel,** and in the very passage whose teaching Rabin rejected — precisely here and related to the issue of Jewish sovereignty over the entire Land of Israel, the Codes refer to Rabin in a most dramatic fashion.

"After sunset...a torch of two bad fires in Rabin" —
(i.e. RABIN WILL BE MORTALLY WOUNDED BY TWO SHOTS).

That is what is encoded in verse 17 and that is what is highlighted above as five distinct and consecutive words in the Torah. Indeed, Rabin was assassinated *after sunset* of Shabbos Vayeira — after sunset of the very day when this passage was read in synagogues throughout the world. You will note that Hashem also specifies the **month** and **year** of Rabin's murder. Additionally, the assassin's **name** and **political affiliation** are spelled **backwards** —איל (black letters in white boxes) probably to indicate that Amir proceeded the **wrong way** in attempting to resolve two issues: the issue of Jewish rights to *all* the Land, as well as with regard to preventing the continued and escalating deterioration of Israeli security. Vigilantism or assassinations are *never* approved actions even when an elected leader is giving away parts of the country, even when that official is jeopardizing Jewish security. Murder of anyone is a heinous crime. There are many legal and effective practices that should *always* be initiated to remedy a situation — **murder is never one of them!!**

This is only one of six references to Rabin in this one small passage, but you'll agree that the point is already well-proven.

Getting back to our first four examples where the word תורה is encoded in the first and last two Books of Torah: the third Book, Vayikra, does not contain the word תורה encoded within the first sentences. Instead, the name of Hashem is encoded when every 8th letter is combined and then read as a word.

מ	ל	א	א	ר	ק	**י**	ו
י	ר	ב	ד	י	ו	**ה**	ש
מ	ו	י	ל	א	ה	**ו**	ה
ל	ד	ע	ו	מ	ל	**ה**	א

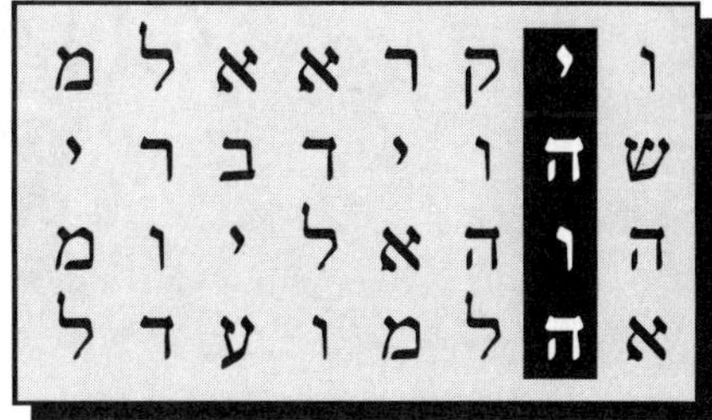

These five Codes are presented visually because, as Oral-Torah emphasizes, the wicks of the Menorah were all directed towards the central wick[17].

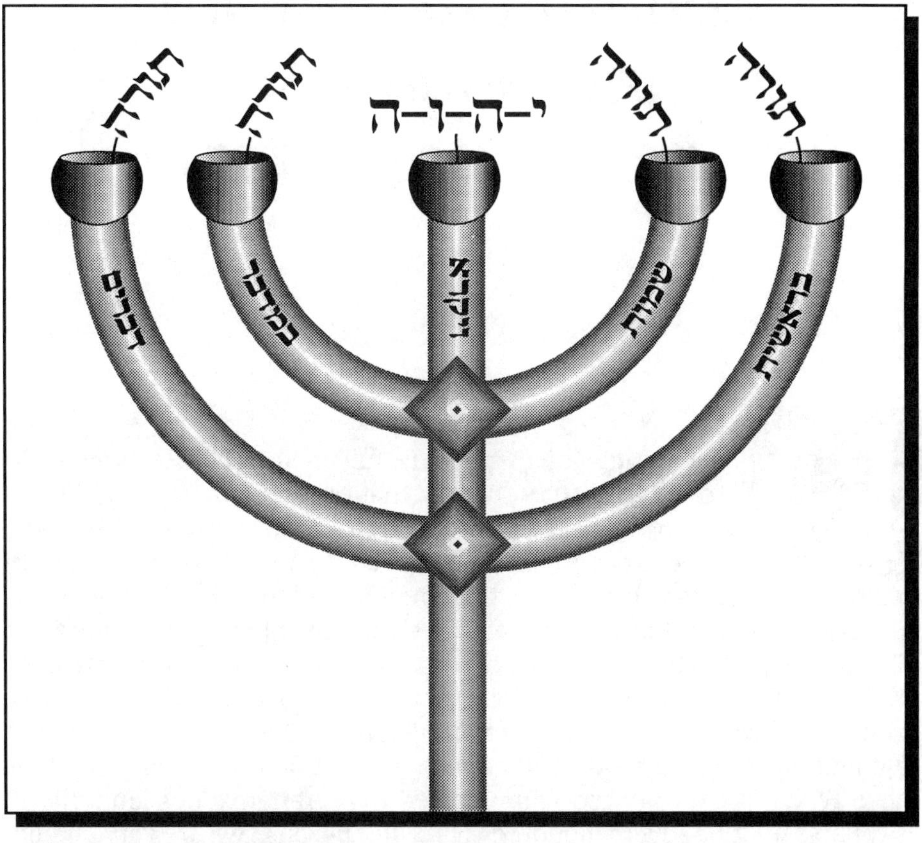

Hashem is truly the source of all light. Nay, Hashem is the source of all life and guides the lives of peoples and nations. Indeed, Hashem wrote the Torah and encoded messages therein.

17. Sifri 60; Talmud M'nachos 29a. This concept would also suggest why, in our earlier examples, the Coded "Torah" in the last two Books are spelled backwards.

CHAPTER
IV

History is a Cycle:
Confrontations with Individuals & Their Descendants

id you ever stop to grasp the full impact of the statement: — "מעשה אבות סימן לבנים," that our forefathers' experiences are prototypes and we, too, as a nation, will share those very same experiences?[1] Most of us do not realize the validity of this axiom of Jewish History; we have never explored the depths of this important concept because we often restrict our thinking in this area to Biblical times. It is true that many of the applications of this axiom are from the Biblical period, but this is only done because everyone is familiar with these events. For example, if Avraham went down to Egypt and then suffered discrimination or had his property stolen — most of us can easily see how these types of experiences were shared by Avraham's descendants in Egyptian servitude several hundred years later because we are very familiar with the facts. But this concept of prototypes transcends time and is not limited to the events of *Chumash*. This axiom of Jewish History, *ma'aseh avos,* means that these events are truly prototypes and that, by definition, these

---

1. Zohar III,149b; B'reishis Rabah 40; Midrash Tanchuma, Lech L'cha 9; and Ramban (B'reishis 12: 6-10). This concept is also mentioned in Koheles 1:9 — "מה שהיה הוא שיהיה"

events are replicated throughout the generations.[2] That is why the Rabbis who are quoted in the Oral-Torah, the *Tannaim,* always searched the weekly Torah readings for insight into local issues, as well as when preparing for international conferences.[3] And understandably, it has always been a very common practice for Rabbis to search the weekly Torah reading in order to gain a proper understanding of current events. But how many of us have been applying this principle to the events of the past 100 years, for example? After all, we, too, are the descendants of that very same Avraham who lived more than 3600 years ago. How many of us actually view an incident in the life of Avraham from the perspective that it might also apply to our times? We are accustomed to applying the prototypes of *Ma'aseh avos* to biblical times, but we ignore the wealth of learning that applies to the very special times of which we are fortunately a part. Getting back to "מעשה אבות סימן לבנים", prototypes, let's examine several aspects of the events recorded in B'reishis, Chapters 16 through 21.

After many years of childlessness, Avraham fathers a child through Hagar, his secondary wife. This child will be named **Yishmael**, we are told. Most people think that the child was so named because Hashem **had heard** the prayers of the pregnant Hagar when she was so despondent (as a result of her feelings of being mistreated). At that moment, Hashem promises her that she would have many, many descendants and that she would be the matriarch of all the Arabs. But there's much more to this because, as a phrase, **ישמע א-ל** is in the **future tense**. Indeed, Yishmael was so named not only because of an event from the past but, just as importantly, Yishmael was so named because of other events that would eventualy unfold in the course of Jewish History. Indeed, Yishmael was so named because of events of the future. There is a second aspect to his being so named because, in the period right before the arrival of Moshiach, **Hashem WILL HEED the prayers of the Jewish people** who will then cry out to Him, because Yishmael's

---

2.   This is why *TaNaCh* has many verbs written in the future tense. To make that verb also refer to a past occurrence, Hashem introduces a "ואו המהפך" as a prefix to the verb. For example,"יאמר" is in the future tense and is translated as 'He will say" while "ויאמר" has the root of the future tense but is rendered "He said" — in the past tense. In other words, an incident of the past is written with future verbs because the incident simultaneously refers to a future event as well as an event of the past. Many translators of *TaNaCh* did not understand this concept and rendered the word "ויאמר" as *And* he said". They confused this concept of "ו" with the "וְ" that has a *sh'va* underneath which is a conjunctive prefix. The former, the "ואו המהפך" does not mean 'and'. The "ואו המהפך" is how Hashem, through the future conversive, indicates that an incident of the future also occurred in the past — that the events of the past are prototypes for the future.

3.   B'reishis Rabah 78:15

descendants will then be acting upon the Jews in a threatening and cruel fashion — so predicts the Written-Torah as emphasized in Oral-Torah.[4] In other words, ישמעאל means literally that

"... שעתיד לשמוע הקב"ה באנקת העם ממה שעתידין בני ישמעאל לעשות בארץ באחרית הימים"

> *"Hashem **will** heed the prayers of the Jews who will be in terrible pain and anguish as a result of what B'nai Yishmael will do in the Land right before the Messianic Era."*

Not only had Hashem **heard** the mother's prayers **in the past**, but the boy was named ישמעאל because Hashem **will also heed** our prayers **in the future** when the Arabs will threaten the Jews of Israel.

Here we see how the clear awareness of just the tense of the word 'Yishmael' can make such a significant contribution to our understanding of an entire chapter in the Torah, as well as helping us see the Divine 'hand' in current events.[5] Now, because of this one *Chazal*, we realize that this entire chapter was also **a description of things to come — in our day**. After all, when else was there ever a situation where the lives of Israeli Jews were threatened by Yishmael or his descendants if not during this century?! For a clear understanding of current events, then, we must take a careful look at the events of B'reishis, Chapter 21.

> *"Hashem remembered Sarah as He had said ... and Sarah conceived and bore Avraham a son in his old age at the exact time of which G-d had spoken to him. Avraham called the name of his son that was born unto him ... Yitzchak. Avraham circumcised his son Yitzchak when he was eight days old, as G-d had commanded him, and the child grew and was weaned. Avraham made a great feast on the day that Yitzchak was weaned. [Several years later], Sarah saw the son of Hagar (i.e. Yishmael) ... acting criminally. [Therefore] she said unto Avraham: "Cast out this bondswoman and her son for the son of this bondswoman [is a distinct danger for Yitzchak and] he cannot be heir ... with Yitzchak. This matter was very grievous in Avraham's sight on account of his son [Yishmael]. And G-d said to Avraham: "Let it not be grievous in your sight because of the lad (i.e. Yishmael) ... in **all** that Sarah says to you, you must listen to her ... Avraham ... sent [Hagar] away [together with*

---

4.   Pirkei D'Rebbi Eliezer, end of Chapter 31

5.   "מי איכא מידי...דלא רמיזי באורייתא" — "Everything is alluded to in the Torah." (Talmud Ta'anis 9a)

*Yishmael] and she departed and strayed in the wilderness of B'er Sheva. The water in the jug was **spent** and she threw the child away under one of the shrubs. She went and sat down very far away ... and G-d opened her eyes and she saw a well of water and she went and filled the jug with water and gave the lad to drink. G-d was with the lad and he grew and he dwelt in the wilderness and trained others in shooting ... He dwelt in the wilderness of Paran and his mother took him a wife from the land of Egypt."*

At the time of this incident, Yishmael was thirteen years old. After many years of childlessness, Sarah finally becomes pregnant and gives birth to a son who is named Yitzchak. Several years after the birth of Yitzchak, Yishmael is involuntarily and permanently sent away by Sarah, although this is a politically unpopular position as is also evidenced by Avraham's reluctance to follow Sarah's wish. Sarah maintains:

"Because Yishmael is a dangerous threat[6] to my son Yitzchak, he cannot live in this Land together with Yitzchak or share in it."[7]

Hashem tells Avraham:

"[Sarah's position of deporting Yishmael probably sounds too radical to you, Avraham, but her solution is the only logical one at this time and under these circumstances because Yishmael is unwilling to conduct his life in a civil fashion.] Listen to your wife[8] because your blessed progeny will be found in the descendants of Yitzchak."

After being deported from the Land by Sarah and Avraham, Yishmael is then cast aside — **abandoned** by his mother and left with no visible means of survival or support. He is now **without food and water, without a home or land**, and just **languishing — neglected** by his guardian and **ignored** by all relatives and neighbors. So how does he survive? Despite the harsh indifference of his mother, this time Yishmael survives outside of the Land and develops into an independent entity while also training others in the use of weapons.[9] He becomes more independent and eventually forms an

---

6. Sh'mos Rabah 1:1 and B'reishis Rabah Chapter 53:11 — Yishmael was also attempting to kill Yitzchak in order to exercise — what would then be, with Yitzchak dead — an unchallenged claim to *all* of the Land. (Not much changes, it seems.)

7. Verses 9 and 10

8. As mentioned (Sh'mos Rabah 1:1), Sarah was a greater prophet than Avraham as noted by Hashem's advising him that "You, Avraham, must listen to *everything* that Sarah tells you." It's just because we read and learn so much about Avraham that we don't realize the greatness of Sarah.

9. See Reb Shimshon Raphael Hirsch, verse 20

alliance by marrying an Egyptian. Do you see the story unfolding in our generation — this time with their respective descendants, the Israeli Jews and the Israeli Arabs?!

But how does Yishmael survive in the undeveloped areas, far from civilization? It is interesting to note that when the Codes are utilized in the three verses which describe Yishmael's receiving sustenance and becoming independent, there are seven references to the U.N. (‎או"ם‎).[10] It should be noted

well that it is unusual to find even one reference — let alone seven identical references from Codes, and in only three sentences.

It is very interesting to note that the Arabs who **ran away** from Israel when the State was founded, these very same Arabs became dependent upon the good graces of the UN and were afforded the status of refugees even though

---

10. ‎אומות מאוחדות‎

44

they **willingly** ran away from the Land at the request of the Egyptians (whom they viewed as their **mother** and whom they listened to in 1948 when she told them to leave Israel because, by the Arabs' leaving Israel, it would then make it much easier for the very considerate **Mother-Egypt** to destroy all the Jews of Israel). No other Arab entities or Arab countries volunteered to support these so-called '**refugees**' while they **languished** in the undeveloped areas, far from civilization — **without food and water, home or land, and with no concerned guardian**. Who is the mother who could abandon a child! What kind of mother can abandon a child? Where else do we learn of a mother doing such a terrible thing?!

Here we see how the clarity of but one word can make such a significant contribution to our understanding of another entire chapter in *Chumash*. Now, because of this one *Chazal*, we realize that **this entire chapter, too, was also a portent of things to come — in our day**. After all, when would there be a situation where the lives of Jews would be more threatened by the criminal behavior of Yishmael or by his ugly and menacing descendants in the Land — if not in our day? Similarly, when else was there ever a time where Yishmael would leave the Land while Yitzchak remained — as Sarah demanded. This is the only other instance of Yishmael leaving the Land *en masse* at someone's request. This is also the only other instance when the criminal-Yishmael has actually been a real danger to Sarah's son, national-Yitzchak — when **both** are **living together** in the Land.

It becomes even more exciting when we examine verses 5 and 6. When the birth of Yitzchak is recorded, the Codes spell out בתש"ח.

Yitzchak will be born בתש"ח 'in [5]708' which is, of course, the equivalent for **1947/8** in the civil Calendar; it is the year when the UN declared its intention to create the State of Israel an independent country with all the 'benefits of membership' in this international body of nations. So, we also have the Torah alluding to the birth of a national-Yitzchak in the year 5708, in 1947 when the UN declared Israel an independent Jewish country.

In an attempt to revise history, Arabs have been referring to today's Israeli Arabs as Palestinians — and they, unfortunately, have been largely successful in perpetrating one of the biggest hoaxes in history. Most people are truly ignorant of the facts surrounding modern Mid-East history, and as uninformed people, they are beginning to believe that the Arabs really do have legitimate rights to the Land which at least rival those of the Jews, and perhaps even supersede the rights of the Jews to the Land. This approach has already been reinforced by the earlier actions of Peres and Rabin. It must be that the Arabs are correct, otherwise why would Peres and Rabin have offered to give them territory?! These are the thoughts of the majority of the world: "It must be that the Arabs really do have legitimate rights to the Land". Think about it for a moment. Suppose that a menacing stranger knocked on your door and claimed ownership of your legally deeded property. Suppose this menacing stranger claimed that you are living in his house. Would you

(a) invite him into your house and offer him a cup of coffee?

(b) offer him the use of a shed (instead of deeding him your house as he demands)?

(c) gladly offer him his own bedroom and allow him to share your living quarters?

(d) begin negotiating with him the extent of how much of your house you will give him?

(e) slam the door in his face and quickly summon the police?

Apparently, Peres and Rabin did not agree with your choice — I assume your response was (e) — and since most people in the world saw Rabin and Peres **giving away land**, it must be (so thinks the world) that Israelis agree with the Arabs that the Land legally belongs to the Arabs; otherwise, why would anyone negotiate with a stranger who has no legal basis for his claim?! We usually describe such a menacing stranger as an **extortionist**. Now several passages from Written and Oral-Torah become alive:

"ותהי האמת נעדרת ... כי אין משפט"

"[During our day] the truth will be hidden ... and there will be no real justice."[11] The masses of people who are untutored in Torah will not know

---

11. Yeshayahu 59:15. See also Talmud Sotah 49b

who is really telling the truth about ownership of the Land. Certainly, at this point in time, even were Israel to be victorious in another war — this military victory would not prove legal ownership. Now, only pure reasoning and logic will substantiate our claim to the Land. So it appears that the battle for Israel and Jerusalem will focus on **truth**, on the issues of true ownership. It becomes very meaningful now to see that Jerusalem is referred to as "עיר האמת", **The City of Truth**[12] — not only because the Torah teachings of Truth emanate from this great and unique metropolis and will continue to increase in geometric proportions, we pray — but also because the theme of our generation is: **In truth, to whom does this city really belong?** And who really owns **all** of Israel? It becomes even more exciting when we take note that Moshiach will have to **"fight with his mouth"**[13] because the battle for Israel's existence now has to be waged in the international arena in view of the entire world. Moshiach will, **with his mouth**, argue our case in order to prove to the entire world that **all the Land truly belongs to the Jews.**

As we become more and more familiar with the related sources, learning becomes more and more exciting. Look, today's Israeli Arabs insist on calling themselves Palestinians without realizing that this term is anglicized from the Hebrew פלשתים (which also gave rise to the anglicized term 'Philistines'). But as everyone knows, פלשתים comes from פלש which is the Hebrew word for *'an entity that invades, seizes, and expropriates with force (i.e. an armed robber)'*. I smile as I think of the *G'mora*[14] that states that we don't even bang a finger by accident unless it's Divinely decreed. The irony is that the Arabs could not have selected a more fitting description for themselves: **Today's Palestinians are indeed invaders, extortionists, and expropriators of a land that is not theirs.** The Arabs describe themselves perfectly when they call themselves Palestinians — **armed robbers**. But *Chazal* always knew that this name *P'lishtim* would be used again. It appears that all of the references to the *P'lishtim* of Biblical days could also refer to the *P'lishtim* of our day. (See page 61 for an example.) The Zohar[15] also states that the Written-Torah is referring to the modern day *P'lishtim* when it states that we'll have to fight a war when we return to Israel.

We pointed out a cute hint, through Codes, that the State of Israel (Yitzchak) was to be born in the year 5708 (from when the world was created). We will also see further that Arabs were given partial rights to the Land but only until

---

12. Zecharyah 8:3 — "Yerushalayim *will be described* as the city of truth"
13. Yeshayahu 11:4 — "...והכה...בשבט פיו."
14. Talmud Chulin 7b
15. On Bamidbar 10:9

World War I. It is an abuse and a violation of their original trust to now try and seize the Land. The truth is that their custodianship of Israel was temporary and those temporary rights have long expired. The truth is that the Land of Israel rightfully belongs to the Jews because Hashem repeatedly said so[16] and not because of a UN vote or a declaration by Balfour or any other person or country — no matter how well-meaning they were at the time of that declaration. Hashem's word is immutable; agreements between people or countries are often broken. The UN can give (in 1947) and the UN can just as easily take away (at some other point). Do you realize how close we are to losing the Land right now, Heaven forbid; did not the UN declare that Zionists are all racists! The UN Commission on Human Rights' Sub-committee on Prevention of Discrimination and Protection of Minorities, during one of their 1995 sessions in Geneva, reaffirmed that "The Israeli occupation of Palestinian and other Arab territories including Jerusalem constituted a gross violation of human rights". They also "reaffirmed the inalienable rights of the Palestinian people to return to their homeland". And what are the implications of such a position?! The handwriting on the wall is very clear to those who possess clear vision. After all, no other country in the world has ever been condemned by the United Nations as many times as little Israel. But as the Oral-Torah indicates[17]

"כיון ששמעו האומות שהקב"ה מגביה קרנן של ישראל ומכניסן לארץ התחילו מתרגזין".

"שלא מלכות אחד או שתי ממלכות באים עליו אלא מאה ועשרים מלכויות"

> *"When the nations see that Hashem is elevating the position and status of the Jews by bringing them into the Land — at that time, the nations of the world will begin to challenge the Jewish rights [to the Land].*

"ויזדווגון כלהון עממיא על ברתיה דיעקב לאדחייא לה מעלמא ועל ההוא זמנא כתיב ועת צרה היא ליעקב וממנה יושע."

> *"And all the nations will band together against the Jews to 'remove' them from [the Land and] the world. About this era it is written: 'It will be a time of trouble for the Jews and from that situation they will be rescued'."*

It is really true — agreements between peoples or nations can be abrogated, but Hashem's promises for good are always fulfilled![18]

---

16. In many, many places throughout *TaNaCh*; see also Rashi (B'reishis 1:1)
17. M'chilta B'shalach 9; Yalkut Shimoni on Yirmiyahu 31, section 315; Zohar ll, 479-481; Zohar l, 32a; ibid., 119a
18. See, for example, Talmud B'rachos 7a.

Talking about promises, who remembers when the United States had a special treaty with Taiwan (remember Formosa)? This treaty precluded American recognition of Mainland China while promoting special status to Taiwan, our eternal and forever ally. What happened to this agreement which was signed shortly after World War II? How long did this treaty last? Now, Mainland China is a powerful member of the United Nations and Taiwan has been ejected from this world body. Indeed, agreements between peoples can be broken at some point; only Hashem's promises are immutable!

Talking of promises — Avimelech, King of the *P'lishtim*, grants Avraham **full title to and citizenship in** a section of the Land[19] but then allows others to seize Avraham's territory in stages, taking one piece after another. Let's examine the text of B'reishis 21:22-34:

> *"And it came to pass at that time that Avimelech...spoke unto Avraham saying 'G-d is with you in all that you do. Now therefore swear unto me here by G-d that you will not deal falsely with me, nor with my children, nor with my grandchildren — but according to the kindness that I have done to you and to the land wherein you have sojourned [as a foreigner].' Avraham said: 'I will swear'. [Then] Avraham criticized Avimelech because of the [territories around a] well of water which Avimelech's followers had forcibly taken away. Avimelech said: 'I know not who did this nor did you ever mention this nor have I heard about this until now'... The two of them made a covenant...[and Avraham said: 'As a token of your agreeing,] take these seven sheep as proof that I have dug this well'. Therefore that place was called B'er Sheva because they both swore there... [After the others left] Avraham planted an orchard in B'er Sheva and had people refer to this location by the name of Hashem, the Master of the world. Avraham lived [undisturbed] in the land of the Philistines for a long time."*

Look, a citizen is experiencing the expropriation of his land and there is no public outcry at this injustice. After a parcel of land had been so expropriated by the *P'lishtim*, Avimelech attempts to justify the taking of the Land by the Palestinians (OOPS, I meant 'Philistines'), by denying that Avraham ever had legitimate rights to the Land. Do you see what's happening?! **The same entity** that bestowed legal rights upon Avraham through an agreement, that very same entity now attempts to abrogate the contract and thus deny Avraham those selfsame rights that he was earlier granted by that identical entity. In fact, no longer does Avimelech consider Avraham a legal citizen.

---

19. B'reishis 20:15

Now, he refers to Avraham as an *immigrant* and *foreigner*[20] — but not as a citizen. No longer is Avraham a citizen of Israel; he is now described as an **illegal settler**[21] — thus essentially denied all legitimate rights to even the Land still remaining in his possession. (This seems to say: once one allows another to take away some land, then ownership of the entire parcel is brought into question.)[22] Finally, after being non-assertive and ignoring the criminal act of land seizure and after having suffered in silence, Avraham [with proof in hand] becomes assertive and publicly declares the true facts:

> *'You have reneged on the Partition Plan and you have allowed your subjects to take away the very land that I was earlier granted.'*

When so confronted, of course, Avimelech initially claims ignorance of all the alleged events, but is quick to state:

> *'Until now, until you explained your position so clearly and so forcefully, I never understood that Palestinian behavior was unjustified and without a legal and historical basis'.*

Avraham does not argue and completely ignores the issue of whether Avimelech was involved in this seizure of territory. Avraham sticks to the point — just the issue of land ownership. When Avimelech finally admits that the Palestinians acted illegally, Avraham demands: 'You, Avimelech, as a national leader, must promise to abide by the original Partition Plan when the Land was deeded to me legally and now, once-and-for-all, you must publicly declare the truth that "THIS LAND IS AVRAHAM'S LAND! No one is to even disturb him. Let him live peacefully on his land!"'

We know that Avimelech makes the requested declaration and that the Palestinians stop harassing Avraham. In turn, Avimelech receives an agreement that he and his progeny will be treated with concern and sensitivity by Avraham's descendants. The land is returned to Avraham and, with the issue of title to the Land resolved, Avraham returns to educating others and to developing the country without any further interference.[23]

Based on our recorded history, and as to be expected, **this treaty was broken badly by the Philistines** several years later in the time of Yitzchak[24]

---

20. בראשית 21:23 — this is what"גרת" means — in contradistinction to"שב" (ibid. 20:15) which means "to reside with equal rights" (i.e. a citizen).

21. It appears that nothing much changes — Jews in their legally deeded property are still being labeled as *settlers*.

22. See the earlier 'hypothetical question' about a stranger who knocks on your door claiming to own your house.

23. Verse 33. See also Talmud Sotah 10 and B'reishis Rabah 54:6

24. B'reishis 26:15-22

and when they massacred Israelites: right before the Exodus;[25] in the days of Shamgar, Yiftach, and Avdon; and, again, in the time of Shimshon[26] just a few generations later — an example of a treaty that others make and break with us. In contradistinction, I cannot remember even one instance where the nation of Jews abrogated a treaty or agreement with another group or nation![27]

The application to our day and Israel's current predicament is so obvious. That situation is an **exact replica** of the present Israel-PLO-Arab situation. We see the PLO stripping Jews of their land; we see Israelis allowing this to happen. Do the Jews own Israel? Weren't they granted the Land in this century through the Balfour Declaration? Weren't these rights reaffirmed by the League of Nations and then again by the UN in the Partition Plan of 1947? Yet, we now experience the horror and fear of having pieces of the Land ripped away from us.

We hear all the time: "But you cannot trust the PLO or the Arab countries". Even moderate Egypt, in the 1994 Casablanca Conference — even 'moderate' Egypt still does not include Israel on the maps of the Middle East — and this is a 'moderate' country that has had a so-called peace treaty with us for the past fifteen years. Furthermore, in practice war games, the Egyptian military still identifies the 'practice-enemy' as Israel. Jordan *did not* have a peace treaty with Israel for the same number of years that Egypt *did* have a peace treaty with Israel and Jordan *did not* make war on Israel during this period — nor has Syria nor any other Arab country. It must be that **the absence of war is definitely not contingent upon a 'peace' treaty**.

In a 1995 poll, the American Jewish Committee revealed that 71% of American Jews maintain that Arafat and the PLO cannot be "relied on to honor agreements and refrain from terrorism". Only 17% of polled Jews felt that the PLO are reliable. The same poll revealed that 37% of American Jews do not believe that the goal of the Arabs is the destruction of Israel. It must be that these 37% of Jews do not read the newspapers, because Arafat was requested twice to amend the PLO documents that call for the destruction of Israel, in both Oslo agreements, and both times he has stated publicly that he will never change the PLO Charter nor The Phased Plan documents, just as the Jews will never amend their Torah.[28]

---

25. Nearly the entire tribe of Ephrayim was murdered by these Philistines when the former left Egypt some thirty years before the actual Exodus. See l Div'ray Hayamim 7:20-21 and Talmud Sanhedrin 92b.

26. Shoftim 3:3-31, and also Chapters 10-16

27. Even with intentionally dishonest people. See Talmud Sanhedrin 91a and Y'rushalmi Shabbos 6.

28. Please review these PLO documents which are found in the Appendix.

What the murdering Arabs could not achieve in their three wars against us, they are now attaining **piecefully** (OOPS, I mean 'peacefully'). Should Jews negotiate with Arabs, in general? Oh, how we now so desperately need the services of a spokesman like Avraham to stand up and argue our case publicly so the rape of the Land will stop, once-and-for-all.

CHAPTER
V

Observance of Circumcision:
It Merits Control of the Land

here are several incredible passages[1] which state that we are entitled to the Land of Israel because of several national characteristics — and the one national attribute that is emphasized repeatedly is that of *bris milah* (religious circumcision). "בזכות דם ברית מילה אתם עתידין לגאל בסוף מלכות רביעית" What's really amazing is that the majority of Jews who went on *aliyah,* who moved to Israel from Russia and Europe during the early 1900's — the vast majority of these Jews were irreligious; Judaism just was not important to them. They did not observe anything. In fact, there was a very significant number who were actually haters of Judaism. They even despised observant Jews — those who observed the *mitzvot.* Many of the early communists and socialists of the country came from this group. This group, of course, did not accept the divinity of Torah nor did they observe the *mitzvot.* In fact, they ridiculed Judaism — as is a tenet of communism. Incredible as it may seem, for some unexplainable reason,[2] these anti-religious Jews maintained the practice of

---

1.   Pirkei D'Rebbi Eliezer 29. See also Zohar II, 32a; ibid., 124a; B'reishis Rabah, Chapter 16

2.   It is interesting to note that *milah* is the only positive *mitzvah* in today's world that carries with it a very severe punishment for those who refuse to be circumcised.

bris milah — which is a behavior that makes no sense whatsoever for one who is a non-believer of Torah and *mitzvot*. Why would such a communist or socialist want to "mutilate" his children with a barbaric ritual; after all, what other type of meaning could *bris milah* have for a person who is so anti-religious?! If a person does not accept the veracity of the Torah and its Divine origin, then it is totally incomprehensible that he would consciously elect to mutilate a child for absolutely no purpose whatsoever. Circumcision, from the perspective of the denier of Torah, must be cruel, primitive, and barbaric. Yet, virtually every single one of these people had their sons circumcised at eight days of age.

Indicating that we are entitled to the Land of Israel because we circumcise our children, this same Zohar continues by also stating that the B'nai Yishmael would be entitled to a modicum of control over the Land for a time because they, too, observe a procedure similar to *bris milah*. It is not a complete *bris milah*, however, because their procedure does not occur when the child is eight days old nor do they effect *priah* which is the removal of the thin membrane from under the foreskin. When Hashem told Avraham that he would father a son through Sarah, Avraham's prayerful response was **"לו ישמעאל יחיה לפניך"**.[3] When Hashem said that the very elderly Sarah was going to become pregnant, Avraham responded: 'It is not necessary to intercede with a miracle'. Avraham prayed: "If only [my already-born son] Yishmael would live [and inherit me — landwise, financially, and spiritually]".

The Zohar points out that Avraham did pray that Yishmael would inherit the Land and so, as a **Tzadik, Avraham's prayer had to be answered** in the affirmative.

ויהב להו חולקא לתתא בארעא קדישא בגין ההוא גזירו דבהון וזמינין בני ישמעאל למשלט בארעא קדישא כד איהי ריקניא מכלא זמנא סגי כמה דגזירו דלהון בריקניא בלא שלימו.

> *"Hashem will give them (i.e. the Arabs) control of the Holy Land because of their bris. And it will be that Arabs will lord over the Holy Land while it is barren [and not in its finished condition], just as their bris is barren and not completed."*[4]

But Hashem compromised: Yishmael would be entitled to manage the Land only in the **absence of its owner** and only **while the Land was desolate**. After a very long time, control would be transferred from the circumcised Arabs to the uncircumcised Esav (i.e. the Christians). Only then could control pass

---

3. B'reishis 17:18
4. Zohar ll, 32a

back to the legal and rightful owners, the Jews, who would then develop the Land and retain it **permanently**.[5] Avraham's prayer, that Yishmael should inherit the Land, was answered by Yishmael's controlling and ruling Israel for a very long time. In other words, for two reasons **Arabs were bestowed with the special privilege of protecting the Land while it was in its desolate condition** (and while the rightful owners were on a world-wide trip in the Diaspora for an extended period of time):

(a) Yishmael is partially circumcised because of Divine influence.

(b) Avraham's prayer (that Yishmael be his true heir) was partially heeded by Hashem.

It is important to remember that Yishmael's management of the Land of Israel is supported by his partial *bris* and by Avraham's prayer. As a result, the Zohar states, their control of the Land will be for a pre-determined amount of time, after which it will be transferred to Christians (who don't demand that their adherents circumcise their children). The Jews can only take back the Land from the British, uncircumcised Christians — but not directly from the partially circumcised Yishmaelites who were granted temporary custodian-ship as a reward for their maintaining a procedure similar to religious circumcision. And so it happened, as we will soon see.

It is even more amazing to note that right here, where the *bris* of Yishmael is discussed and where Avraham prays that Yishmael should succeed him and where Hashem states that Yitzchak's descendants will inherit the Land — this is the only place where Yerushalayim with a *yud* (ירושלים) is encoded in the Torah in equal intervals of less than 100 spaces. Here the spacing is 71 letters and, no doubt you are saying to yourself:

'Wow! 71, that's close to 70. **The number 71 is very close to 70 [nations of the world].'**

And you are probably correct. It appears that the Torah is hinting to us **that there will be a conflict between the 70 [nations] and the one (i.e. the Jews).** These '71' countries will vie for control over Jerusalem, too. To emphasize this point, that there is going to be a very serious conflict about control over Jerusalem between the Jews and the 70 nations — led by Yishmael who is supported by the nations of the world — Hashem encoded in the same chapter another Yerushalem (ירושלם — the more common spelling that is without the *yud*). It is just so unusual to have two Codes intersect each other

---

5. Amos 9:13-15 — ‏"הנה ימים באים...ושבתי את שבות עמי ישראל...ונטעתים על אדמתם
‏**ולא ינתשו עוד** מעל אדמתם אשר נתתי להם אמר ה' א-להיך"

in such a precise fashion — even sharing a letter. As we have noticed in Chapter 3, a repetitious Code in one passage is indicative of a serious and/ or grave situation.

א ש ר ת ש מ ר ו ב י נ י ו ב י נ י ב מ ו ב י נ ז ר ע ב א ח ר י ב ה
ל א ו ת ב ר י ת ב י נ י ו ב נ י כ מ ו ב נ ש מ נ ת י מ י מ ו
כ ל ב נ נ כ ר א ש ר ל א מ ז ר ע ך ה ו א ה מ ו ל י מ ו ל י ל י ד ב
ת ע ו ל ס ו ר ל ז כ ר א ש ר ל א י מ ו ל א ת ב ש ר ע ר ל ת ו ו נ
ו י א מ ר א ל ה י ס א ב ר ה ס ש ר י א ש ת ך ל א ת ק ר א א ת ש מ ה ש ר י
ל ד ן ו ב ה כ ת י ה ו ה י ת ה ל ג ו י ס מ ל כ י ע מ י ס מ מ נ ה י ה י ו
ו ה ל ב ן מ א ה ש נ ה י ו ל ד ו א ם ש ר ה ה ב ת ש ע י ס ש נ ה ת ל ד ו י
ל פ נ י ך ו י א מ ר א ל ה י ס א ב ל ש ר ה א ש ת ך י ל ד ת ל ד ב ן ו ק ר א
ר י ת ע ו ל ס ל ז ר ע ו א ח ר י ו ו ל י ש מ ע ש מ ע ת י ד ך ה נ ה ב ר כ
ד מ א ד ש נ י ס ע ש ר נ ש י א ס י ו ל ג ו א י ד ו נ ת ת י ו ל ג ד ו ל ו א
מ ו ע ד ה ז ה ב ש נ ה ה א ח ר ת ו י כ ל ל ר ב ר א ת ו י י ע ל א ל ה י ס ם
א ת כ ל י ל י ד ב י ת ו ו א ת כ ל מ ק נ ת כ ס פ ו כ ל ז כ ר ב א נ ש י ב
ס ה ז ה כ א ש ר ד ב ר א ת ו א ל ה י ס ו א ב ר ה ס ב ן ת ש ע י ס ו ת ש ע ש

Both codes share the same *Shin*; both entities will have to resolve the Jerusalem issue: who owns Jerusalem and Israel and can they be shared?! The fact that Yerushalayim is encoded twice in the section dealing with Yishmael's *bris milah* indicates the seriousness of the confrontation and how it will involve so many diverse countries — diverse except when it comes to ownership of Yerushalayim. When it comes to Yerushalayim, however, all the 70 nations of the world insist that Yerushalayim not belong to Jews, but that ownership of Yerushalayim revert to one of the recent custodians.

CHAPTER
VI

Don't Judge by Externals:
Nations Have Come in Peace Before

he theme of this *Galus* is very different from all other exiles. It is very interesting because when Hashem wants us to know about the different countries that will rule us, the prophet is shown a vision of four immense and terrifying beasts, each one different from the other.[1] The first is like a lion with eagle's wings, the second like a bear that acts not in accordance with its usual behavior, and the third is like a leopard with four wings on its back. As *TaNaCh* and Oral-Torah indicate, these first three beasts refer to the kingdoms of Babylonia, Persia, and Greece and their respective treatment of Jews. But it is the fourth beast that I would like to discuss with you because it is described as creating the most horrifying and cruel exile for the Jews. The presented image was different from all the other beasts because this fourth monster had ten horns and because it was the most horrific. Suddenly, as the Prophet Daniel is observing, a small horn springs up and uproots three of the already established horns. And then comes the big clue: in this newly erupted horn are

---

1. Daniel, Chapter 7

eyes like human eyes and a mouth which speaks great ideas. Who or what is Hashem describing here? A smart approach would be to search for ruling entities that look like human beings and speak of great ideas and a ruling power whose exterior facade hides a reservoir bursting forth with such tremendous power and aggression that it is capable of uprooting three previously established kingdoms.

You know, when one thinks of Rome *vis-a-vis* Jewish history, one recalls that they invaded Israel in the year 70 CE and proceeded to destroy the Temple and kill nearly two million Jews. What we fail to note is that the Romans were actually invited into Israel earlier by two Maccabean grandsons who did so in order to have Rome resolve the issue of which brother should be king of Israel. Historians claim that it was very nice of Rome to resolve a Jewish problem and help Jews make peace amongst themselves. However, it did not take long for Rome to be awakened from their slumber[2] and lash out at the Jews and eventually destroy the entire country and murder two million Jews and exile tens of thousands of the surviving Jews. Indeed the Romans were barbaric and very cruel to us. But what should be noted is their facade. They came to Israel in the spirit of friendship and helpfulness. They were invited into the Land to help resolve an internal problem. First impressions were certainly positive. But within a short time their true colors became obvious as they rampaged throughout the Land.

A power that controlled our destiny during the Middle Ages was the Catholic Church. This religion appeared very nice; they spoke so beautifully about loving people. As a matter of fact, they call themselves the 'Religion of Brotherly Love'. They appeared so thoughtful and caring of others. They cared so much that they wanted to save all non-believers from their religion's purgatory. But it didn't take long; throughout the Middle Ages they showed their true colors when the Catholics murdered nearly three million Jews[3] (besides the other 'non believers' whom they wished to save from damnation — as they saw it). So, in their eyes, it was morally correct to murder millions of human beings in the name of their 'religion'. They certainly spoke like fine, concerned human beings, but they acted like the most violent of animals — devouring and destroying everyone who didn't believe and practice exactly what they espoused.

---

2. Jews must never consult foreign powers — not even for advice, let alone to intervene. Such consulting is likened to bothering a sleeping dog. While the dog is sleeping, we're in no danger; once aroused from sleep the dog is likely to attack those very same people who bothered him by awakening him. (See B'reishis Rabah 75:3.)
3. See the specifics in "Foot of Pride" or "Europe and the Jews" by Malcolm X. Hayes

Russia was precisely the same. The early communists spoke so glowingly of equality for all — it was great. After such a long history of experiencing cruel anti-Semitism throughout the world, Jews were promised equality. What a hopeful sign. As a matter of fact, my brother has a *sefer* which was printed around 1922 and was "dedicated to the new Russia — a secure and safe home for Jews". Those first communists — they certainly looked like human beings, but they became a force of continuous oppression and cruelty and murder for seventy very long and bitter years.

The British, too, appeared as though they were going to administer Palestine in a benevolent fashion, in accordance with the Mandate of the League of Nations and its eventual successor, the United Nations. It looked good for the Jews of the Land; soon they would have their own country. But the sheer cruelty of the British is unforgivable. The litany of their dastardly acts is very well known by now:

* They restricted Jewish immigration to the Land while allowing massive and unconditional Arab immigration;
* They confiscated weapons from Jews and transferred them to Arabs;
* They assisted the Arabs in the murdering of Jews;
* They executed Jews for carrying weapons;
* They prevented Jews from entering the Land during the Nazi years;
* They sent escaping Jews back to the Nazis for scheduled murder.

The British certainly appeared respectable, but they were no different than the beasts of earlier days. In fact, they were the lowest of the low.

So, it seems that all the dominant countries during this current exile which began around the year 3830 (70 CE) — all these nations, all the ten horns of the fourth monster share at least one common factor: they, the dominant powers, treated the Jews in the same fashion. Although all these powers initially appeared very civilized — beneath the facade was an intensity of hate and murder, the horror of which was beyond the imagination and machinations of most evil people. The German Nazis were also members of the era of the fourth beast. This fourth beast had human eyes and spoke beautiful words of conciliation, love, and equality; this beast was also the ugliest, most terrifying, and most destructive of all the beasts. And so have the nations treated us, throughout this period of 1900 years of forced exile: initially, a warm invitation to settle in their country **soon** to be followed by barbaric cruelty and awesome destruction.

We have a tradition from the Vilna Gaon that Psalm 20 refers to the last seventy years of *Galus*. As a matter of fact, there are seventy words in that chapter for that very reason.   These were to be the harshest and most diffi-cult years, a time when the very survival of Jews and Judaism would be threatened with total destruction and extinction — the seventy years that would threaten to destroy us physically and spiritually. One of the themes of that chapter is that the cruel countries will *not* have to be defeated in battle.

"אלה ברכב ואלה בסוסים ואנחנו בשם ה' אלקינו נזכיר. המה כרעו ונפלו ואנחנו קמנו ונתעודד".

We are told that during these seventy years, these cruel powers will just fall and disintegrate all by themselves without the Jews even having to lift a finger to fight these 'host' countries in a war.

Who could have ever envisioned that the greatest source of fright for America would just disintegrate overnight?! That is exactly what happened to Russia, the cruel bear; overnight, it just fell apart. The Jews were severely oppressed in Russia for nearly seventy years and Torah was nearly forgotten — the reins on the Jews were very much like the treatment by the Egyptians more than 3300 years ago. And then like a miracle, after nearly thirty years of protests by Western Jews, the gates opened up and one million Russian Jews were able to leave the country — many to Israel. It is interesting to note that, when speaking to Avraham, Hashem says[4]

> *"I [protected you from life-threatening dangers when you were all alone and] took you out of Ur Kasdim and [brought you] and gave you this Land as a legal inheritance."*

Nothing is impossible for Hashem. Hashem can do anything. In this passage, which also speaks of the terrors[5] that would **eventually** befall the Jewish people and the exodus from those countries, we find *Russia* (רוסיה) spelled out in a backwards order in a coded fashion.

---

4. B'reishis 15:7

5. As evidenced also by the horrifying fright which overcame Avraham upon learning that such violent and massive massacres will eventually befall his children in the Diaspora. See B'reishis 15:12, Tanchuma Tazria 11, and B'reishis Rabah 44:15. See Chapter 3, above, for the names of other cruel nations that are also encoded in the very same passage.

It is spelled **backwards** because that exodus from Russia will occur at the **back-end of Galus**. We will see many times, that whenever Hashem is referring to the period of time called *B'achris ha'yamim* (באחרית הימים), at the **end** of the Exile, the Codes are often written *backwards*[6] when the Torah is referring to those events that are to occur at the *back-end* of the Diaspora.

Who can ever forget how the British boasted that "The sun never sets on the British Empire" because prior to World War II, the British Empire extended into every time-zone in the world. But after their total cruelty directed against the Jews of Israel, the British also received part of what was due them: **they lost their entire world-wide empire — all without a war**. But that is exactly what Hashem said to Daniel (7:12): **"העדיו שלטנהון"**— **"Their dominion will be taken away."** And that is exactly what the above-quoted selection from Psalm 20 emphasizes:

> *"They will fall [by themselves] while we will stand up and become independent."*

Today, B'nai Yishmael appear to the world as downtrodden human beings and as 'refugees' — without a home, without a land. These 'unfortunate' people only beg for one thing: all they want are equal rights, rights to a land that they claim was once theirs and that was stolen away by some Jewish foreigners. It sounds so tear-jerking; who could be so heartless as to deny such a pitiful people their home and land; they sound so believable and truthful. Who could not but feel their pain? They have the eyes of a human and they speak so well; they explain their position so logically. As a matter of fact, they have even persuaded most of the nations of the world to support their cause for ownership of what has always been acclaimed as Jewish land — until this generation. Yet, underneath their human facade is an intensely monstrous beast which is lurking, just awaiting a successful first-opportunity to destroy all the Jews and make Jerusalem the capital of their own country which they have already announced as Palestine — may Hashem prevent these events from befalling us.

Contrary to the terms of *both* Oslo agreements, the PLO Charter has never been changed. The PLO Charter with its 1974 amendments calls for:

❖ NEGOTIATING for as much territory as possible from the Israelis and then, as the second step:

❖ To use this newly acquired territory to launch an INVASION into Israel in order to murder all the Jews and expropriate and seize the entire Land.[7]

---

6. The names 'Nazis' and 'Peres' are similarly spelled backwards when in coded form.
7. See Appendix for excerpts from this infamous document.

Arafat has already stated his position publicly; **HE WILL NEVER CHANGE THE PLO DOCUMENTS JUST AS THE JEWS WILL NEVER AMEND THEIR TORAH.**

Hamas wants to destroy Israel in **one step;** they are called extremists. The PLO want to accomplish this destruction in **two steps.** Is this why the world describes them as **moderates?!** But certainly, they have a nice appearance; they speak with tears; they evoke pity from the world. The nations ignore Arafat's open threats to destroy the Jewish People and take control of all of Israel. The world (and many Jews) believe that the PLO are nice people who have been 'mistreated by the bad Jews'. But underneath the facade is a barbarism and cruelty that rivals the Romans, the Church of the Middle Ages, the Spaniards, the British, the old Russia, and the Nazis — all combined!

The PLO have certainly revised Middle East history through the oft repeated Big Lie. The Arabs have already persuaded the world into believing that Arabs have legitimate rights to the Land. And the world has affirmed these 'new facts' as truths. These Arab arguments and accusations have to be refuted in an expert fashion because the entire world is paying very careful attention now. That's why Hashem describes Moshiach as "‏והכה...בשבט פיו‏" — **"fighting with his mouth".**[8] Moshiach has the gift for acting in an equitable and just fashion. Moshiach possesses the skills of a successful debater, and the entire world needs to recognize the Arab distortions and be alerted to the evil that is being covertly planned against the Jews of Israel, Heaven forbid — and the entire world at-large. The entire world needs to hear all the real facts; a brilliant spokesman is needed in order to dissuade the populace from accepting distorted and falsified 'facts'.

The last horn of the fourth and most monstrous of the dangerous beasts is the horn that erupted from out of nowhere. This horn is the last hostile component of our final *Galus*, the *Galus* of Edom — the exile that began with Rome in 70 CE and continues uninterruptedly for all these centuries. This exile which was brought into existence by Rome has a final period that is a little different in appearance from all the preceding periods in the specifics of how Jews are to be oppressed. This last horn, the final segment of the Roman exile will have a human-like appearance. After all, B'nai Yishmael do not appear to be as beastly as their predecessors. Yishmael has human eyes and a mouth; it has strict standards of morality, is monotheistic and not pagan, and speaks alot about Allah. They also, now, talk a great deal about living in peace. What could be better? Who could envision a better host-coun-

---

8.　Yeshayahu 11:4

try or a better neighbor? As a matter of fact, they really do appear human. So much so that they are described in *TaNaCh* in human terms:

> *"If not for Hashem who was with us when an* **"אדם"** *arose against us, we would have been consumed by their rage."*[9]

Since **"אדם"** means 'human being', what enemy could be described as being a human being, a term we reserve for only nice people? It must be that they only present themselves as human beings, because two sentences later we are told:

> **"אזי המים שטפונו"** — *[Even though they look so human in appearance] this is an enemy who is THREATENING TO DROWN US in the sea.*

It is not coincidental that the motto and rallying cry of the present-day Arabs is exactly that same threat that is predicted in T'hilim, namely — **"to throw the Jews into the sea"**!! This all fits together even better when we note that the Torah[10] also refers to Yishmael as **אדם** [פרא], as a person. But, the Torah states, he also possesses a second nature, *perra:* an **uncontrollable** [aggressive] drive to hurt others as the Torah continues: **"ידו בכל"** Is it coincidental that the threat they present is not obvious to about 25% of the Israelis and to most of the world?[11] They certainly do look like an **אדם**, like people with peaceful intentions. But underneath this human facade is an uncontrollable rage that is intensely murderous — *Hashem Y'rachem,* may Hashem protect us!

All the preceding governments were easily and immediately identified as beasts, murderers and pagans. Today's Yishmael is called **אדם**, because, to many people at present, they do not appear destructive on a quantitative level. Arabs do not appear dangerous at all — as a matter of fact, it is very popular these days to refer to most Arabs as "moderates". For almost 1300 years and until this century, the Arabs were indeed less barbaric than the other 'host' countries for Jews. Come to think about it, almost any government would be an improvement over the unmerciful behavior of the vile Church of the Middle Ages. Certainly, the Arabs did discriminate; they were indeed hostile towards the Jews during their rule over us, but there were very few murders

---

9.   T'hilim 124:2

10. B'reishis 16:12

11. It is obvious that what is presently transpiring in Israel is bereft of logic. The very same situation that Zionists and Torah Jews view as a *threat* to national security is seen by many non-Torah Jews as *vital* to Israel's security. It should also be noted that the pre-war German Jewish community could not see what was about to happen to them nor could most of the non-Torah community of those days see the handwriting on the wall. There's no question about it — Hashem is planning something extra-ordinary and spectacular!

and pogroms in the 1300 years of their control of the Land.[12] The Arabs differ from all the other custodians of the Land in this manner:

❖ The cruelty of all our host countries was apparent very soon after they assumed control of the Jews.

❖ The intensity of Arab hatred has not yet become apparent to the world and this is after 1300 years, in addition to three recent wars within a period of only 26 years. Despite Arafat's many open threats to destroy all Jews and take control of all Israel, this view persists.

So, indeed, the most difficult *Galus* will be with an אדם who will try "to throw us into the sea". It will be the most difficult period of this *Galus* because:

(a) We will have to contend with a world who sees Yishmael as an אדם who is so downtrodden and whose lot is so pitiful.

(b) We will have to expose his monstrous plans to destroy the Jews and prove that his civil announcements in the West to co-exist peacefully with the Jews in the Land contradict his calls in the Arabic media for the murder of all Jews in a *jihad*.

(c) We will have to disprove his alleged claims to the Land while concurrently demonstrating the legal rights of Jews to this land.

This project is a formidable one and probably the most difficult that we have ever faced. This is not a confrontation over a piece of candy. This era will be so depressing that most of us will feel totally impotent to act against the dictates of an entire world. We won't even be able to determine the appropriate steps to take,[13] or envision how this life-threatening saga could possibly end with the Land safely and securely in the hands of Jews.

In Bethlehem, two weeks before the end of 1995, Arafat announced: **"First we will kill the Saturday people, then we will kill the Sunday people."**[14]

"אני שלום וכי אדבר המה למלחמה"

"Even though we, Jews, really want peace, when we do speak of our aspirations, the Arabs speak of war and prepare for it."[15]

This is such a serious battle and it cannot be fought on the battlefield. To resolve issues of ideology and legalities will require the services of an out-

---

12. Yes, one life is as important as one million lives; but we're merely describing the extent of a devastation on a *quantitative* level — not necessarily the way Torah Jews usually evaluate a situation, but it is certainly descriptive of the extent of the destruction.

13. Compare Talmud Sotah 49b

14. The umbrella group for Israeli Christians begged their co-religionists to boycott Bethlehem during their holiday, because they do believe all his pronouncements.

15. T'hilim 120:7.

standing spokesman and an articulate debater who is, more importantly, a brilliant Torah scholar. It is such a serious battle; we will need the help of someone very special, who with his mouth and language, will dazzle the entire world with his cogent arguments.[16]

---

16. Yeshayahu 11:4

CHAPTER
VII

Arabs Will Control the Land:
How Long?

he first few times that we understand various prophecies of Written or Oral- Torah — when we see where the prophecies are fulfilled, we are speechless. But the prophecies become clear to us because we are looking back into recent events,[1] and have the advantage of hindsight. But we shouldn't be amazed at all. After all, *TaNaCh* and Oral-Torah with its accompanying illuminations, clarifications,

---

1. As M'tzudos David indicates (Daniel 8:14): In the area of prophecy, we understand a particular prophecy and we possess insight only when we look into the events of the recent past; most of us would be unable to properly analyze a prophecy that has not yet unfolded — sometimes because of terms that society has still not invented. For example, when Targum Yonasan explains that Chapter 28 of Yeshayahu is referring prophetically to a time when *"m'chablim"* would be negotiating a false peace with Israel, it would not mean anything much until we realize that this term was just 'invented' in modern Hebrew 40 years ago to describe *fedayeen* murderers, now known as PLO. The Codes that refer to the UN by name — this would mean nothing to a person living in 1925, way before the emergence of the UN. Doesn't **"כעב תעופינה"** (Yeshayahu 60:4-9) — that Hashem will return us to the Land by moving us quickly like clouds — take on a special meaning now that we have air travel? Also, the passage referring to Jews traveling in from very distant countries to pray on Rosh Chodesh in Jerusalem and then still being able to return home that very same day before sunset — this prophecy could not be understood by the average person before the advent of airplanes (see P'sikta Rabsi, page 11 of section on Shabbos and Rosh Chodesh).

paraphrasings, and underscorings (which are known as *Chazal*)— all this is Torah and it is given to us by Hashem and Hashem, being omniscient, has foreknowledge of every event. So why should it be mind boggling that Hashem knows everything? More than seventy times a year we declare in public that not even one iota from all the Biblical prophecies will be lacking, that every single detail will be fulfilled and realized. Actually, we truly become excited because we are learning something new and when we understand it we realize that we have secrets that the rest of the world lacks and are privy to information that unfortunately most Jews are unaware of. After understanding a passage of Oral-Torah or a passage or two in *TaNaCh* — the real excitement comes about because we also realize on a sub-conscious level how proud we are to be Jews who appreciate and love to learn and because these powerful experiences motivate us to learn more each day. These experiences are intellectual and emotional as well as the fulfillment of the *mitzvah* of learning Torah — a sense of real accomplishment. And maybe, at the same time, we feel very disappointed that many of our co-religionists are unable to share and/or appreciate our excitement.

Keeping in mind that all of Torah is Divine, it is expected and it is axiomatic that every prophecy will be accurate and fulfilled to the last detail. Knowing this, we still find it amazing when we first understand a prophecy whose meaning escapes most people. Oftentimes, it's only because people are not expending enough effort in learning. They are reading instead of studying. *"Mir daf harevin"*. We can't just *read* Torah on a superficial level. We must perservere; we must study and expend effort in this direction. And, in our situation, we must also be alive in this special Epoch when we can review the events of the recent past and the special circumstances behind these monumental occurrences.

In other words, study combined with the experiences of having lived through the prophecized events that are described in a coded and mystical fashion enable us to understand what previous generations could not. And that's why *Chazal* say[2]

וכד יהא קריב ליומי משיחא אפילו רביי דעלמא זמינין לאשכחא טמירין דחכמתא ולמנדע ביה קצין וחושבנין. ובההוא זמנא אתגליא לכלא

> *"In the period before Moshiach, [all people,] even children will have the ability to understand many mysteries whose explanations eluded even the vast majority of yesteryear's Torah-studying adults and they will also be able to know with certainty exactly when Moshiach will arrive. In that time, everything will be revealed to them."*

---

2. Zohar I, page 118a

By way of example, this will become clear. Hashem tells Daniel[3] that the last horn of the fourth beastly ruler over Jews — the last ruling entity in our final *Galus* will be, potentially, the most dangerous of all the rulers of the Land. Hashem says[4] that these last rulers of the Land will have dominion over the Land for "עד עדן ועדנין ופלג עדן"

> *"one [constant[5] in the measurement of] time,*
> *two [constants in the measurement of] time, and*
> *half a [constant in the measurement of] time".*

In other words, the last custodial rulers will have jurisdiction in the Land until the completion of a span of **3 ½ constants of time-measurement.** What measurement of time is referred to in this section? It can't be seconds and it can't be minutes because both these measurements are not utilized in *TaNaCh* as precise units. This section is obviously referring to a precise Biblical unit of time which is also very common.

All students of Torah realize that the most common measurement of time in *TaNaCh* is the **year.** Even the word עדן is related to "year" (B'reishis 18:14). And so there must be a constant in this measurement that Hashem is referring to. The only common 'constant' which is precise and never changes, the only constant that I'm aware of: there are **365 ¼** days in the solar year.[6]

To be more precise, in a solar year there are **365 days, 5 hours, 48 minutes, and 46 seconds.** It must be that Hashem is referring to **3 ½ times the 'constant' of 365.24** [days in a year]. Well, 3.5 x 365.24 = 1278 ⅓.[7] This means that the domination by the Land's final non-Jewish custodian will **span over a period of 1278⅓ years** from when they **begin** their care of the Land **for the first time** (up until their rule is completed). This means that the custodial care will end precisely 1278 ⅓ years after domination begins for the first time. So, now, all we have to do is determine when this 1278 ⅓ year span begins and then we will know when it ends.

We demonstrated earlier in Chapter 5 that B'nai Yishmael had been given temporary custodial care of the Land after the Roman destruction and only

---

3.   Daniel 7; ibid 8:1-10

4.   ibid 7:25

5.   The specific term "constant" is a mathematical term which refers to a specific number that is unchanging. For example, in the phrase "2y = 6", the numbers '2' and '6' are both described as 'constants' because they remain fixed and *unchanging.*

6.   The solar year is really the basis for our Jewish calendar; after all, Pesach must occur during the spring time, a solar phenomenon. So, the solar year is really the basis for our intercalating, for making leap years according to a 19 year schedule. Besides which, the lunar calendar is not constant at all since there are 6 different lengths to our lunar calendar ranging from 353-385 days, depending on how many months have 30 days and as to whether we're in a leap year or not.

7.   Actually, it's 1278.34 years, but for our purposes, we've rounded it to one-third.

while it was in its desolate condition. In the previous chapter, we saw that the last horn of the fourth beast refers to Arabs. So, when did Yishmael begin 'caring' for the Land and when did their custodianship end for the last time? Omar, the successor to Mohammed, conquered Jerusalem in 4398 (638 CE). Hashem says that Arab control of the Land will end 1278⅓ years after it first begins [in the year 4398]. So the calculations would look like this:

> 4398   *marks the first time that Arabs gained control of the Land*
> +1278⅓   *years later, control will finally be wrested from the Arabs*
> 5676⅓   *marks that moment when Arabs lose control of the Land.*

Hashem says that the period of **Arab domination will end after 5676** (i.e. during the first third of 5677) which is 1278⅓ years after the first time that the Arabs gained control of the Land. Hashem says that the Arabs will be the custodians of the Land over a span of 1278⅓ years starting from the very first time that they conquer Israel.

And so it happened. The Land remained in the hands of various Moslem entities until the British and French took it away from the Ottoman Empire under the military leadership of Lord Allenby during World War I. The Land was under the control of the Moslems for a period spanning 1278⅓ years, except for a brief cosmic moment when the Crusaders temporarily gained the upper hand during a short tug-of-war. Except for this momentary lapse, the Moslems were the sole custodians of the desolate Land for a period that spanned 1278⅓ years — *exactly*, from start to finish. After conquering Gaza in November, Lord Allenby captured Jerusalem from the Moslems on December 9, 1917 — all during the first third of the year 5677. **With the routing of the Ottoman Turks, the prolonged Arab domination over Israel ended — exactly 1278⅓ years after it first began.**

It is so amazing to see; we are fortunate to live in a period of time when we can understand a passage in *TaNaCh* that could not be understood by most adults from yesteryear but that is so easily understood today by ordinary people like you and me — with just a little effort.

What do I hope to accomplish by sharing this information with you? Certainly, we just learned a little bit of Torah and we understand it and feel great. But, the secondary benefit which is almost as important is knowing where we are; at what point in Jewish History do we find ourselves. Truly, the most important secondary benefit is knowing that **we are not floundering** in the middle of an ocean, on a ship without a captain. We have not been abandoned! **We should not be anxious or despondent or frightened by world events.** After all, when we travel in the cabin of the ship, we can't possibly see the captain steering the boat. We don't even know where his office is or where the helm is. Most of us have never even seen him at work.

How do we know that there's a captain aboard? Well, we have clues that there's a navigator aboard because of the pre-printed itinerary; our ship docks at every port **exactly as scheduled and printed.** We, too, have not been abandoned! We know that Hashem is intervening in history because everything He said that's recorded, **everything** is happening to us **exactly the way He stated it** and exactly as scheduled and printed. And Hashem also tells us that the **world will soon evolve into a really nice place.** So why should we worry?! **We have not been abandoned!!** We may not under-stand the purpose of all events. But we do see that they were predicted and that every prophecy is being fulfilled — down to the very last detail.

We are not finished yet, not by a long-shot. Hashem also tells Daniel[8] how long the physical *Galus* will last and for how long the Jews will be without their own place of refuge. But before we discuss this issue, we first must define certain concepts that are used by many people, some in an imprecise or in-correct fashion.

---

8.   Chapter 8

CHAPTER VIII

The Two Stages of *Galus*

There are two aspects to every *Galus* (exile from Israel) and it makes sense, because why else would there be a *Galus* if not for the fact that we, as a people, have serious shortcomings. So, the estrangement aspect of *Galus* is **"...ומפני חטאינו גלינו"** — that of a *spiritual Galus.* The entire reason for our exile is that we have not acted in the manner befitting a Kingdom of *Kohanim* and an exclusive and unique[1] people. The entire purpose for possessing the Land is that it allows us the freedom to be unhindered in our quest to lead the qualitatively unique life of a Jew. If we are not interested in acting according to Torah principles, then we can live anywhere but we don't require a special Land.[2]   If we do

---

1. We are not translating **"קדש"** as 'holy' which is too abstract; besides which *"kadosh"* does mean 'exclusive' and 'unique' as in **"הרי את מקודשת לי"** — where the unique relationship between husband and wife excludes other men.

2. This concept is found in many places in *TaNaCh* including Vayikra 26 and D'varim 28. T'hilim 105: 44-45 captures the spirit very succinctly — **ויתן להם ארצות גוים ועמל לאמים יירשו בעבור ישמרו חקיו ותורתיו ינצרו,** "Hashem gave the Jews the Land ... in order for them to observe His statutes and keep His Torah."

not perform in accordance with Torah doctrine — if we are estranged, then we do not deserve the Land either. This is the spiritual component of *Galus.* Hence, our exile from the Land.

The physical aspect is more readily observable; those Jews who do not live in the Land are still in *physical Galus* while those Jews who have returned to the Land are no longer in *physical Galus.* This form of *Galus* is most easily recognizable.

The problem is that some orthodox people confuse the issues. While it is true that the majority of Jews, unfortunately, do not observe all 613 *mitzvot,* this has little to do with the fact that there does exist a physical Land which offers unlimited Jewish opportunities for Jews who desire to be observant and which offers all Jews a place of **refuge**. The mere existence of the physical Land of Israel in Jewish hands bespeaks the end of physical *Galus* and points to the first step of the redemption process — physical independence in the Land of Israel.

Hashem never said that both forms of *Galus* have to end together at the same exact moment — they certainly do not even begin in the same instant. Isn't it true that **first** the Jews acted inappropriately and then some time later, they were exiled from the Land; this phenomenon has occurred twice. The prophets talk about this aspect throughout *TaNaCh.*

Isn't it also true that there were two forms of *Galus* in Egypt which were cast-off at two different points in time?! The **geographical Galus ended** the moment the Jews left Egypt. The estrangement, the ***spiritual Galus* ended** in a very slow and deliberate fashion as the Jews moved from the lowest point, the 49th level of *tum'ah* (corruption and impurity) until they were able to **receive the Torah and become observant** some **seven weeks later.** But both *Galuyot* did not end at the same moment. Both ended in a serial fashion — first the physical *Galus* and later the spiritual.

Similarly, it is obvious from many passages in Torah and *Chazal*[3] that in our scenario, we are to experience the physical redemption before the spiri-

---

3. This is in the "בעתה" mode in contradistinction to the "אחישנה". See Talmud Sanhedrin 97, wherein is discussed two different possible scenarios of how Moshiach will arrive:

    a) in the *designated* time **("בעתה")** which is the natural way, where one event follows the other in a natural and developmental fashion and without stupendous miracles (e.g. establishment of the State of Israel through international permission).

    b) *sooner* than the designated time **("אחישנה")** which is with stupendous miracles and when overwhelming numbers of Jews are observant (e.g. the creation of a Temple with absolutely no human effort and through stupendous Divine intervention).

tual. First we will arrive in the Land and develop it, and then will come the spiritual rebirth in a rather natural fashion. A few quotes should suffice to prove the point.[4]

> *"I will take you from the midst of the nations of the world, I will gather you from all the lands, and I will bring you to your land ... THEN you will become virtuous. I will [then] give you a new heart ... and I will arrange it so you will follow the laws and observe the regulations."*

> *"Though you were waste and desolate, a land in ruin, now you shall be too small for your inhabitants ... Your children ... shall yet say 'The place is too confining. Move over for me so that I may settle here' ... Thus Hashem says, 'Behold I will raise My hand to the nations ... and THEY shall bring your sons in their arms and your daughters on their shoulders [to Israel] ... AFTERWARDS ... you will know that I am Hashem (i.e. that you will be observant) and my followers will never be disappointed."*

As a sampling, these two passages point to the fact that complete redemption is a two-stage process. This process whereby redemption evolves in a natural fashion is the very scenario which is emphasized throughout the Oral-Torah.[5]

❖ **First the Jews will return to the Land** (i.e. geographical *Galus* ends).

❖ **Afterwards, they will become observant** (i.e. spiritual *Galus* ends).

It is not that the present series of Israeli governments are the ultimate and best governments for Jews. No sane person can maintain such a position. No educated and observant Torah-person would ever attach such meaning to the political entity that currently governs the State of Israel. But even without a proper spiritually-based state, the **Land does exist** and it affords Jews a **physical freedom** which surpasses that which Jews experience in all the various lands of their dispersion. More important, as it is stated:[6]

אם ה' לא יבנה בית שוא עמלו בוניו בו

> *"If Hashem wouldn't want the Land to be rebuilt, then all human efforts would be in vain."*

In other words, the only reason that a place of refuge exists is because Hashem endorses our efforts to create that physical entity called "The State of Israel."

---

4. Yechezkel 36:24-27 and Yeshayahu 49:19-23

5. As a sampling — Talmud Sanhedrin 97-98; Talmud Y'rushalmi B'rachos 1:5; Midrash T'hilim 18:36; Zohar Vayishlach

6. T'hilim 127:1

If Hashem would not want such a country, it would not exist — no matter our efforts. Jews tried to rebuild the Land for thousands of years; in the past, **all their efforts were futile.** The Land remained barren and desolate until this century. Hashem supports our initial efforts. But we must strive to work and pray for a Torah-governing entity. More has to be done — not only to solve some of the physical issues, but also to develop a country that is based on Jewish principles, on a Torah way of life. We pray for this day; we have to also work and do our share — and not just sit back and complain.

CHAPTER
IX

The Arabs' Infamous Legacy in the Land

id you know that there is not even one Jew who lives in Jordan. It is against the law for a Jew to live there. As a matter of law, selling property to a Jew is a capital crime. Death for a person who sells real estate to a Jew? Jordan is a moderate Arab country, and these laws exist today — after their 1995 'peace' treaty with Israel.

I remember that shortly after the Six Day War in 1967, I had purchased a book that was printed in Israel. It showed pictures of the terrible destruction the Jordanians had perpetrated in the Land that they conquered in the 1948 War of Independence. It was an awfully depressing book. The Jordanians built roads on top of graves; they took monuments from our cemeteries and built urinals and sidewalks with them. They took synagogues and converted them into barns. Other synagogues, like the Churva Synagogue, they destroyed. Hundreds of synagogues and yeshivot were similarly destroyed. It beats me as to how any Israeli government would trust Jordan — how any Jewish government could ever think about appointing Jordan as a custodian of holy sites in Jerusalem. But this is exactly what Peres and Rabin have accomplished with their 1995 treaty with Jordan. That book was so depressing that I have not been able to read it more than once, when I quickly glanced at it. Now that I'm writing this *sefer*, I began searching for it. It's gone. It's gone and I do not really miss it. To look at the pictures at this time would be so devastating. Yet, I wanted to share with you, my dear reader, the extent of this intensive hatred that "moderate" Arabs harbor for Jews. That book showed it all. But, you know something — that is exactly what was supposed to happen, as it says: "Half the City of Jerusalem will be exiled".[1]

Chazal[2] explain that the descendants of Yishmael will cause certain very specific things to happen in the Land of Israel during the time of their control and they will be associated with these fifteen mostly-infamous 'events':[3]

רבי ישמעאל אומר, חמשה עשר דברים עתידין בני ישמעאל לעשות בארץ באחרית הימים. ואלו הן, ימדדו את הארץ בחבלים, ויעשו בית-הקברות למרבץ צאן אשפתות; וימדדו בהם ומהם על ראשי ההרים, וירבה השקר, ותגש האמת, וירחק חק מישראל, וירבו עוונות בישראל, שני תולעת כצמר, ויקמל הניר והקלמוס, ויפסל סלע מלכות, ויבנו את הערים החרבות, ויפנו הדרכים, ויטעו גנות ופרדסים, ויגדרו פרצות חומות בית-המקדש, ויבנו בנין בהיכל.

1) [During their negotiations with Jews] they will measure the Land exactly — where the parties are literally fighting over inches, the amount that can be **measured with ropes** [as was done: in the *UN Partition Plan*, in the various so-called treaties beginning in 1979 with Egypt, in the ongoing 'negotiations' with PLO and Jordan—as is also described in *TaNaCh*].[4]

2) They will convert the cemetery into a dunghill.

3) They will profane the tombstones by using them on the hills [for sidewalks, roads, and urinals].

4) They will cause the truth to become elusive and they will propagate and teach falsehoods [like the stereotypical Arab propaganda and hoaxes: their revisionist history about the 'imperialistic' Jews of Israel and about the poor Arabs who are being uprooted from the very land that they have 'always' owned] and about the so-called 'evicted Arab refugees'.

5) They will create a lawless society [where Jewish society will be chaotic, where Jewish law and Torah values will be discarded and remain foreign, and where government leaders will violate basic laws].

---

1. Zecharyah 14:2
2. Pirkei D'Rebbi Eliezer, Chapter 30 (in the uncensored edition)
3. Only eleven events are translated.
4. Amos 7:17 and Yoel 4:2

6) [Because of the Arab presence in the Land and because of their demands and movements], Jewish sins will increase [as Jews stop acting like Jews *vis a vis* owning the Land].[5]

7) The printed word will be worthless and ignored (i.e. they will create new facts).

8) The Israeli-Arabs will have no independent currency of their own [because they will have no independent economy but will be dependent upon the Jews for their livelihoods].

9) The Arabs will plant gardens and orchards.

10) The Arabs will close up the walls around the Temple Mount in Jerusalem and prevent Jews from entering the area.

11) The Arabs will erect a building (i.e. Dome of the Rock) on top of the *Heichal,* on top of the exact site of our Holy Temple in Jerusalem.

If someone wanted clearer proof that there is a Master of the Universe who is in charge and who is guiding the events and who announced them in advance — especially as they concern Jews and the Land — this *Chazal* tells it all. There does not even have to be further comment; these descriptions stand on their own. Most of the descriptions need no further amplification.

Besides those already discussed elsewhere in this *sefer,* there are many other signs given to us. I would like to show you several signs that are listed in three other places.[6] But I want to remind you that these are only several of the many events that are mentioned in Written and Oral-Torah that pertain to Jews and the Land of Israel during this century. That is why this *sefer* was written so easily; the references are 'all over the place' and 'free for the pickin'.

The Talmud mentions that

> *"Jews will not have to fight a war against the non-Jewish custodians in order to take possession of it from them."*

> *"The creation of an independent country will be done through the joint efforts of the nations of the world."*

This is another Principle of Jewish History. *Chazal* also state[7] that the Land will be given to the Jews 'on a silver platter',

---

5. Giving away even a tiny, tiny piece of the Land is such a serious crime (D'varim 7:2). See also our discussion about giving away the Land in Chapter 18.

6. Talmud: M'gilah 17b; Sanhedrin 97-98; and K'suvos 111a

7. Yalkut Shimoni, Ekev, paragraph 852; see also Yeshayahu Chapter 66

כי לעתיד לבוא יתנו רשיון לבני ישראל להתישב בארץ ויעזרו להם לרשת אותה

*"The nations of the world will give the Jews permission to settle in the Land and will help them establish **independence** there."*

Additionally, this is a major principle in Jewish history, as stated[8]

ובכולן השביע הקדוש ברוך הוא את האומות שיעזרו לבנותו –

*"Hashem established a **fixed and immutable principle** of history that the nations will help the Jews develop the Country."*

These very nations will grant Jews independence in the Land. Only Hashem could accomplish the overall task of creating a world that would vote for a Jewish State in 1947 — the very same world that would no longer support a Jewish entity several years later and that would never, ever vote for the creation of the State of Israel again — at least not for Jews. What an Architect of History; what a Master of History is Hashem.

Unfortunately, to get to this point, *Chazal*[9] describe a ghastly destruction that will take place before we will be able to proceed with the resettlement of the Land. A Holocaust and a horrific darkness will engulf the world right before Jews develop the Land as an independent entity.

Then will begin the period of serious *kibbutz galuyot,* when Jews will be returning to Israel in huge numbers. As a matter of fact, Hashem describes the process as happening so very **quickly and through air travel.**[10] Look how the population grew in such dramatic and amazing proportions. There were only 56,000 Jews in the Land in 1918. We already saw that the Jewish population hit 600,000 shortly before the War of Independence and 700,000 one year later. It took thirty years, until 1948, for the population to increase to 700,000. But during the next twenty years, the population would grow quickly and miraculously through air travel. By 1972 there were already 2,500,000 Jews in the Land. An impossible feat — the Jewish population had **quadrupled** in less than 24 years. Yet, twenty years later the population would increase another 2 ½ million; by 1996, the Jewish population had already increased with air-travel speed to **nearly 5 million.**

But the happiness and excitement of an independent Jewish country will be short-lived, Hashem continues, because only half the city of Jerusalem will be in Jewish hands. The other half will be taken away with the Jews being exiled from the City. Remember always what the Jordanians did to the half

---

8. Shir Ha'Shirim Rabah 8:4

9. See the beautiful explanation provided by *Chazal* about the father and son who are traveling and the latter asks when the Land of Israel will be rebuilt (Midrash T'hilim 20:2).

10. Yeshayahu 60:8

that they conquered in 1948. That part of the city that Jordan captured is now even called East Jerusalem with some people now believing that it had always been an Arab city. How easily we forget that it was a Jewish city and that thousands of Jews lived there until 1948 and that the Jordanians imprisoned every Jerusalem Jew that they captured and that thousands of Jews fled from the City that was captured by the Jordanians in 1948.

And even when the city will be recaptured, Hashem tells us that our happiness will be tempered by much aggravation and tension emanating from the nations of the world who will then begin to pressure us to surrender the entire City — either to internationalize it or give it to Arabs. But either way, unbelievable pressure will be brought upon the Jews to surrender control of the City.

Additionally, there will be more pressure brought upon Jews to divvy up the entire Land, to take away other parcels of land from the Jews.

While all of this is happening, the desolate area around S'dom and Amorah will become a viable and valuable asset for the Jews. The Dead Sea area, ghastly barren since the time of Lot, will be restored as a habitation for Jews. For nearly 4000 years, this area was forbiddingly desolate. In our special era, we have witnessed that even this area is bringing forth its 'fruit' — that from what was very 'salted' earth, there now comes forth precious minerals to 'feed' the Israelis and so this prophecy is also fulfilled as it says[11]

> *"I will return your captives ... and Sodom will be restored to its beginnings [and be revitalized as it was originally]."*

Stay tuned for three more developments:

a) How all these tensions and murderous acts will be replaced by comfort and optimism;

b) How the Jews will improve themselves, become proud [as Jews], and how they will become observant;

c) How Moshiach — may he arrive today — will create a better world and an observant, committed, and proud Jewry.

---

11. Yechezkel 16:53-55; see also Sh'mos Rabah 15:21

CHAPTER
X

Disrespect at the Holy Sites:
How Long Will Jews Be Denied Control?

The Torah tells us[1] that the Jews of the Land of Israel must never allow polytheists or pagans or criminals to dwell therein. Only believers in monotheism and only people who observe the **Seven Basic Laws of Morality**[2] are permitted to dwell in the Land. *TaNaCh* discusses the era when we will be in a position to legislate against polytheism; the period when Jews will be able to control their own destiny (if we choose to exercise this option); and when Jews will have the capacity to allow only *civilized* non-Jews to live in Israel (i.e. people who behave in accordance with the Seven Noachide Laws of basic morality).

The eighth chapter of the Book of Daniel discusses the specific period when Jews would be unable to control how others treat the holy sites, when Jews would not have the power to prevent people from trampling on our holy places. Daniel requests that Hashem disclose when these terrible conditions will come to an end.

---

1. Sh'mos 34:12-17; D'varim 9:15 and 12:29-31
2. The שבע מצוות בני נח include respect for Hashem, human beings, and animals.

I will never be able to forget the first time that I peered through a second story window overlooking the *Har Habayit*, the Temple Mount. I saw a most upsetting and terrible sight. Animals and dirty, barefoot Arab children were running about our holy place.[3] I have, from that day, been unable to comfortably view the Temple Mount for fear that I would again witness such disrespect and trampling. When will the Jews assert their authority and put a stop to these abominations? When will they have this option?! Essentially, this was also Daniel's question of Hashem.

"When will these terrible conditions no longer exist?" asks the Prophet. This is the question that Hashem addresses in verse 14.

"עד ערב בקר אלפים ושלש מאות ונצדק קדש"

Daniel is told that after 2300 years from ונצדק קדש, a certain point in time,

> *After these 2300 years have passed, there would be no more trampling of Jewish holy sites'.*[4]

To quote Hashem's answer to the prophet:

> *"UNTIL the EVE of the MORN of 2300 [years from the time that] v'nitzdak kodesh".*

From what time? A little later we will come back to *v'nitzdak kodesh,* the starting point for counting the 2300 years. But let's stay with the first part of the response.

There is a rule that the word 'until' (עד) is an exclusive term — and not inclusive; 'until' (עד) *does not* include the endpoint (ולא עד בכלל). For example, the phrase '*until* Wednesday' does not include Wednesday; '*until* Wednesday' really means '*through* Tuesday'. '*Until* Wednesday' means '*one [day] before* Wednesday'. In other words, in this passage of *"until 2300"*, we're talking about *one [year] before* the completion of 2300 years from *"v'nitzdak kodesh"*, our starting point. So, because of the exclusive term **"until"**, our period of counting is now **2299 years** from that starting point. Additionally, '*Erev*', translated as 'eve', always means the unit of time *right before*. For example, '*Erev Shabbos*' always means Friday, '*one [day] before* Shabbos'; similarly, '*Erev Sh'mita*' always means '*one [year] before* the Sabbatical Year'. Therefore, in our verse, **"erev 2300 years"** really means **"one [year] before the 2300 years"** are reached [after our starting point of *v'nitzdak kodesh*]. So far, then, with **"until"** and **"erev"**, we have **2 years less** than the originally

---

3. Yet I was somewhat comforted by the words of Rebbi Akiva who points out that after this type of desecration there will follow a complete rebuilding of Jerusalem in Jewish hands (see Talmud Makos 24b).

4. Nor trampling of Jews — see Reb Saadya Gaon, ibid.

stated 2300 years — that is: now we have **2,298 years from** *"v'nitzdak kodesh"*, that certain starting point. It can be seen from what Hashem tells the prophet Daniel that the period of our inability to govern the holy sites will terminate exactly **2,298 years after the starting point of** "ונצדק קדש". After these 2298 years elapse, the Jews will be regaining the capacity to ensure that **all holy places** will be treated with respect. Whether the Jews exercise this option at their first opportunity is not being discussed — only that Jews will regain the capacity to exercise the option in order to maintain a degree of proper decorum at the holy sites. The Jews will have the power to decide.

Let's return to our calculations and the starting point for these 2298 years. Suppose for a moment that the phrase "ונצדק קדש" means

> *"[when it is obvious that] the holy ones are [reaffirmed as] a righteous people".*

Some years before Daniel's query, the Jews were exiled by Nevuchadnetzar, after suffering a terrible destruction at his hands. The Jews had also suffered through the destruction of the Holy Temple in Jerusalem. The 2298 years would then begin at the point when it is clear that the Jews, who had earlier discarded Judaism and who, as a consequence, had earlier suffered the destruction of the Temple — when these Jews will be forgiven. It will become obvious that these Jews are exonerated when they are allowed to return to the Land and rebuild the Temple. That moment in time when the Jews return to the Land — at that very moment it is obvious that Hashem has forgiven His people and that Hashem has vindicated the Jews and reaffirmed them as a righteous people. This is precisely what the phrase "ונצדק קדש" means: **The Jews are reaffirmed as a holy people at the very moment when they returned to the Land and rebuilt the Temple.** That is how we know when the holy ones are reaffirmed by Hashem.

We know that the *Galus* of Daniel's time ended with the rebuilding of the Second Temple which, in-turn, lasted for 420 years and which was destroyed in the year 3830 AM (70 CE). This means that the Second Temple was completed 420 years earlier, in the year 3410 (or 350 BCE). Thus, the starting point of *v'nitzdak kodesh* refers to the year 3410, when the Second Temple was completed and when it became obvious to the world that the Jews were reaffirmed as a Holy People with a rebuilt Holy Temple. So if this is our starting point, then the calculations would look like this:

3410 (350 BCE) is the year when the forgiven Jews return to build the Second Temple, the starting point of "ונצדק קדש"

+ 2298 years of Jewish powerlessness to control desecrations at the holy sites

5708 (1947/8 CE) is the year which ushers in the end of this era of inability to control decorum at various holy sites. This is also the beginning of a new period when Jews are able to halt all disrespectful acts at the holy sites.

The period of Jewish powerlessness at the holy places ends in the year 5708 (1947/8 CE). **In 1947 the State of Israel is born; no longer must the Arabs maintain exclusive control over the holy sites.** 1947/8 initiated the period when Jews could regain the ability to ensure that all holy places are treated with respect.[5]

We are not finished yet because Hashem has given us one more precise detail. The passage also indicates that this will be in the *'boker'* part of the year as it says: **"עד ערב בקר אלפים ושלש מאות"**— "until the eve of the *morning* of 2300 years." Of course, *"boker"*, morning, is the **very early part** of a day and according to *halachah,* **boker** is the **very first quarter** of the day.[6] Similarly, the **boker** of a year, the **very first quarter of a year** contains the months of *Tishrei, Cheshvan,* and *Kislev* which **always** correspond to October and November.[7] Not only are we told **the year** when desecrations (at the holy sites) can come to an end, but we are also directed to the specific **season**. Rhetorically, what occurred in October or November of 1947 that was so significant?! But, of course, the 29th of November 1947, corresponding to 16 *Kislev* 5708 — that is the day that saw the creation of the State of Israel by the UN. Certainly, **16 *Kislev* 5708** occurs in the **morning of the year** and 5708 is 2298 years after the Jews returned to Israel to build the Second Temple. The year 5708 certainly ushers in a period when Jews are finally able to maintain an atmosphere of respect at all the holy sites under their control, if they should so desire.

For some strange reason which we will discuss later, the Israeli Jews have not yet decided to exercise control over these holy sites. But the truth is that this is the first time, from the period of the Second Temple — 1947 is exactly 2298 years from the time of the building of the Second Temple — a time when, if they wish, Jews are able to control all movement at the holy sites of the Land.

What a powerful passage! What a great feeling to understand such a seemingly difficult prophetic passage.

---

5. Full control would have been regained had the Jews rejected the Arab initiated plea for the UN cease-fire proposal — as advised by Menachem Begin and many others in 1948. Additionally, the fact that Moshe Dayan surrendered control of the Temple Mount in 1967 to the Mufti is one of the gravest errors to have been committed. With Hashem's help, this sin will be undone soon.

6. Talmud B'rachos 9b

7. Some years, parts of September and December might be included in the first quarter of the Jewish year, but October and November are *always* included.

Israel's Rescuers:
Can Secularists Create & Govern a Jewish Country?

efore we discuss some more of the current events that were predicted with regard to the development of the Land and its People in our day, I would like to emphasize a very important point: Hashem never stated that the Land would be redeveloped by the orthodox, **nor does it state anywhere that the newly created country will be led by observant Jews from its very outset.** As a matter of fact, we already saw to the contrary — how both Written and Oral-Torah describe a generation who are generally unobservant except for *bris milah.*[1] We will soon see how both Written and Oral-Torah describe how a governing body with no real values will be ready to give away the entire country to Arab murderers and make an alliance with two beasts that have an infamous history of murdering many Jews — how this Israeli government will be the actual creators of an alliance between Yishmael and Esav in order to strip

---

1. *Chazal* also indicate that, additionally, Jews, providing refuge for others, will be caring and protecting of each other. These actions possess unbelievable merit beyond anyone's imagination — probably **the most important mitzvah** (see Seder Eliyahu Rabah, Chapter 25).

away real estate from Jewish possession. No! No! No! Indeed, the Oral-Torah tell us that the redevelopment of the Land is not initially based on Torah values — not at all.

I would like to share with you one thought from *TaNaCh* that will show clearly that redemption can develop through non-observant Jews — sometimes even through sinners. More importantly, if nothing else is learned from this *sefer* — we must never, ever sit in judgment on another and claim that he/she/they are unworthy and do not deserve a miracle nor would a miracle ever be performed on their behalf. We are, each and every one of us, far from being perfect and far from being omniscient and all-knowing. Specifically, I refer to some Jews who incorrectly claim: 'Hashem would never perform a miracle for Jews who are mostly non-observant nor would Hashem create a State of Israel for Jews who are mostly secularists or anti-religionists'. They continue: 'So the State of Israel should not be supported and it is not right for Jews to own it at this point in time'. By the way, are these critics certain that Hashem would create a country for them if they would desperately need it? Are they certain that Hashem would save them if their lives were being threatened?

Since some of these critics are vocal enough to be quoted in the media from time to time and to enable you to understand that their thoughts are not Torah concepts, I would like to merely present two passages from *TaNaCh* and *Chazal* to refute their prejudicial views which are also 100% unsubstantiated and which find no support whatsoever in Written and Oral-Torah — the only source for a Jewish position on any matter. Certainly, the country, in its present developmental stage, is not our dream country, but it is the best we have so far, and it has saved millions of Jews from certain death. The State of Israel *does* serve as the basis for us to go forward and create that which should be created. We are to recognize that, in its present form, the State of Israel is only the beginning — but it is part of the unfolding of the Divine plan. Granted that the State of Israel in its present phase is far from the ideal Jewish State and granted that many governments have been morally bankrupt, but how does the State of Israel fit into Hashem's plan?

My Rebbi, the Gaon Reb Ahron Soloveichik *shlita*, emphasized the following two points in class several times — from the story about the four lepers.[2] After Gaychazi created a terrible embarrassment and sullied the beauty of Judaism, he and his three sons were involuntarily isolated from the Jewish people. They were sent away from the centers of Jewish life; they became *m'tzoraim*, spiritual lepers. As *Chazal* point out, their behavior was extremely unscrupulous and offensive; they caused damage that was irreparable and so they

---

2.   II M'lachim, Chapter 7

were denied a share in the World to Come. You can well imagine how terrible their actions must have been if they were to lose a share in the World to Come. Gaychazi was extremely wicked.

Some time after Gaychazi committed this terrible atrocity and was isolated from society, the Israelites suffered through a terrible famine — they were dying from hunger. There was absolutely nothing to eat and there was no sign of any let-up; there seemed to be no hope for the Israelites; they became resigned to their deaths which seemed imminent. To exacerbate the situation, as if it was not sufficiently critical and dangerous, King Hadad was advancing with the army of Aram to destroy the northern part of the Land. Suddenly, the Israelites were rescued by the four most wicked people of the generation. Are you paying attention? Can you believe it — four people who were so evil that they had to be excluded from social contact with other Jews — these four evil people are about to rescue the entire kingdom! Take note: these four spiritual lepers discovered a tremendous source of food and were about to miraculously save the lives of all the Jews by directing them to this life-sustaining source. Can you imagine this: **the greatest of miracles is about to be performed and it is through the efforts of the most wicked of Jews.**

Rebbi pointed out further: When these two miracles occurred for the Israelites — that an invading army of Aram suddenly fled and the Israelites were being led to an enormous supply of food — an assistant to the King started denying Hashem's involvement. 'It is not a miracle' he maintained. He shouted, 'Hashem does not perform miracles through intermediaries who are non-observant'. He also insisted that this particular generation, because they were not observant, had not earned the right to have Hashem perform any miracles for them at all, and certainly not through wicked people.

> *'This can't be a miracle', he shouted. 'The fact that the Aram army suddenly fled from the Land and the fact that there is now a storehouse of food to save the lives of all the Israelites — these are not miracles.' 'Stay away,' he continued. 'Wait for a miracle that Hashem will perform through observant people. We must also wait until all Jews become observant in order for Hashem to save us.'*

The position of the King's assistant is precisely the position of some Jews who are not very well-educated in Judaism — the Jews who maintain that the State of Israel did not evolve through Hashem's desire since most Jews appear non-observant and thus, they claim, non-deserving of Divine intervention. By the way, how do these omniscient critics know who is deserving and who is not deserving?! **Rubbish!!** Where does one have the gall to judge another's situation or character!![3] These Jews, who are so critical of others — these Jews do not even understand a simple story in *TaNaCh*; how could they be considered as quotable when they do not even know the *aleph bais* of Judaism, a simple story. The truth is: [יבוא] הנס מכל מקום

Miracles occur because Hashem wants them to occur. There are no prequalifiers or prerequisites. Hashem has a plan; events occur according to this plan. Nothing happens by accident. Nothing happens against Hashem's will. ומי]-עביד רחמנא ניסא לשקרא]—"Hashem only produces miracles that are valid and just."[4]

Nowhere does *TaNaCh* or *Chazal* ever state that Jews cannot be saved by irreligious people or by wicked people. As a matter of fact, several times Hashem emphasizes in *TaNaCh*[5] that the saving of lives is never reserved as the exclusive assignment for only observant Jewish intermediaries. Indeed, Hashem states very clearly:

יכין וצדיק ילבש

"Any person will prepare in order to enable the righteous to benefit from that work."

רב מחולל כל ושכר כסיל ושכר עברים

"The Great Master of the world [brings everything to fruition and to help Him accomplish these tasks, He] enlists the assistance of the fool and the sinners."

More than this, the Talmud emphasizes: not only does Hashem have fools and non-observant people accomplish constructive tasks, but **Hashem actually performs miracles through the very efforts of even the most wicked person.** Hence, these four wicked people saved the entire country from imminent death. One can certainly use the principles of logic to state unquestionably, as a principle of Jewish History: Hashem intervenes through miracles by using *any intermediary*, any means, any person — even the most wicked. This incident with Gaychazi serves as another important axiom of Jewish History.

The State of Israel was created by Hashem to initially save the lives of Jews. This is not the first time that Hashem had to protect Jews through the mechanism of using their homeland as a refuge for them against adversaries — especially when they had no allies or when the entire world remained

---

3. Talmud Avos 2:5 and 4:10
4. This concept is emphasized in Talmud B'rachos 58a.
5. Iyov 27:17; Mishlay 26:10

unconcerned. *TaNach* already records that during the reign of the extremely cruel and wicked Yarav'am ben Yoash,[6]

> *"Hashem saw that the troubles of Israel were very bitter...and there was no helper for Israel. And Hashem never said that He would erase the name of Israel from under the Heavens. So He saved them."*

This is a corollary, an extension of the previously cited axiom. World conditions are such that after the horrific experience of the Nazi holocaust, it again became obvious that a Jewish homeland was going to be indispensable for the physical survival of the Jews. In such an aggressively dangerous world, the Jewish people can only survive if they have their own homeland with their own defenders. And so it is declared in *TaNaCh*[7]

וירא כי אין איש וישתומם כי אין מפגיע ותושע לו זרעו...

> *"When Hashem will notice that there are no worthy people and when He is astonished that there are no intercessors [from any non-Jewish country], then Hashem will extend His arm in order to save the Jews..."*

When the threats to annihilate Jews become a reality and no country in the world is there to intercede and protect Jews, then Hashem intervenes to protect the defenseless Jews. The Nazi Holocaust testified to this condition. The State of Israel is a direct result of this condition. The State of Israel was created by Hashem to save the lives of Jews — in the present and in the immediate future — in a world that mostly harbors murderous intentions against Jews or that is indifferent to our plight, to say the least.

The most noble action is to save a life.[8] To save the lives of millions of Jews is the most important *mitzvah* imaginable. On the contrary, each and every Jew who dedicates himself to saving human lives, either by creating the State of Israel and by being willing to sacrifice one's very life in order to protect others — that Israeli Jew has done the greatest good. There is no one more important than the Israeli Jew who helps create a place of refuge or the Israeli who is willing to sacrifice his very life in order to protect

---

6. ll M'lachim 14:26 -27. Also, see Talmud Sanhedrin 94. It's very important to keep in mind that this king was extremely cruel and evil and his **only merit** was his concern for the size of the Land and its integrity. You also see from here how important the *mitzvah* is to keep **every inch** of the Land. Not surprisingly, the *mitzvah* of preserving Jewish ownership of the Land far overshadows every imaginable evil which could be committed.

7. Yeshayahu 59:16

8. המקיים נפש אחת מישראל כאילו קיים עולם מלא — "To preserve one life is equivalent to preserving an entire world."

others — **that Israeli Jew is a far, far better person than we could ever be**, relaxing at home in our easy chairs. *Chazal* state it very succinctly:[9]

"[יבוא] הנס מכל מקום"

> *"Miracles occur from any place"* — *even through the efforts of the truly wicked* — *and the present Israelis are far, far from that point of being truly wicked.*

By the way, you may ask, in our story of the four spiritual lepers: whatever happened to the critic who claimed that the Jews were undeserving of miracles, and that the intermediaries were not qualified because of their wickedness? Well, it seems that while the Jews were rushing to be saved from death (through the very miracle that the critic denied) — ironically, this critic was accidentally trampled to death by the very Jews he had just denigrated. The Jews themselves — what happened to them? **Hashem intervenes through any intermediary;** they were all saved.

This is another Principle of Jewish History that most people are unaware of. As usual, in emphasizing a principle of *TaNach*, Oral-Torah discusses[10] the circumstances where Hashem suspends certain rules, laws, or other principles. Specifically, when there is **no protector** for defenseless Jews and when the physical existence of the Jewish entity is threatened with extinction and when **no country** in the world is willing to protect the Jews — during this period, **Hashem intervenes!** In these instances, **Hashem considers absolutely no other circumstances or conditions.** It is totally irrelevant whether the Jews are deserving or meritorious nor does it matter who the Jewish leaders might be. **The prime concern is the saving of lives.**

It is totally irrelevant to judge whether the Jews of the State of Israel were deserving or not. That was not a consideration for Hashem; it must not even enter into human conversation. Hashem created a country of refuge to protect Jews from being murdered by the non-Jewish world — because Jews were threatened with extinction and there was no other way to save their lives — not then and not now and not for the immediate future. Hashem created a place of refuge where every Jew could seek shelter and protection from the unfortunate evil that abounds in this world.

[ומי] עביד רחמנא ניסא לשקרא

> *"Hashem never produces a miracle that is [accidental, misleading, purposeless, premature, or] fraudulent."*[11]

---

9. Talmud M'ilah 17b
10. D'varim 32:36; Yeshayahu 59:16; ll M'lachim, Chapter 23; Talmud Sanhedrin 94 & 97a
11. Talmud B'rachos 58a

CHAPTER
XII

Multi-faceted Inundations —
Why Now?
General & Technological Advancements

he period of time in which we live is phenomenal and unique; it is a period that cannot be compared to another. And this phenomenon exists on so many levels. I remember when computers were first being mass marketed on the retail level. For Chanukah one year, we purchased a Magnavox Odyssey video game and it brought the family so much enjoyment for years to come. I learned the strategies for Backgammon from the computer — to the point that I was able to consistently beat the computer. Then we purchased a Commodore 64 which I was never able to master — I couldn't understand the symbolic language which appeared unrelated to the actual action that the computer was to perform. But I envied my young children who were able to teach themselves how to program and operate the computer 'like champs'.

Some years earlier, in the early 70's, I remember visiting a large department store and I noticed how their display of calculators were chained-down to the counter. I also noticed that their tags carried prices in excess of $200 per calculator — then the equivalent of an entire week's salary. Those machines could do a string of mathematical calculations in seconds. As a high school student, I remembered how long it took for us to learn how to utilize a slide-rule and the answer, after careful adjustments, was only an approximation of the true answer. And here, with the new calculators, the answer was precise to nine digits. Then I remembered hearing that one of the scientists who was sequestered for years working on the Manhattan Project (the 1940's project to create the atomic bomb) — one of these scientists extolled the virtues of the calculator. He stated that a string of mathematical calculations that took him and his assistant an entire week to complete could now be executed by one unsophisticated youngster with just a calculator; the average teenager could now complete these very same calculations in an hour — and with complete accuracy. What required a staff of scientists one week to complete could now be accomplished by a child and a calculator in one hour. Most of us can't picture what the world was like without many of our recent technological advancements. Many of us may not be able to truly appreciate their importance because we grew up this way; they were never absent from our lives.

What's fascinating is that, now, from one generation to the next, so much happens; so many new inventions eventually become necessities. The scope of this phenomenon only becomes apparent when we compare our generation to the experiences of any generation that lived before 1840. You know, you can take any person who lived in colonial America and transport him through time to 1840 and he would find that much remained the same. The civilization of the 1600's was also very similar to the civilization of the mid-1800's. With few exceptions, not much would be different for him either. Life was to a large extent the same. Tools were basically similar, operating on the same principles as the earlier societies. As a matter of fact, even a person from before the Middle Ages would not experience culture shock were he to be transported to the 1800's. We can go back even further — we can analyze the civilization of the Israelites when they first arrived in Israel more than 3000 years ago and compare it to the civilization of the 1800's: essentially, nothing of significance changed. People could only be employed during day-light hours. The family spent evenings together with few distractions. Clothing was rather simple and functional. Food was fresh and prepared daily. Societies were generally agriculturally-oriented. Land transportation utilized animals for all those thousands of years. Life was very simple, with hardly any trappings that weren't organic. Mechanical devices were made from the materials of nature and were minimally processed; people were generally self-sufficient. The external appearances of the two different societies were also similar. Communities were usually small and enveloped the center of town. Until the mid-1800's most homes had very few rooms. Plumbing, electricity, communication, news dissemination, fire departments, mail distribution, universal pricing of goods, machines — these are but a few characteristics that were absent from every society until they were introduced or discovered or invented within the last 150 years. One-room school houses and a few types of simple wooden toys were commonplace.

Inventions were not related to each other in any manner; one invention did not hasten the invention of another. Each invention was indeed isolated from every other invention. Today, however, every invention requires the foundation of previous inventions; each invention depends upon a previous one. For example, there could be no television without the prior discoveries of: electricity, radio, and Forest's three-element vacuum tube (triode). Each and every familiar object of Twentieth Century life was made possible only by a long series of prior inventions and with each of these earlier inventions being important on their own but much more important now, because each is a building block from which greater and more stupendous inventions evolve. For example, what served as fireworks for centuries — this very same rocket technology now propels the modern jet airplane.

Then I remembered the *Chazal*[1] that describes the information explosion and the technological advancements and the scientific discoveries that will begin to inundate our society. The simile that is utilized is '**like the floodgates** that are finally opened in order to release immense amounts of water'. The Zohar goes further and is very specific. This Zohar also indicates the specific era when these "floodgates" will be opened.

ובשית מאה שנין לשתיתאה יתפתחון תרעי דחכמתא לעילא ומבועי דחכמתא לתתא ויתתקן עלמא לאעלא בשביעאה כבר נש דמתתקן ביומא שתיתאה מכי ערב שמשא לאעלא בשבתא

> *"In the **600th year of the Sixth Millennium**[2] (i.e in the year 5600 since the creation of the world which corresponds to 1840 CE), the gates of Torah knowledge will open **from above** simultaneously with the wellsprings of secular knowledge **from below**... as it says in the Torah: 'all the wellsprings of the great deep burst forth [from below] and the floodgates of heaven were [also] opened'."*

The Zohar states in such colorful language, how the floodgates of knowledge will be opened in order to benefit mankind and prepare us to enter the Seventh Millennium. I didn't fully appreciate this passage until I studied some history — after all, we do know that in order to understand Torah, one

---

1. Zohar I,117a
2. We count millennium as we do with centuries — the **Eighteenth** Century refers to the 1700's and the **Sixth** Millennium refers to the 5000's

must have secular knowledge, to the extent of "one who lacks even one measure of secular knowledge will be lacking in 100 measures of Torah knowledge".[3] There is only just so much Torah knowledge that is attainable without a prior mastery of secular knowledge. With secular knowledge, the world of Torah opens wide. So, taking this sage advice, I began to research the significant events that occurred in the 1800's and early 1900's. Something had to be there. I just knew it. But what I discovered was truly earth-shattering.

I began to really understand precisely what the Talmud says: 'If you do not have the necessary secular background, you will not understand Torah to its fullest'. I discovered that while there were some discoveries in the Middle Ages, these discoveries either tended to be isolated or had limited practical application. The discovery was made, but no one was able to apply it or market it for mass consumption. In addition, the innovation, at best, remained just that — an innovation in a specific area with no spill-over into other areas. I discovered the following 14 inventions — but they were over a span of 300 years.

Year	Invention	Year	Invention
1450	*printing press*	1650	*vacuum air pump*
1520	*rifle, spiral grooves*	1657	*pendulum clock*
1589	*knitting machine*	1705	*atmospheric steam engine*
1590	*compound microscope*	1709	*piano*
1598	*thermometer*	1752	*lightning conductor*
1608	*telescope*	1764	*spinning machine, jenny*
1643	*barometer*	1765	*condensing steam machine*

Certainly, they did make life easier for a few isolated individuals. These are all important inventions, but they didn't change the face of the Earth.

When we examine the nature of the discoveries beginning in the mid-1800's, however, there emerges an inundation, a radical transformation. Life in the 1840's was very similar to the life of the previous 3000 years. But beginning in the mid-19th Century, the world began advancing in geometric leaps and bounds which was to be expected — after all this Zohar says that now the pace of discoveries will become so very accelerated. The chart above indicates fourteen major inventions in 300 years. Let's now explore a few of

---

3. Our Rebbi, the Gaon Reb Ahron Soloveichik used to stress this as did the *GR"A*, as also quoted by Reb Yehuda Leib Maimon in *Sefer HaGR"A*. (See also Talmud M'gilah 13a; Zohar: B'reishis 204 and Vayikra 81, as well as Malbim on II Divray Hayamim 1:10-12.)

the major scientific advancements for just the **seventy years around 1840** — I've purposely ignored the routine inventions like **typewriter, battery, sewing machine, bicycle, photography, reaper, dynamite, and countless other inventions** in order to demonstrate that this period experienced **immense knowledge infusions** besides the 'normal' dose of inventions that occasionally had surfaced in the centuries preceding the 1800's.

Year	Discovery	Year	Discovery
1803	*Dalton's Atomic Theory*	1845	*Boolean algebra*
1823	*Ampere (electricity)*	1857	*Pasteur and immunization*
1825	*Laplace formulae*	1859	*spectroscope*
1829	*electric motor*	1860	*incandescent lamp*
1832	*electric telegraph*	1865	*Mendel and genetics*
1834	*Faraday, electrochemistry*	1869	*periodic table of elements*
1842	*Joule's 2nd Law of Thermodynamics*	1873	*electromagnetism*
1842	*Doppler Effect*	1876	*Koch and microbiology*
1842	*Radio*	1876	*Bell and telephone*

It's not only that there was an increase of scientific activity during this unusual period. The nature of activity was unknowingly directed to discovering major principles that would advance human understanding and progress beyond the wildest imagination. For example, Boolean algebra serves as the basis for the operation of today's computers. Without Boolean algebra there are no computers. Truly, the **floodgates from below** (of secular knowledge) burst forth and inundated the entire humanity.

There was a simultaneous opening of the **floodgates from above** (in the area of Torah advancement) as demonstrated by the discoveries of many hidden or lost manuscripts that were written by the *Rishonim,* the great Torah sages from the early Middle Ages and that now could finally be printed and disseminated throughout the world for the first time. The Yeshiva of Volozhin, the schools of the Torah giants of The Vilna Gaon, Chasam Sofer, Rebbi Akiva Eiger, Reb Shimshon Raphael Hirsch, and many other greats of such magnitude that the generation has been described as דור דעה[4] — all fortunately for us who benefit from these remarkable influences.

---

4. The same appellation ascribed to the generation who left Egypt and experienced Hashem's revelation.

Think about it: our generation is one of the most amazing generations. We have experienced so much and so quickly. Just consider: the Jet Age, the Atomic Age, the Space Age, the Computer Age, etc. — **more technological advancements in 50 years than in all of the previous history of the world,** advancements that have literally revolutionized the entire world.[5] Social movements and civil rights movements of the 1960's — where do you think they came from? What events caused these movements to evolve? The world had just recently discovered the horrors of the murder of the Six Million Jews and the destruction that could evolve from discrimination and hatred. Then came an anti-war movement. It is the first time that there was a moral awakening of mankind to the horrors of war, horrors that could exist in a world that is not acting and thinking properly. And it all began with the death of the Six Million Jews and with the rebirth of the Jews in our homeland after 1840 — many years of suffering and slavery and exile and nearly twelve million Jews murdered.[6] Indeed, the world is developing in many different ways. We are certainly not attempting to justify or understand what Hashem does or did; it is something beyond's man's ability. We are merely making an observation that humanity is also in the process of maturing. Indeed, the world's current development is not restricted to the scientific arena.

What is even beyond the realm of coincidence is that in that very same year of 1840, a monumental sociological movement was beginning for Jewish people, a movement that would eventually affect the entire world. In 1840, there began an energizing of a trend that until then had only been slight. Until that point in time, there were always trickles of Jews who would leave their countries in the Diaspora and move to the Land of Israel. But it was always just that — a trickle. Beginning in 1840, the *aliyah* movement began to increase in geometric proportions; from an annual trickle of Jews, the *aliyah* movement would increase into the thousands and eventually into the **hundreds of thousands per year.** The years of 1992, 1991,1950, and the period of the 30's into the late 1940's showed an immigration to Israel of hundreds of thousands of Jews from Russia, from Arab countries, and from Europe, respectively.[7] Since advancements in science were occurring as *aliyah* was increasing dramatically and since there are no coincidences, could it be

5.   Zohar (l, 117a) emphasizes: in order to prepare for Moshiach and to develop a truly advanced society.

6.   See "Europe and The Jews" by Hayes where many of the murders and massacres are documented.

7.   There is, as of this writing, no country in the world where a significant Jewish population remains and where they are also being oppressed or enslaved or murdered. Hopefully, and with G-d's continued protection, we will never again see acts of inhuman barbarism against Jews. **We pray that there be no cruelty anywhere in the world against anyone.**

that the opening of the floodgates was designed to ultimately benefit the Jews of Israel in making it possible for them to quickly transform the country from a malaria-infested devastation into the potential for a blossoming oasis in the midst of an awful world?! Well, that's what this Zohar says!!

One can easily conclude, since nothing in this world happens by accident or coincidence,[8] one can safely and justifiably conclude that the relationship between scientific advancement and the mass influx of Jews into Eretz Yisrael are significantly and truly related to each other.[9] It certainly appears that the purpose for all these technological advancements is to help foster the development of the Land in the shortest time possible.[10] What Jews accomplished in the Land, in converting a desolate desert into a blossoming and thriving country, has amazed the world. Never in recorded history has a people been able to transform a desolate country into a viable entity in such a short time. The world has consistently described this magnificence by saying that 'the entire birth of modern Israel is a miracle'. But that's what Hashem already told us[11] — and that is how and why we benefited as a result of the efforts of other people — beginning in the 600th year of the Sixth Millennium (i.e. 1840).

I'm smiling and tears of joy are welling up within me as I write these words. Feelings of nostalgia; when I remember with pride, how I long for the days when Father and I would spend so much time together. I miss those days because I've 'grown some'. They are also tears of sadness; I miss those days because I will never be able to again experience those moments of closeness with my father, *zal*. We would spend many evenings together going from house to house, trekking from store to store with the JNF charity box. We were collecting money so the Jewish National Fund could buy saplings and plant them in Israel. My father was an unusually non-assertive person outside the family, yet Father resorted to **extorting money** for JNF — and in my presence. I couldn't understand it. Though I was only about 6 or 7-years-old at the time, I already understood that he was out-of-character and acting

---

8.   Talmud Chulin 7b

9.   See also Zohar ibid.

10. As early as 1952, the Rav *zal* taught us that the sole purpose for the formation of the League of Nations and the UN was in order to create the State of Israel. Think about it — what good has the UN brought? What did the League of Nations ever accomplish for mankind? The UN is a den of wolves and has always been so — except for one 'unexplained' moment when **even Russia** voted to admit the State of Israel as a member in this world body. Russia? Catholic countries of South America who protected the escaping Nazi murderers? Unbelievable! But not a coincidence at all. See the Zohar (ibid.) which, in discussing all these advancements, states specifically that, during this period, the Land of Israel will arise from its desolation because of these advancements.

11. Yeshayahu 49:23; Yirmiyahu 2:3

very aggressively with others, to say the least. Father, who was so ethical and honest, was extorting money from other people — I couldn't believe it. But like a respectful Jewish boy, I didn't challenge; I just became a more astute observer.[12] And then I understood; it seemed that Father only threatened the storekeepers who wouldn't give him enough money, according to *his* assessment. To those merchants he would say, "I'm looking for a $5 donation for Israel. I'm not here to argue, but if I don't get that amount, your store will never again do business with my family." In those days, do you realize how many pairs of pants my overly active brother and I 'went through' in a week? The merchants saw that Father meant what he said; Jew and Christian alike, every merchant immediately 'saw the light' and gave. Father (and I) collected alot of money for Israel. What a sense of accomplishment. What a wonderful feeling spending quality time with Father. Treasured moments that I shall always cherish and long for. They are only memories now — but powerful ones, at that. They are powerful because we devoted so much time and effort, like so many Jews throughout America, in supporting the fledgling new Jewish country. What a feeling of accomplishment to assist — each and every one of us — according to our respective abilities. The caring that Jews showed for the *chalutzim*, the pioneers — the concern, the prayers, the heartache. We didn't know any Israelis but Jews we were — everyone — and Jews help each other in every way possible. The Talmud states clearly and emphatically:[13]

כל ישראל ערבים זה לזה — *"Every Jew is responsible for the welfare of every other Jew [in the world]".*

So work we did — Israelis in developing a country and Diaspora Jews supporting them in every way possible. Many Jews sent entire paychecks to Israel. My friend Avraham's Staten Island home was converted into a base-station for Israeli diplomats to transmit shortwave messages to Israel.[14] It is essential to indicate that J. Edgar Hoover became obsessed with Avraham's father, Reuben Gross *zal*, and was determined to decipher these coded Hebrew messages that were being transmitted overseas. Try as he could,

---

12. Later on I was to understand that these types of coercive techniques are permitted if they're utilized to generate money for noble causes. (See Talmud Baba Basra 8-10; Rambam, *Matnos Aniyim*, Chapter 10.)

13. Talmud Sh'vuos 39a

14. In those days it was illegal to communicate in codes with certain foreign governments. See "The Pledge" for more details of this true adventure story that would defy your imagination — an extremely suspenseful and terrifying and proud moment in American-Jewish history as Reuben Gross, Avraham's father, survived a life-threatening battle with Hoover, the infamous and all-powerful FBI dictator. Many of these frightening facts are now first being discovered, as these FBI files have recently been 'declassified' and can now be reviewed upon request under the "Freedom of Information Act".

Hoover was unable to get even one American Jew to translate the Hebrew messages into English. Not one Jew could be so engaged. No Hebrew-speaking Jew would volunteer if it meant possibly jeopardizing the life of another. That is the way it was and that is **the way it is supposed to be ALWAYS. The degree of Jewish unity was stupendous** — perhaps only the second time in thousands of years of Jewish history that Jews united and devoted all their time and energy to support other Jews, the proper and intense response which emphasizes the glory of the Torah principles of life.

Other people shipped clothing and supplies; my sister-in-law's mother, Amelia Seif, once described in detail how she and so many others shipped weapons and ammunition which they hid in breads and cakes. Sure it was illegal, certainly they could have been imprisoned for many years, but what Jew was willing to stand by idly and allow Arabs to murder defenseless Israeli Jews. What Jew was going to sit idly as every single country in the world refused to sell arms to Israeli Jews. In this case, the Torah value of saving lives *must* take precedence over an illogical law that says you can sell weapons in any local hardware store, but you cannot sell weapons to Israeli Jews. No Jew is to condone the death of another person. Neither is a Jew allowed to claim impotence when observing life-threatening dangers confronting another. A Jew must do what a Jew must do in order to protect another Jew.[15] There are **never** justifiable reasons for not helping another Jew whose life is in peril.

Here in real-life action and drama is the principle of unity and caring *(Gemilas Chesed)* displayed in all its glory and as Oral-Torah indicates:[16] 'It is through acts of *chesed* that we will inherit the Land'. Not only because Hashem officially rewards our efforts in helping others in-need (by giving us the Land), but also because if we would not have been united with Israeli Jews, there could be no physical country of Israel today. The Israeli Jews just could not have done it by themselves.

Every Jew who worked on behalf of Israeli Jews — every single one of these precious Jews was *gomel chesed* and helped create the country. We were each indispensable — every one of us. Certainly, the 'pioneers' were there for heroic action — to fight malaria, to reclaim the deserts, and to defend against Arab invasions. And we were their support behind the front lines. But no entity consists of only a front line; the support staff helps complete the team. One without the other cannot accomplish the task. While critical for any business, the front line sales force cannot singlehandedly sustain any company for long, if there is no accounts receivable department, no new products division, no

---

15. Vayikra 19:16
16. Seder Eliyahu Rabah, Chapter 25

personnel department, and no back office. A team is effective when all the people work together — each according to his/her ability and each in a specific area of specialization. So, too, with *Gemilas Chesed,* with a great deal of work, we were all able to merit the creation of modern Israel and ensure its continued survival in the face of enormous odds. And with Hashem's help, we succeeded according to plan and on-schedule.

And so Hashem reminds us[17] that we are approaching the Messianic Era, a reminder which will be noticed by the entire world. The Land which had been desolate for thousands of years will blossom again. Hashem tells us that even the hills and mountains will blossom. And in case a person reads this verse superficially instead of studying it attentively, the Talmud[18] emphasizes the fact there is no more impressive a proof than the rebirth of the Land — there is no greater proof that we are getting very close to the Era of Moshiach. When you see it happening, you will know that we are approaching the end of menacing times and that soon we will be ushering in a period of true universal brotherhood — a time when undisturbed learning will abound, with a desire to apply this learning to create ethical and moral life styles for us and for our families and for our communities — with only peace and relaxation for all people. It is clear and obvious that we are getting close. The Talmud emphasizes that the best evidence is as Hashem already stated:

> *"The hills of Israel will give forth blossoming branches and yield its luscious fruit in preparation for the Jews who are about to return to the Land."*

This has happened; you can check the itinerary and know where we are in the course of Jewish and world history because **this is the only time in the past 2000 years that the Land is blossoming.** No matter who lived in the Land, no matter who was in control of the Land, the Land could not sustain its inhabitants because of the pervasive desolation and its stubbornness in not allowing itself to be developed.[19] Even the Jews who dominated the country during the Middle Ages and even through the early 1900's — even these Jews were constantly perishing because of serious water shortages and devastating famines that occurred so regularly and frequently. Indeed, **this century is very special — it is the first time that the Land has become fertile, the first time in thousands of years.**

This is the most obvious proof that we are about to experience something very, very special — there is nothing more conclusive!! אין לך קץ מגולה מזו

---

17. Yechezkel 36:8
18. Sanhedrin 98a
19. Vayikra 26:32

The Creations of Israel and the Sixth Day:
Exact Parallels to the Hour & Year

ne of the most difficult concepts to understand is the concept of time. Many of us have struggled to understand the Creation of the world. Were the "days" of Creation the same as six human days? Were these 'Divine' days — whatever that means? Or were these six stages in creating the world? Then again, once we accept the notion that Hashem created the world and Hashem is omnipotent, then it stands to reason that Hashem is able to do anything. Since Hashem is also not bound by time, it also means that Hashem can do anything we call complicated and complete the task in a millisecond — nay, less than that. If so, then we've probably wrestled with this concept, with trying to understand Divine creation in human terms — we, the finite, trying to fathom the workings of the Infinite.

As many questions as we asked in this last paragraph, we are now faced with one more critical question. As we already know from Torah,[1] Adam was created on that first Friday, the Sixth Day of Creation. *Chazal* fill us in on

---

1. B'reishis 1:26

some details[2] by telling us that on the Sixth Day of Creation, Hashem created Adam in the following sequence:

❖ At the end of the first hour of that first Friday, Hashem had already gathered earth from throughout the world.

❖ At the end of the *second hour*, Hashem had already shaped this pile of dirt into the general outline of a human being.

❖ At the end of the *third hour*, Hashem had already formed the limbs for the very first human being.

❖ At the end of the *fourth hour*, Hashem had already breathed life into this mass and Adam became physically alive with a soul.

❖ At the end of the *fifth hour* of that first Friday, Adam stood up.

❖ At the end of the *sixth hour*, Adam had already invented names for all animals.

❖ At the end of the *seventh hour*, Adam begins to live a normal married life.

Why does it take Hashem an entire hour to travel throughout this planet to gather earth. A whole hour? Why so long?

I remember learning this passage several times. When I was a young teenager and unsophisticated like all teens, I didn't even attempt to understand the details of Adam's creation. I just knew that it was beyond my reach at that time. As a young adult, I knew that this passage was still too advanced for me — but I suspected that I needed to understand more physics. If I could only understand Einstein's concepts of physics and time.... I put aside this passage, in the same way I approach all difficult passages, and said, 'On another cycle through the Talmud and with more scientific knowledge, and with Hashem's assistance, I'll be successful in discovering the meaning of this very mysterious passage'.

So I devoted some energy in this direction. Understanding the measuring of time still required more effort than I was willing to devote to this one passage. But the real connection came about when I began to understand concepts in supersonic travel. One of the first phenomenon I discovered was that if a person is traveling at the speed of sound, at 600 miles per hour — whenever such a traveler speaks, his words are heard *after* he speaks them. It's not what we usually experience. Generally, when we recite a word, we *hear* that word at the exact moment that we *pronounce* that word through speech. When planes or rocket ships travel at supersonic speed, speech is heard *after* the fact; we're 'there' *before* the spoken word.

---

2. Talmud Sanhedrin 38b

But once one travels faster than the speed of light then he's truly traveling back in time. On a sophisticated level, we know that Hashem doesn't travel, but on a very elementary level, this helped me begin to understand that Hashem is not bound by time. However, as a young teenager, I thought that Hashem could just travel so fast that Hashem could be anywhere in time at any human moment. Hashem is not bound by time. Hashem is thus able to create the Exodus from Egypt while simultaneously observing us read this passage thousands of human-years later; simultaneously, Hashem can be a part of events 50 years from now. No, Hashem doesn't travel, but it was the start of how I began to understand in a logical fashion that Hashem is infinite and unaffected by time.

Since Hashem is unaffected by time and because days are related to revolutions of different planets including the sun, and since there was no sun until it was created on the fourth day, our previous question becomes even more powerful. How could the Torah talk about hours and days on those first three days — even before there was a sun that functioned as it does today?[3]

Then one Shabbos, I studied a verse that we recite at least once a week:

"A thousand human years approximate one day for Hashem."[4]

That was the key I needed to unlock this puzzle, the puzzle that remained a mystery for so long.[5] *Cosmic* days, Hashem's days are *not equivalent* to human days at all. As a matter of fact, 1000 human years only approximate one *Cosmic* day since *Hashem is not bound by time at all.* Not that the above relationship is a scientific statement or a precise equation, but this is the only ratio that we are given, so we will utilize it for some insight.[6] Let's follow the logic:

We're told that ...... 1000 Human-years = 1 cosmic day

This means that ...... 41²⁄₃ Human-years (1000/24)= 1/24 cosmic day = 1 cosmic hour

Similarly, ... 1 Human-year = 1/41.6 of a cosmic hour

And finally .... 1 Human-hour = .2367 cosmic seconds

In truth, Hashem does not require an entire human day to create. Hashem's "one hour" of creation is more nearly like ¼ of a human second. Since Hashem

---

3. See Talmud Chagigah 12a

4. T'hilim 90:4

5. This is not to imply that this is the only passage that I didn't understand; there's much more that escapes me than this one passage; I'm only trying to share the excitement of developing a Torah insight with someone — while demonstrating how some passages require effort, lots of time, secular knowledge, and a modicum of maturity and Divine assistance.

6. We're justified because דברה תורה בלשון בני אדם (i.e. The Torah has to sometimes resort to human language to express concepts that relate to Hashem and defy finite language expression).

is omnipotent and infinite and not bound by time, *Hashem does not require any human time to accomplish anything.* Truly, Hashem did not require any human time to create this [humanly] complicated world. From Hashem's perspective, nothing is complicated and nothing is easy[7] for Hashem is omnipotent. Hashem created a world in how long? Our human day is like a tiny fraction of a tiny second for Hashem. Divine creation is instantaneous. Essentially, 1000 human years are like *no-time* for Hashem. He created the entire universe in six stages (we call them days) — but, remember, for Hashem there is *no-time.*

This relationship of 1000 human years to one 'day' of cosmic time is brought to life by the Zohar[8] when it states that **the six *cosmic* days of creation parallel the six millennium of *human* history.** Six cosmic creation days parallel the first 6000 years of human life. In other words,

❖ On the Sixth Day, Adam was created as a person.

❖ During the Sixth Millennium, there will be another creation.

Adam was not created all at once but in several stages (hours). Similarly, this 'other creation' (during the Sixth Millennium) will also develop in several stages over a period of years. During the *daylight hours* of that Sixth Day of Creation (i.e. for the *last* twelve cosmic hours on the Sixth Day), the following activities occurred in a successive fashion:

During Cosmic Hour #1,	Hashem gathered material from throughout the world in order to create.
During Cosmic Hour #2,	the material began to take shape — although not yet viable.
During Cosmic Hour #3,	limbs become noticeable.
During Cosmic Hour #4,	the mass of material becomes physically alive.

---

7. That's why Rambam (Moreh N'vuchim I, Chapters 51-60) maintains that Hashem cannot be described with positive characteristics (e.g. smart, caring, etc.). If Hashem, for example is described as happy or angry, then our statement implies that Hashem is limited by emotions and possesses deficiencies; if so, Hashem is "finite" — a position which is illogical. With this in mind, Rambam suggests that descriptions should only emphasize the negative attributes (e.g. Hashem has no emotions or no body or Hashem is not affected by any external influences nor is Hashem subject to physical conditions). In other words, Hashem possesses no [limiting] qualities nor does Hashem possess any properties or attributes which describe the essence of an object because this implies composition — a condition which is certainly limiting and finite; Hashem is limitless and infinite. All anthropomorphisms detract from Hashem's uniqueness. Essentially, we're saying that if *we* performed in this manner, then others would describe us as happy, satisfied, angry, etc. This is the only way we can justify the use of positive descriptions for Hashem.

8. Zohar Chadash 16b; see also Talmud Sanhedrin 38b

During Cosmic Hour #5,   Adam stands up on his own and becomes an independent entity.

During Cosmic Hour #6,   Adam recognizes the true nature of the world.

During Cosmic Hour #7,   Adam begins to live a normal married life.

Cosmic-sunset which ended the First Thursday and which ushered in this First Friday would be the equivalent of the human-year 5000 — the Sixth Millennium. Similarly, after twelve Cosmic-night hours pass, *mid-point* of the Cosmic-day arrives. Sunrise, **halfway** through that First Friday, would then be equivalent to the human-year 5500, **halfway** through the Sixth Millennium. In other words, *sunrise* marks the passage of *half* the day. Also, keeping in mind that our only clue is that each cosmic hour is equivalent to $41\frac{2}{3}$ human-years,[9] the above chart can be translated into non-cosmic time in the following manner — remembering that the events of the First Friday have a counterpart and are exactly paralleled by the events of the Sixth Millennium:

Cosmic Hour #1   begins with 'sunrise' and parallels the *Human-years* of 5500-42

Cosmic Hour #2   spans the *Human* years of 5542-83 ($41\frac{2}{3}$ years later)

Cosmic Hour #3   spans the *Human* years of 5583-25 ($41\frac{2}{3}$ years later)

Cosmic Hour #4   spans the *Human* years of 5625-67 ($41\frac{2}{3}$ years later)

Cosmic Hour #5   spans the *Human* years of 5667-08 ($41\frac{2}{3}$ years later)

Cosmic Hour #6   spans the *Human* years of 5708-50 ($41\frac{2}{3}$ years later)

Cosmic Hour #7   spans the *Human* years of 5750-92 ($41\frac{2}{3}$ years later)

Since most people are more familiar with the common calendar used throughout the world, we will now add the secular civil dates:

Cosmic Hour #1   ends with the Human year of 1781/82 (5542) and parallels **the gathering of material from throughout the world in order to create.**

Cosmic Hour #2   ends with the Human year of 1822/23 (5583) and parallels **the material taking on shape — although still not viable.**

Cosmic Hour #3   ends with the Human year of 1864/65 (5625) and parallels **the limbs becoming noticeable and detectable.**

---

9. Though scientifically exaggerated, ‏אלף...כיום‎, meaning "1000 ... is like one day", is still the only 'time' relationship that we, humans, are provided.

Cosmic Hour #4	ends with the Human year of 1906/07 (5667) and parallels **the mass of material becoming physically alive.**
Cosmic Hour #5	ends with the Human year of 1947/48 (5708) and parallels **Adam becoming an independent entity.**
Cosmic Hour #6	ends with the Human year of 1989/90 (5750) and parallels **Adam recognizing the true nature of the world.**
Cosmic Hour #7	ends with the Human year of 2031/32 (5792) and parallels **Adam beginning to live a normal married life.**

To sum up, here are the Divine activities of that Sixth Day of Creation with their significant counterparts from the Sixth Millennium:

Cosmic Hour #1 parallels the period ending in 1782 (5542)

(Hashem gathers material from throughout the world in order to create.)
During the 18th Century, the Vilna Gaon and Baal Shem Tov were inspiring their followers to emigrate to Israel — from other parts of the world.

Cosmic Hour #2 parallels the period ending in 1823 (5583)

(Material is taking on a shape — but still not viable.)
Jews of France are granted equal rights; the desire for Jewish emancipation grows throughout the world, as well as the notion of nationalism for all people — a combination of 'circumstances' which invigorates Zionist strivings. The followers of the Vilna Gaon and Baal Shem Tov begin moving to Israel. Indeed, Israel is beginning to take on a shape.

Cosmic Hour #3 parallels the period ending in 1865 (5625)

(Limbs and infrastructure are becoming noticeable and taking shape.)
In the mid-1800's, Rabbis Kalisher and Alkalai start persuading people, through their publications, to move to Israel — as do Hess, Pinsker and others including many influential British Christians who maintain that the Holy People should be restored to the cradle of its birth. The first large group of European Jews come to settle in Palestine which triggers the start of the modern Zionist movement. On the world scene — Montefiore and Rothschild initiate a program of purchasing much land from the ruler of Syria and Palestine; significant scientific and technological advancements prevail — in order to ultimately benefit the future State of Israel.[10] Indeed, the limbs are becoming noticeable.

---

10. See details and references in the previous chapter.

Cosmic Hour #4 **parallels the period ending in 1907 (5667)**

(The mass of material is becoming physically alive.)

On the world scene around the 1900's, riots and State-sponsored pogroms 'motivate' many Jews to settle in the Land. Meanwhile, an agricultural school is established followed by a period where settlements are developed. The 1881 May Laws and a series of pogroms shatter Russian Jewry's illusions of equality, engendering the slogan: "Flight from persecution offers the key to Jewish survival". The First Aliyah of 25,000 Jews begins in 1882. The First Zionist Congress meets in 1897. The *chalutzim*, the pioneers who are mostly from the Russian areas, start draining marshes and developing cities and the Land starts shaping-up. The masses are becoming physically alive. The infrastructure is in-place to prepare for the next stage.

Cosmic Hour #5 **parallels the period ending in 1948 (5708)**

(Adam stands up and becomes an independent entity.)

Jews begin to assume responsibilities for their own self-defense. The Second Aliyah, ending in 1914 brings 30,000 Jews to Palestine, many of whom are unable to tolerate the terrible conditions in the Land; many of these people return to Europe or move to America. Those who remain espouse a reverence for physical and agricultural labor and are determined to rebuild their nationhood by the sweat of their brows. The Balfour Declaration and the British Mandate from the League of Nations call for a Jewish Homeland in Palestine. Independence for the State of Israel: the UN approves the creation of a Jewish homeland in November 1947 and the Jews formally announce their independence in May 1948 — both occurring during the year 5708.[11]

Cosmic Hour #6 **parallels the period ending in 1990 (5750)**

(Adam recognizes the true nature of the world.)

This period will be noted by the emergence of the quest for truth and the discarding of bankrupt values!

Cosmic Hour #7 **parallels the period ending in 2032 (5792)**

(Adam begins to live a normal married life.)

We pray that Hashem will help us achieve the seventh Cosmic hour — where Jews in the Land will be able to settle down undisturbed, where we can all live normal, natural and peaceful lives — lives that are founded on the observance of Torah and *mitzvot*.

---

11. Tikunay Zohar (on Yeshayahu 60:23) provides us with the very year and season when the Land will be redeemed (i.e. the first third of the year 5708).

The Solution Before the Problem: *Advance Preparation to Welcome & Sustain Returnees*

One of the most unbelievable situations that has ever occurred, a situation that is probably unique in the annals of world history is the following: usually, when a country is conquered, the conqueror relocates its own citizens there and the country is developed through these newly transplanted citizens. Thus, the conquered country becomes an asset for the victors. When the Romans or Greeks conquered a country, they repopulated the vanquished territory with their own citizens. When America conquered the various Indian territories, they similarly repopulated the areas with their own citizens. When America conquered parts of the Southwest from Mexico, they also repopulated the area with American citizens. In each of these instances and throughout history, the conquerors then developed the country and made it into a productive colony for the mother country. All one has to do is look at California, New Mexico, or Texas to see how each of these territories are blossoming with productivity — residential, commercial, agricultural, cultural. In every way these areas are now thriving as integral parts of the United States. Indeed, the conquerors take possession and redevelop the region.

However, this seemingly natural development did not occur with regard to the Land of Israel. As a matter of fact, this takeover could not occur, as we shall soon see. There were, however, other similarities in the conquest of the Land of Israel that were shared by other countries in all their conquests. But, for some very special reason,[1] the Land of Israel was never to be a productive entity for the invading conquerors. Yes, the Assyrians, Babylonians, and Romans each exiled many Jews. However, after being conquered, the Land of Israel remained virtually unpopulated and unproductive as we know all too well. The Land was never an asset for the non-Jewish conquerors.

This phenomenon is actually a Principle of Jewish History[2] as spelled out in Oral-Torah.[3] The Written-Torah[4] says:

ולא תתן ארצכם את יבולה ... ושממו עליה איביכם הישבים בה

"The Land will not produce [not for you and not for the non-Jewish occupiers who supplant you]...and your enemies will be astonished [because] ... The Land shall lie so abandoned and unproductive."

Hashem also describes this situation elsewhere as[5]

"this place that is devoid of people ... and cities ..."

The Torah states a Principle of Jewish History: after it is destroyed by the invaders, the Land will become barren and will remain in this desolate condition. No people will be able to develop the Land. No people will be able to fight this Law of 'Nature'. This Land will "devour its inhabitants". **No one** will be able to thrive in this Land. No one will be able to survive the 'natural' elements of the Land. During the Jewish exile from the Land, other principles of nature will prevail in the Land. While countries throughout the world may experience cycles, the Land of Israel will remain uninhabitable and it will experience only desolation and famine. The Land will produce one continuous period of barrenness and desolation — with not a moment's respite. No other country in the world has ever experienced such constant and extreme

---

1. Torah and *Chazal* explain that this phenomenon has several purposes, one of which is to make it easier for the Jews to return to Israel and reclaim a wasteland from the custodians, because those temporary guardians will be prevented from making any real investment during all the years of their domination. See Sifra (B'chukosai 6) wherein continued desolation in the Land is explained as a great thing for the Jews who, upon returning to the Land, will never have to supplant a dynamic and industrious people in a highly developed Land of Israel that also has a vibrant culture.

2. We will only discuss several of the principles — there are quite a number.

3. Sifra on Vayikra 26:32

4. Vayikra Chapter 26 — especially verses 20, 32, and 43.

5. Yirmiyahu 33:12 (as well as in many other locations in *TaNaCh*).

desolation. Countries have certainly experienced bad times, but never for 2000 years straight — unrelenting and continuous.

But it's a principle of Jewish History:

> *'The Land shall lie fallow and not produce for anyone. The Land shall lie abandoned while the Jews remain dispersed throughout the world."*

No one can survive — not even Jews can survive while their presence in the Land is so minuscule a percentage of their total population [in the world]. To fully understand the extent of this devastation, we need only take a look at **three eyewitness accounts.** In 1267, Ramban writes to his son about how difficult it was to find even ten Jews for a *minyan* in order to *daven.* He continues:

> *"What shall I tell you about the Land? There are so many abandoned places and the desolation is all encompassing ... The more sacred the site, the more it has suffered. Jerusalem is the most desolate; Judea more than the Galilee."*

In 1249 while giving away the City of Jerusalem to Frederick II (the Roman Emperor), al Kamil (the Moslem Sultan) stated:

> *"I have ceded nothing but ... wrecked buildings.."*

Mark Twain, visiting the Land in the 1860's which was nearly 600 years later, had this to say about what he saw:[6]

> *"... the soil is rich enough but is given wholly to weeds ... A desolation is here that not even imagination can grace with the pomp of life and action ... We never saw a human being on the whole route. We pressed on toward ... Jerusalem. The further we went the hotter the sun got and the more rocky and bare, repulsive and dreary the landscape became ... There was hardly a tree or shrub anywhere. Even the olive [tree] and the cactus, those fast friends of a worthless soil, had almost deserted the country ... Jerusalem is ... lifeless. I would not desire to live there. It is a hopeless, dreary, heartbroken land ... Palestine sits in sackcloth and ashes. Over it broods the spell of a curse that has withered its fields and fettered its energies ... Palestine is desolate and unlovely. Can the curse of the Deity beautify a land? Palestine is no more of this work-day world."*

---

6.   "The Innocents Abroad or The New Pilgrim's Progress", Harper and Row, NY, 1922, pp. 216-359

As an aside, but **very crucial to an understanding of current events,** Arafat in his 1974 speech to the UN declared:

> *"Palestine was a verdant area ... inhabited by an Arab people dynamically enriching its indigenous culture."*

We have just seen that every observer had **unanimously marveled at the extreme barren wilderness** and the very poor and sparse population in the Land, but **Arafat begins teaching 'new facts'** to people who are unfamiliar with history. As a matter of fact and of very great importance, we see that Arab culture did not dominate the Land at all. For all their long years of custodianship over the Land, **the Arabs left nothing of significance as a legacy** or even as a hint that could possibly suggest that they had once lived there. In fact, the Land remained desolate, as all observers have recorded for posterity and for anyone who has an interest in discovering the truth — contrary to the 'new facts' of Arafat and his revisionist history.

The failure of non-Jews to settle in the Land and develop it was remarkably noticeable during the Turkish rule. For the first fifty years of Turkish rule, the non-Jewish population in the Land had quickly surged to 300,000. The population was increasing with such speed that it appeared that the Land would be established with a massive non-Jewish majority. But since Hashem stated that the Land would remain desolate while the Jews were in exile, Hashem sent locusts to Israel that destroyed all plant life and subsequently brought widespread famine in its wake. Hashem also brought earthquakes, invading armies, and plagues that killed thousands upon thousands. The reconstruction of the Land under Turkish rule was halted through this series of 'natural' disasters which totally decimated the Land. The survivors fled and, denuded of its people, the Land again returned to a condition of total desolation and waste that had prevailed for hundreds and hundreds of years — as Hashem predicted.[7]

And so it was throughout these last two thousand years — Jews in the Land died of famine and disease; a trickle of Jews replaced them, only to ultimately perish from the very diseases and famines that had just thinned out the ranks of the more seasoned immigrants. Yes, there was always a Jewish presence in the Land but it inevitably consisted of new immigrants because the previous generation would invariably perish. Thus it continued for two thousand years — trickles of Jewish immigration but only in so far as Jews were

---

7. For a land that sits on a major fault in the earth, earthquakes were indeed a common occurrence. Is it not a result of Divine protection and intervention that, for the past century, since the Jews returned and redeveloped the Land, there have been no devastating earthquakes in Israel that have killed people?!

essentially replacing dead Jews — with absolutely no increase in population or in land development. It's totally mind boggling!!

There's another Principle of Jewish History that becomes clear when we stop to examine recent events in the Land of Israel. For years, beginning with the late 1950's, I remember protesting and writing letters and praying so hard for that momentous day when the doors of the Iron Curtain would open wide enough to allow Jewish emigration into the Land. That glorious day finally arrived. The New York Times interviewed half a dozen people, amongst whom was the former Chief Rabbi of Israel, Rav Shlomo Goren, *zal.* The question asked was how could the State of Israel deal with such a huge and sudden influx of Jews into the country. It would be a tremendous financial burden that might ruin the Israeli economy — that was the implication. The interviewer was a non-Torah person. No Torah person would ever imply such a ridiculous position or ask such a stupid question. This is absurd because there is no other consideration when it comes to saving a life. Rav Goren, as a matter of fact, emphasized that of paramount importance is the saving of lives; when it comes to saving lives, economics are never considered — not even for one second.

From the Hell of the Russian furnace of anti-Semitism we were at last able to snatch lives that miraculously survived oppression, hatred, and lack of education. Anti-Semitism was so intense — you can't imagine the intensity unless I tell you of a Russian emigre to the United States who was sixteen years-old when I first began to supervise his treatment. When I first met him, he disclosed that he hated Jews. He hated observant Jews even more — with a passion. My dear readers, this young man was born to Jewish parents. Can't you see the effects of Russian propaganda?! The Russian propaganda machine was unfortunately effective even to the extent of teaching Jews to hate Jews. To study Torah was not possible then; for this young man, to learn Torah in America, far from Russia, was not going to happen because of the far-reaching effects of that most powerful Russian propaganda machine.[8]

Of course, Rav Goren continued, it won't be easy to accommodate an influx of one million Russian Jews within a span of two years; of course that will tax us economically. But show me a Jew with true Jewish values and I'll show you a person who will ignore the issue of economics in order to save the life of another Jew.

Rav Goren made another important point. He stated that had Russian Jews been allowed to emigrate at a much earlier period in Israeli history there might have been another problem. But since 1967, the size of the Land doubled.

---

8. Three years later and after much work, this young man is now becoming observant.

After the Arabs invaded in 1967 and subsequently lost the areas of Judea, Samaria, and Golan — after that war and with the newly acquired territory, it is now very easy for the Land to accommodate all the Russian Jews, in addition to all the Jews of the Diaspora. **Hashem prepared the Land in advance** to gracefully receive the new immigrants. Before the spoils of the Six Day War, it would have been very, very difficult to accommodate such a large influx of Jewish emigres in such a short period of time. Now, with newly expanded borders, Israel will resettle all the Russian Jews without a problem because: אין הקב"ה מכה את ישראל אלא אם כן בורא להם רפואה תחילה

> *"Hashem provides the solution even before the problem is presented."*[9]

Making room for the new immigrants is not a new phenomenon. This is not the first time that such an unusual phenomenon has occurred. As a matter of fact, it's the second time in less than thirty years. We just are not used to utilizing our eyes and no one has taught us the principles of Jewish History.[10] Two of the truly great miracles that have taken place in our days have gone unnoticed, unfortunately. Perhaps that is why so many people cannot experience the excitement of the day. We go through life with eyes that see but do not perceive. Of course, everyone is fully aware of the three major Arab wars and the miracles performed on our behalf. Not only were we protected but, after each war, the victorious Israeli Jews emerged with double the size of their pre-war territory.

But most people did not pay attention to the nearly **one million Arabs** who had moved into Israel during the first half of the century. The British restricted Jewish immigration to Israel while Arabs were free to migrate in a massive and unrestricted fashion. While the Jews were miraculously successful in defending themselves during the 1948 War of Independence, there was a huge problem facing these very same Jews: in this little piece of truncated Land, how do you make room for the **two million Jewish immigrants** that are about to arrive from the Displaced Persons Camps in Europe and from the other European and Arab countries?! By 1947, the Land was inundated by a recent influx of nearly one million Arabs; there will now be no room for the two million Jewish immigrants who survived the Arab, Russian, and Nazi venom. It would not be easy to remove Israeli Arabs in order to make room for, what was to be, a mass and sudden influx of Jews into the Land. Besides

---

9. Talmud M'gilah 13b

10. Our Rebbi, The Gaon Reb Yosef Dov Soloveitchik *zal* often said in the name of his grandfather, Reb Chaim Brisker, that most people don't realize that stories and events that are recorded in Torah (i.e. *agadeta*) contain the principles of Judaism in action.

which, the world would never tolerate the forcible displacement of one million Israeli Arabs, nor could human beings deport people who are seen by the world as 'peaceful'.

Obviously, the Jews would not be able to solve this problem by themselves. Nay, normal people do not deport another people who are living so 'peacefully' in that country. But this very problem found a miraculous solution — no less a miracle than the glorious Jewish military victory against the hordes of mighty Arabs who were bent on destroying every last Jew — but, nonetheless a miracle, only that it went unnoticed and did not register. **The solution to the problem of the Arabs** who were 'in the way' — that solution **came from the Arabs themselves.**

In order to easily identify the Israeli Jews in 1948 and then murder them easily and quickly, Mother Egypt asked the Arabs of Israel to leave the country. This occurred during the first Arab invasion — in the year 5708. The tremendous, unsurmountable obstacle to repopulation by Jews of the Land was solved in one second. The problem that defied human imagination and solution was solved by the Arabs themselves! The miracle occurred so naturally and so easily that most Jews didn't even see the Divine intervention; most people did not appreciate the Hand of Hashem at work. Hashem was creating miracles all over the place and they were largely unnoticed. The unsurmountable was resolved without the use of any force. In 1948 Mother Egypt addressed the Arabs living in Israel: 'Please move out of the country to enable us to kill all the Jews quickly and easily'. And move the Arabs did — **permanently.** The Land was now able to accommodate what was to be one of the largest mass migrations of Jews to date. The Jews of Europe and Arab countries found an open invitation to settle the Land wherever their hearts desired. **About 500,000 resident-Arabs voluntarily left**[11] **in order to make room for two million Jews, soon to arrive from 'the four corners of the world'.** Stop for a moment to consider the magnitude of this miracle: Arab farmers were working the land; Arab workers came to the Land to find employment and were in fact, as a result, gainfully employed by Israeli Jews. These same Arabs who were hitherto unemployed in their former lands and who were now gainfully employed in Israel — these Arabs were now giving up their entire livelihood and moving voluntarily from the Land of Israel to languish in refugee camps and to return to their former lives of

---

11. Although the Arabs claim that two million Arabs were forcibly deported by the Jews, they're wrong on two counts: (a) only about 500,000 Arabs were involved; (b) Egypt requested that they leave — weeks before the State was even declared, weeks before the War of Independence. Verification of these facts are provided by every single historian who has done original research of UN documents and correspondence for the years 1947 to 1950.

abject poverty. That Arabs should leave their jobs in order to establish lives of abject poverty and that Arabs should give up their farms and homes in order to hand them over to new Jewish immigrants to Israel — is this normal or is it beyond the realm of the natural?! An unbelievable solution! But the Land is called *Eretz Tzvi* because the Land is expandable as it is stated[12]

יצב גבלת עמים למספר בני ישראל

> *"Hashem moves the boundaries of adjacent countries [thus making Israel larger] in order to accommodate the increasing numbers of Jews."*

Such a quick and easy solution and, yet, just another Principle of Jewish History.[13]

This Principle of Jewish History is verbalized by *Chazal*[14] as follows:

בזכות ישראל גזירין אתכנעו שנאיהון תחותיהון וירתי אחסנתיהון ...כי אוריש גוים מפניך והרחבתי את גבולך דהקב"ה עקר דיורין [דעכו"ם] מאתרייהו ואתיב דיורין [דישראל] לאתרייהו ... ההוא דאית ביה קיימא קדישא דדכיר לון מלכא בכל יומא

1) "... the Jews will humble their enemies and retake their legal inheritance because of their observing the *mitzvah* of religious circumcision ...

2) [and Hashem also promises that the Jews will also experience] the expansion of their borders.

3) [Since Jews generally observe the *mitzvah* of *bris milah*], Hashem will also uproot an entire population [of Arabs] from their place and replace them with Jews in that very same area."

This Principle of Jewish History, succinctly stated, is that

> *Hashem will replace the Arab population with a Jewish presence.*

T'filah, Jewish prayer, attained its present form through the efforts of the last of the prophets amongst whom were such notables as Ezra, Daniel, and Mordechai. These are not mere words that were compiled by people of an earlier generation. Almost the entire service on any particular day is composed of quotes from *TaNaCh*[15] or is based upon Torah concepts that were emphasized and publicized through the efforts of *Chazal*. The Talmud[16]

---

12. D'varim 32:8

13. Regarding the current threat of an Arab takeover of Israel through the Oslo fiasco and through the cries of *jihad*, Hashem says that the 'solution' will come from the Arabs themselves. Hashem says that we will be extricated from this debacle — suddenly and because of what the Arabs will do!

14. Zohar II,124a

15. See Avudraham for the specific Biblical references for each and every phrase in the Siddur

16. M'gilah 17b

stresses this point when it calls our attention to The *Sh'moneh Esray,* the main weekday petition of *Eighteen* prayers.[17] Within this section, we analyze our thoughts, motivations, and actions, and/or inactions. Have we improved from yesterday? What have we accomplished today? Have we studied? Are we truly interested in self-improvement? Have we prayed for the recovery of those who are emotionally and/or physically involved?

In addition, we petition Hashem on behalf of the nation. We pray for evil governments to desist from their ways. We pray for the establishment of a Torah government in the Land. But the point I wish to discuss with you is the fact that all the prayers received their final form from this last generation of prophets through Divine inspiration. The Talmud emphasizes that each of the petitions are in a specific order because, in the pre-Moshiach years, this is exactly the sequence of how these very events will unfold — precisely in the order that is found in the weekday service. The Talmud states that **first we pray for the redemption process to begin.**

Chazal emphasize:

> Redemption of Jews will begin with a blossoming of the stubbornly desolate Land which will be followed by a massive ingathering of Jews from throughout the earth.

So we first pray to Hashem:

> "Bless the Land so that, from its goodness, it will become fruitful enough to satisfy all our needs."

Then we pray:

> "Please sound the great shofar to herald the ingathering of the dispersed Jews."

But as you must realize by now, *Chazal* did not invent any concepts; they only emphasized concepts that are already found in *TaNaCh* — concepts that we may have missed if we were too superficial in our learning or not sufficiently attentive in our studies. Yechezkel states that right before the Messianic Era:[18]

> "The hills of Israel will give forth blossoming branches and yield its luscious fruit in preparation for the Jews who are about to return to the Land."

Hashem says that first the earth will be developed; afterwards, the Jews will return to the Land.

---

17. Originally eighteen prayers, but which are now expanded to nineteen because of the inclusion of an additional prayer.

18. 36:8

Yeshayahu[19] states that:

> *"[In the pre-Messianic period] the Jews will inherit a land that will sport the growth of Hashem's plantings".*

Hashem tells Amos[20]

> *"I will bring back the Israelites and they will build the desolate cities and live in them and they shall plant vineyards and drink its wine. They shall create gardens and eat its fruit. [Then] I shall plant them in their land and they shall never again be uprooted from their land..."*

This prophecy is even more miraculous because, as we know too well, the Land had been impervious to all human attempts at development for nearly 1900 years.[21] These facts must be clearly understood so that we may truly 'see with our eyes', in order to appreciate the magnitude of the miracles surrounding the People of Israel and the Land of Israel.

---

19. 60:21
20. 9:14-15
21. See the earlier quoted descriptions of Ramban and Mark Twain.

CHAPTER
XV

Arabs Want the Land – Why?
There is an Arab-Palestine Already

hy do the Arabs want a Palestinian state with Jerusalem as its capital? After all, 260 million Arabs have a total land allotment of five million square miles which is **625 times the size of the Land of Israel.** The present State of Israel occupies the equivalent of 0.16% of the total land in the region which is less than ⅙ of 1%. That's correct: 0.16%; that's the equivalent of a dot on the map of Arab countries. If they were really smart and could operate without *Hashgachah,* without Divine Providence and intervention, they could probably wind up with almost the entire State of Israel. If they were smart, they could have received as a Peres-gift almost the entire country except for certain select areas. They asked for Jericho — and they got it. They asked for Gaza — they received it. They asked for Judea and Samaria — and, Heaven forbid, plans were being made to transfer this area to them, also. Someone is asking for Golan — and plans were being made to accommodate the request, but there was a big delay; the delay was only because Peres was stubbornly holding out for permission to install very sophisticated monitors on the Golan Heights to detect the next Syrian invasion of Israel. That's crazy, but if you're taking pieces — I mean if they're talking **'peace'**, why should Peres have been concerned about an **imminent invasion** from a peace-partner? Either they trust Syria or not. Either Syria has peaceful intentions or not. But more importantly, Peres had agreed to present almost the entire Golan to an Arab country — as Rabin used to say, "The depth of the withdrawal is dependent upon the depth of the peace". All an Arab had to do was ask and Peres was there with a counteroffer initially; when that's rejected by the Arabs, Peres negotiated a little and then acceded to their original demand — exactly as initially demanded by the Arabs. This appears to be the history of the 'negotiations' since 1993 in Oslo and before that at Camp David when Begin gave away the entire Sinai with the oil wells that Israel discovered there, as well as the $2 billion a year oil industry that Israel also developed there.

So it's obvious that what the Arabs have demanded in the way of territory — what they've demanded, they've always received. So why do they insist on getting Jerusalem? What does it mean to them? But more importantly, why do they insist on receiving Jerusalem — which is evidently a much hotter issue than all the other areas of Israel?

Not long ago, I evaluated an Arab teenager because she was exhibiting academic deficiencies. As part of the assessment process I asked her many personal questions. In response to the question about her birthplace, she mentioned that she was born in "Palestine". I couldn't believe what I just heard; so I asked her again, and again she responded "Palestine". I raised my voice purposely, and in a planned fashion asked, "I don't understand. *Where* were you born?" Again she responded with "Palestine". Emphatically, I rephrased my statement-question and said, "But there's no place in the world with that name. Tell me the truth. Where were you *really* born?". Clearing her throat, she then meekly said: "I was born in Israel". A small victory for the sake of truth, I thought, getting her to use the word 'Israel' and seeing her choke as she said that 'dirty' word.

Some days later after I had discussed the results of the evaluation with her father and our professional conference was completed, I asked him to explain to me why the Arabs want Jerusalem. He responded: "Weren't there alot of prophets there?" "Sure there were", I responded, "but they were Jewish prophets". The client's father then retorted so nonchalantly and so automatically and with words that I shall never, ever forget: "So aren't we all cousins"?!

Don't you understand what he was saying?! **Jerusalem is not intrinsically important to Arabs** — not at all. It possesses no inherent value for them. Jerusalem is significant for the Jews and because it is significant for us — that is why it is important for Arabs and that is why they want to take it away from us. They want to take away Jerusalem from us because they are our cousins. The statement, by itself, lacks internal logic. The father's response makes absolutely no sense. But it is the cry of the Arab: 'Jerusalem belongs to us because it is holy and unique for our Jewish cousins'. In other words, **'If the Jews have it, we want it'**.

Who can ever forget the inflammatory speech Arafat made in the South African mosque on May 10, 1994. He said to his Moslem brothers:

> *"The **jihad** will continue. Jerusalem is not for the Palestinian people. It is for all the Moslems. You are responsible for Jerusalem ... Our main battle is Jerusalem. Jerusalem is the fourth shrine of the Moslems".*

(By the way, Arafat then continued by inviting the South African Moslems to join him in the *jihad* to murder Jews and gain control over the entire country. And mind you — this is just a half year after the well-publicized and infamous handshake of peace between Rabin and Arafat in Oslo and shortly before Arafat was to receive the Nobel *Peace* Prize.)

This position is ridiculous; it is lunacy; it is pure and unadulterated falsehood. Lies! **In the Koran, Jerusalem is not mentioned even once in a positive manner.** Mohammed forbade any recognition of Jerusalem; he forbade his followers from attaching any significance whatsoever to it.[1] The Moslems are ordered to pray to Mecca and turn their back on Jerusalem. As a matter of fact, in 1249 the Moslem Sultan, al Kamil, gave Jerusalem as a gift to Frederick II, the Roman Emperor, and stated to him: "I have ceded nothing ..." Truly, do these words describe a city that is holy for Moslems?! **The Koran says that the entire Land belongs to the Jews.**[2] It's a lie! Jerusalem is not the fourth holy city for Moslems; it's not a Moslem city at all. Mohammed forbade his followers from paying any homage to the City of Jerusalem because he stated that **Jerusalem is a city that belongs to Jews.** In fact, according to the Koran, the entire Land belongs to the Jews.

Every intelligent person knows that Jerusalem is not a revered Moslem city nor was it ever. All historians agree that Mohammed did not even step foot in Jerusalem towards the end of his life. All historians agree that the folk tale of him jumping heavenward in order to die is exactly that — a folk tale. He stated that only Mecca is significant for Moslems. **Neither Jerusalem nor the Land have any importance whatsoever for Arabs.**

"If the Jews have it, we want it." This typical Arab response may appear illogical and irrational, but *Chazal* state[3] that when the Jews begin

---

1. Especially after the Jews refused to be converted to his new religion.
2. Chapter 5
3. Pirkei D'Rebbi Eliezer, Chapter 29

returning to Israel in full-force — at that point in time, the Arabs will try to prevent the Jews from developing the Land any further. The exact method that Yishmael will utilize in confronting the returning Jews is also specified. They are going to attempt to wrest the Land from the Jews through the method of lying. All the while that Yishmael confronts the Jews, the truth will be ignored and hidden as it says,[4] "וְהָאֱמֶת נֶעְדֶּרֶת". So their response may appear illogical; Hashem wants them to hide the truth. And now, non-Moslems are believing the Arabs, too — despite the truth, despite the facts that were well-known for centuries that the Land belongs to Jews; despite the fact that the UN already took away 80% of Palestine from the Jews and partitioned the Land into two parts — the small part for Jews and the larger part, Transjordan, as the designated Arab homeland; and despite the most important basis for Land ownership: **Hashem designated Israel for the Jews and declared it so!**

And who will be the **partners of Yishmael** in trying to wrest control of Jerusalem from the Jews? *Chazal* state,[5]

זמינין בההיא זימנא לאתערא עם כל עמין דעלמא למיתי על ירושלים

the partners of Yishmael will be the *entire world*. Yishmael will be joined by the non-Moslems to come against Jerusalem in order to take away the City and Land from the Jews. You know what is most amazing? Excluding the Jews, the Moslems hate the Christians the most. It's obvious that the Arabs could not have gotten this far with their revisionist history without the help and acceptance of the Western countries. Divine Providence, the *Hashgachah*, is so obvious: the Moslems united for a project with their other sworn enemies, the Christians. Divine Providence allows the union of the Arabs with their hated Christian enemies — united in order to strip the Jews of their Land.

In the course of this last decade or two, the West has allowed history to be revised by the Arabs with absolutely no dissension whatsoever. It is totally preposterous, but the world has recently come to accept the notion that the Land of Israel belongs to the Arabs. Interestingly, I recently found several encyclopedias which were printed in 1963 — which is 15 years after the State of Israel was created and 15 years after the so-called Palestinian refugee problem was 'created'. The only reference to Israeli Arabs was a superficial comment to the effect that **some Arabs fled to Jordan on their own.**[6] Nowhere is it even implied that Arabs are able to claim title

---

4. Yeshayahu 59:15 and Talmud Sotah 49b
5. Zohar I,119a. See also: Sifri on D'varim 33; M'chilta on B'shalach 9; Yalkut Shimoni on Yirmiyahu 31
6. The World Book Encyclopedia, volume 9, page 390

to even one inch of Israel. All books and historians of that era stated unequivocally that **Israel belongs to the Jews.**

It's totally mind boggling. The Arab 'refugees' were created by Egypt in the 1947-48 period when they requested that the Arabs of Israel vacate the Land in order to facilitate the planned slaughter of Israeli Jews. The Arab 'refugees' could have been resettled by other Arab countries who had similar cultures; they would have easily blended into a civilization with a language that was already familiar to them. Legally, they should have been absorbed by Transjordan, the part of Palestine that was set aside exclusively for the Arabs who had lived in Palestine through the 1940's.

Are you aware of the fact that after World War I, both Arabs and Jews simultaneously asked for independent countries for themselves. Are you aware that the Arabs received 21 countries that encompass more than five million square miles. In 1922, the League of Nations recognized the right of Jews to their homeland — this included **both sides of the Jordan River and also comprised Jerusalem, Judea, Samaria, and Gaza.** However, two decades later in its Partition Plan, the UN took away 80% of the Palestine that was promised to the Jews as their homeland. The UN took 80% of the Jewish homeland and gave it to the Arabs for the 22nd Arab country to be created in the region during the 20th Century.

According to the Balfour Declaration of 1917, the **entire Land of Palestine,** as it was called then, **was to belong to the Jews.** The League of Nations reaffirmed that the entire Land of Palestine was to belong to the Jews. But after much underhandedness, the world reneged on their agreement and **took away 80% of the Jewish Land and transferred it to the Arabs** — with the blessings of the UN. To this newly designated Arab territory, they gave the name Transjordanian Palestine, which was subsequently renamed as Jordan by Abdullah, grandfather of the present king. What a demonstration of Divine intervention: can you imagine if the original name was retained?! There could be no revisionist history. Every time people would hear the name Transjordanian Palestine, they would immediately be reminded of the fact that this is the part of Palestine that's on the other side of the Jordan, the side that's reserved for only Arabs.[7] This Arab country is on the other side of the Jordan River (because that particular side was partitioned from the original Palestine and was reserved as a homeland for only Arabs), but the base for measurement is the western side which was given to the Jews. Everybody would have been constantly reminded that there were two homelands already — Israel for the Jews and Transjordanian Palestine for the Arabs.

---

7. Did you know that no Jews are permitted to dwell in Transjordan to this day?

Everyone would have noticed that the Arabs already had their own country. There would be no talk of another Arab country to be carved out of 'the dot on the map' which is all that remains of the original Palestine.

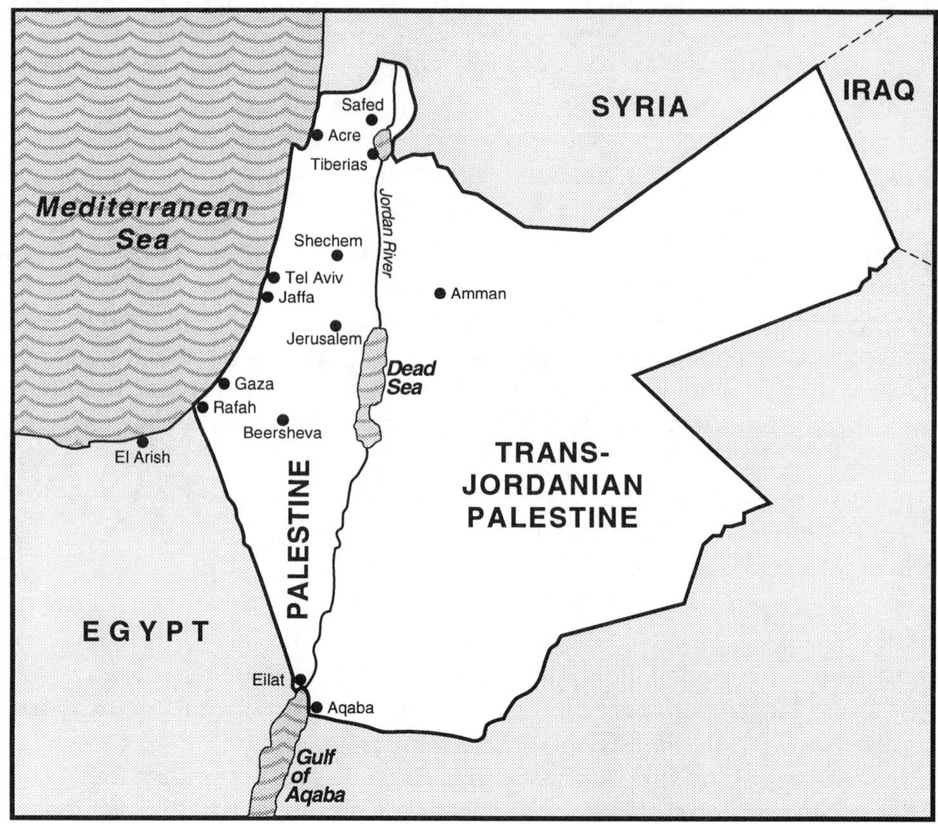

But Hashem has His own plans for us. The Arabs have presented a Big Fat Lie which has been accepted by the entire world — ironically by a world that prides itself in its scientific advancement, in its command of logic, objectivity, and careful observations and rigorous proofs. Having already received Jordan is not enough. What the Arabs are really demanding is a **second Palestinian homeland** at the cost of displacing the Jews, murdering them, or "throwing them into the sea" — whatever.

Before the redevelopment of the Land, before the Land began to blossom for the first time in almost 1900 years[8] — before this time, the 80,000 Arabs who lived in Israel regarded themselves as nomads[9] with absolutely no ties

8.   From the time of the destruction of the Second Commonwealth by Rome in 70 CE.
9.   See Harkabi's *"Palestinian Covenant and Its Meaning"*, Vallentine, 1979.

to the Land of Israel, with no national aspirations, with no identity whatsoever. They saw themselves as nomads who lived in various places in the
Middle East — one day here, tomorrow elsewhere, but never closely
associated with any particular territory. As a matter of fact, most of the
Arabs moved to Israel after the Jews began redeveloping the Land, because
the Arabs saw this as a golden opportunity for employment. Most of the Arabs
moved to Israel because they were hoping to find jobs with the Jewish
pioneers. But there was never a "Palestinian Arab People". There was never
an Arab entity that felt that the Land belonged to them. As a matter of fact,
a quick glance at any history book that was written before 1960 will describe
Jews as the Palestinians. The biggest hoax of the century is what has been
perpetrated on the world to get the world to believe that Arabs are the real
Palestinians! Yet, when the Western world now speaks about the national
aspirations of a Palestinian People, they are referring to Arabs even though
the Arabs of Old-Palestine were already given Jordan as their homeland.

So it's obvious that the focus for the Jews will now have to involve
disclosing the true facts ONCE-AND-FOR-ALL. The focus of Jews and the focal
point of Jerusalem, as a city, is *truth*. **The battle is for control of The City
of Truth.**[10]   The Arabs try to capture the City of Truth (by perpetrating
untruths) in order to distort truth; the Jews will have to ultimately prove the
truth. From this city of Jerusalem will come the proof that the Land belongs
to Jews.

If this is not depressing and frightening enough, Peres, in his infinite
wisdom, also negotiated with the Vatican. He was obsessed with having the
Vatican take control of Jerusalem and I'm certain that he must feel that this
arrangement will accrue benefits for Israeli Jews.[11]   At the same time, it
appears that Jews will now allow the Church to missionize. Missionize for
whom? For tourists who are already Christian? or for non-Christians — like
Jews?! Who will be the target of this missionary work if not our own
brothers? The bankruptcy of Peres' thinking is demonstrated by his inviting
potential kidnappers into Jewish homes to 'spirit away' our kin. Is there anything more threatening to the continuity of Judaism then inviting missionaries
into Israel in order to kidnap Jewish souls?[12] Peres is obsessively desperate
to give the Arabs physical control of the entire country — to destroy the
physical Jewish ownership of the Land while simultaneously destroying the
spirituality of so many weak Israeli Jews who are so vulnerable to the

---

10. As indicated in Zecharyah 8:3
11. See his book, "The New Middle East".
12. See opening paragraphs of the Schema from the Second Ecumenical Council to see that
    the thrust of modern Christianity is to convert the Jews.

evangelical overtures of the Church. This entire scenario defies all logic. It is essentially self-destructive. It is one of the most ridiculous and frightening moments in all of Jewish history. And of course, the *Har HaBayit*, the Temple Mount, the foundation for the symbol of our physical independence and of our spirituality — can you believe that a Jew would so willingly surrender ownership of such an important site? It is more dramatic and traumatic than if the United States were to surrender control of the White House to some menacing foreign power that would, in turn, forbid the President and his staff from using their offices and forbid all Americans from even stepping foot into the building, or from even stepping on the grounds of the White House.

Can you imagine a more self-defeating, self-destructive behavior than Peres' inviting Arab murderers to govern parts of the Land and 'protect' Jews from being murdered by other Arabs. **The PLO are not terrorists; they are murderers** who promise to wreak physical destruction on all Jews — as the PLO Charter demands.[13] It is totally ridiculous to expect that a stalking murderer will 'protect' his designated victim and prevent that Jew, his designated victim and sworn enemy, from being murdered by another Arab murderer — where the two Arabs are cousins or friends. Yet, the Jewish Press of 27 January 1995, reports that Peres and Rabin were *begging* the PLO to protect Jews in a more responsible fashion. It sounds to me like a return to 19th Century Poland where we depended upon non-Jews to protect us — and, boy, did they take care of us ...!! I suppose, if you're not a Torah Jew, it's not surprising that you could make yourself blind to the principles of evasive action, self-preservation, and preemptive action as expounded by *"Haba l'hargicha"*[14] and *"Lo Sa'amod."*[15] I suppose one could dream of peace and one could even fantasize that the PLO want to live in peace, but an awake and alert and normal person cannot ignore logic and reality.

The Arabs have also promised to strangle Israel economically through the medium of a boycott which has been in effect for decades and remains largely observed by each of Israel's 'peace partners'. Can you believe that Egypt and Jordan, our brothers in peace, have still not officially rejected this boycott and that Jordan complains that not enough Jewish money is being spent by Israeli tourists in Jordan?! **Chutzpah!**

---

13. See Appendix for excerpts from the PLO Charter.
14. Sh'mos 22:1-2; Talmud Sanhedrin 72a
15. Vayikra 19:16

CHAPTER
XVI

The Oslo Alliance:
Predicted & Described

ashem talks about the *Erev Rav* and criticizes Moshe for accepting them and allowing them to accompany the Israelites at the time of the Exodus from Egypt.[1] *Chazal* emphasize this point:[2] 'The *Erev Rav* were not true converts'; they merely felt that Hashem was another god, but that this god was stronger than their Egyptian gods. These Egyptians were both frightened and moved by the awesomeness and the extent of destruction caused by the Ten Plagues — but they were superficial Jews; only their outward facade appeared Jewish. Essentially, they were opportunists who saw a golden opportunity to 'go with the best'. They were not truly serious about being converted. They were a Fifth Column who eventually made much trouble for the Israelites. They were the ones responsible for constructing the Golden Calf[3] and they were

---

1. Sh'mos Rabah 42:6 and 7; D'varim Rabah 3:11; and Zohar ll, 46a
2. Zohar I, 119a and Pirkei D'Rebbi Eliezer 28
3. That's why they shout: **"אלה אלהיך ישראל"** or "Israelites, this is *your* god." They don't shout 'This is *our* god' because they aren't Jews addressing their kin. See Sh'mos 32.

the group who 'broke rank' at every opportunity in order to advance their own private and pagan agendas[4] — far from the Torah agenda! The Zohar also states that before Moshiach arrives, this *Erev Rav* will form an alliance with Esav and Yishmael that, if successful, would delay the arrival of Moshiach.

"יתיצבו מלכי ארץ ורוזנים נוסדו יחד על ה' ועל משיחו"

> *"The nations of the world will arise ... against Hashem and against Moshiach."* [5]

ותלת קרבין יעבדון בני ישמעאל בהדי משיחא דא

> *"There will be three wars that the Yishmaelites will wage against this Moshiach."* [6]

Who is this *Erev Rav* that is described as follows:

ובהון נטיל נוקמא מעשו וישמעאל וערב רב, דערב רב מעורבין בעשו ישמעאל

> *"Hashem will seek to avenge the actions of Esav, Yishmael, and Erev Rav — the Erev Rav that is mixed-up with Esav and Yishmael."* [7]

More mind boggling — Esav and Yishmael are arch enemies; they have hated each other for more than 1200 years; they fought many violent wars against each other; the Koran spews forth hatred against Christians. What entity is powerful enough to bring these two arch enemies together and unite them under one banner in order to attempt harm to the Land and its people?! Their alliance is described as so awesome that they have the ability to intimidate and control the entire world — and destroy it if they wish.[8]

Until several years ago, I was confused because I envisioned the *Erev Rav* as a people who were insincere converts to Judaism; additionally, the name of their leader, "Armelus", sounds Latin — like, Romulus, one of the founders of Edom which is the traditional Torah representation for ancient Rome and its successor the Roman Catholics and their outgrowths, the Christians. Recently it struck me: there were two reasons why I was experiencing difficulty understanding this *Chazal*. Firstly, I was learning a prophetic *Chazal*

---

4. As a matter of fact, this is also a prototype that whenever there will be trouble with neighboring countries, there will be a group of superficial Jews who will 'break rank', change sides, and patronize the enemy. For example, it was the Hellenists, a Jewish-born group, who instigated Antiochus to murder Jews and outlaw the observances of Judaism. Sure Antiochus was cruel, but an *Erev Rav* motivated him to the point of cruelty; it was their idea and not the initial intent of Antiochus. See Book of The Maccabeas I & II.

5. T'hilim 2:2

6. Zohar Chadash, Balak, Passage: *Darach Kochav Mi'Yaakov*

7. Raya M'hemna, Pinchas, 246b

8. Zohar l,119a and Pirkei D'Rebbi Eliezer 28

before the event actually occurred and the understanding of the specifics of prophetic messages are never revealed to the average person before the events actually occur.[9] The second factor interfering with my understanding this *Chazal* is that I kept assuming that Armelus was a European.

Then in 1993, the Oslo negotiations between Peres, Rabin, and the PLO... Sure, that's it! They are called the *Erev Rav* because they are the *rav,* the political *leaders* of the Israeli Jews.[10] Then I thought, after all, if the *Erev Rav* is minimally Jewish and they are the political leaders of Jews, then it stands to reason that the individual leader of the political group must also be a minimally committed Jew. The actual leader (Armelus) and his political group *(Erev Rav),* the entire political leadership — all these people are only superficial Jews; they must be the entities of superficial Jews who 'break rank'. Indeed, this *Chazal* states that when the Jews will be persecuted by Esav and Yishmael, there will be an *Erev Rav* group who will 'break rank' and form an alliance with Yishmael.

בההוא זמנא יתער נשר ויתפרש גדפהא על ערבובי דאומין ועשו וישמעאל דאינון עמלקים וערבוביא בישא דישראל וטריף לון דלא ישתאר חד מנייהו לקיים מה שנאמר בישראל ה' בדד ינחנו ואין עמו אל נכר

On the surface, the Peres-Israeli government may be described as being comprised of Jews, but underneath the facade of a Jewish leadership is a government that subscribes to British Law and to Ottoman Law,[11] a government that has never developed their own legal system or even written a detailed constitution. Theirs is a proxy government run by people who, by accident of birth, are Jewish. They don't appear to be making decisions that further the advancement of Judaism or that protect Jews. As a matter of fact, every one of the 200 Jews that have been murdered by Arabs during their reign has been described by this government as "the price for peace". They certainly do appear callous and indifferent to the pain suffered by Jews. To understand the situation better, I would like to remind you of a story that the Maggid of Yerushalayim is fond of telling.[12]

> *One day he noticed that a little boy had fallen and was crying because he had hurt himself while playing in the neighborhood. Rabbi Shwadron quickly picked up the child and began running through the streets with a crying and bleeding youngster.*

---

9.   M'tzudas David on Daniel 8:14

10. See Tikunei Zohar 111a

11. That's why Israel has never developed their own legal system; they're merely enforcing the laws that Turkey and England enacted — which, in certain situations, happen to be pro-Arab and anti-Semitic. How ironic!

12. Krohn, P. "The Maggid Speaks", Mesorah Publications

A neighbor, who saw the Rabbi running so quickly, shouted out to the Rabbi not to worry because the child will be OK. The Rabbi didn't respond but kept on running. As he got closer, the neighbor began screaming, "Mayer'ke! My Mayer'ke." You see, the crying, bleeding child was that very neighbor's child. When she realized that the child was her own son, she began screaming and praying. She was calm and in a comforting mode when she assumed that the child belonged to someone else.

The Peres Government and their leaders are not really wicked people. They are many things, but they are not wicked or cruel. It is true that something close affects us more. When we see our child hurting, we cry and pray with real devotion; a neighbor's child in pain evokes some prayerful emotion. Unfortunately, in too many instances, a stranger in pain goes unnoticed. This Government is just not affected when Jews are hurt or murdered by Arabs, because, by their very nature, there is no real connection between them and other Jews. They feel no special affinity for Jews. They are being completely manipulated by Esav. Yes, certainly, many previous Israeli governments were pressured by Western countries; even Begin, the opposition leader for more than thirty years, succumbed to Western pressure after he assumed leadership. But every previous government had always felt a connection with Jewish history; every previous government identified proudly as Jews even though they were secularists. Each and every single previous government, without exception, felt a **strong connection** to other Jews.

"דערב רב ומנהון ... אפיקורסים משומדים לעבירות שבכל התורה כלה וישראל דאתתמר בהון ויתערבו בגוים וילמדו מעשיהם"

The present governing body feels nothing special about other Jews. The present Government does not even identify with Jews of the past.[13]

Therefore, one of the first 'innovations' of Rabin's Educational Minister was to discontinue the mandated study of Jewish History in Israeli schools. Furthermore, when Rabin signed that infamous PLO Agreement of Principles, he addressed the entire world but referred to a **Jewish struggle** for Israel that was **only seventy years** old, of a dream of Israel that Jews have only had for seventy years, of a Jewish presence in the Land that does not go back beyond seventy years. Don't you see how desperate they must be to mold other Israelis into a group that has no relationship to any other group that lived before. That is why foreign diplomats will no longer be 'exposed to the

---

13. Raya M'hemna, Pinchas, 246b — Here, the populace is described as assimilating and the leaders, much worse.

depressing site' of Yad Vashem, the Holocaust Memorial. That is why they announced that foreign diplomats will no longer tour Massada where Jews fought and died for this Land 1900 years ago. Massada, does call attention to a Jewish historical connection to the Land, which preempts any current spurious and dishonest Arab claims.

The New York Times

Israelis Ask If Holocaust Is Right Image

Memorial No Longer On Official Itinerary

By CLYDE HABERMAN
Special to The New York Times

JERUSALEM, JAN. 13 – For years it has been an almost unvarying ritual for visiting foreign officials: soon after landing they are automatically taken to Yad Vashem, the memorial in Jerusalem to the 6 million Jews killed by the Nazis.

No longer.....

Ministry officials explained that they simply wanted to stop telling visitors what to do. But critics across the political spectrum accused the Government of having lost its sense of Jewish history and identity.

Yad Vashem is not the only site affected. Also off the must-see list is Masada, the mountaintop fortress where Jewish rebels committed mass suicide during a first-century revolt against Rome. And a once-standard tour of the disputed Golan Heights will be made only if a visitor specifically asks for it.

Golan settlers call it political maneuvering by a government that may be ready to give back the strategic area, which was captured in the 1967 Arab-Israel war. Often, the settlers note, visitors leave the Golan convinced that Israel cannot relinquish the area without damaging its security – which is not the Government position these days. Foreign Ministry denials of political motives ring hollow on the heights.

The real emotional chord, though, was struck with Yad Vashem, whose Hebrew name, taken from the Old Testament book of Isaiah, is commonly translated as Everlasting Memorial.

Deputy Foreign Minister Yossi Beilin, architect of the new policy, says he has nothing against Yad Vashem – or Masada or the Golan. But compelling people to visit a particular site, no matter how evocative, is "Bolshevik" behavior, he says, and Israelis must stop thinking that "we know better than you what you should do."

Forced visits to the memorial discomforts some Israelis for other reasons. They see the tours as perhaps overemphasizing Jews as victims in the national self-definition, and suggest alternative sites that show modern Israel's accomplishments. like desert farms or science centers.

But those people may be a small minority. On both the political left and the right, critics accused the Foreign Ministry of trifling with painful collective memories.

Yad Vashem is "an identity card and gateway to Israel," said Shevah Weiss, Speaker of Parliament and a Polish-born survivor of the Holocaust.

Efraim Zuroff, Israel director of the Simon Wiesenthal Center, notes that many countries have monuments that they demand foreign visitors see. "For anyone to understand what this country's all about, why it's important to have a Jewish state, it's obvious that they must learn about the Holocaust and its implications," he said.

Israelis are still smarting from an embarrassment last summer when the visiting Egyptian Foreign Minister, Amr Mahmoud Moussa, practically had to have his arm twisted to stop at Yad Vashem. Even then, he pointedly skipped the main Hall of Remembrance, where he would have had to put on a yarmulke, and went instead to a memorial dedicated to children killed by the Nazis.

Some critics suspect that a hidden agenda in the new policy is to make it easier for Israel to lure other Arab figures, including President Hosni Mubarak of Egypt, who has stayed away despite the peace treaty between the two countries.

The newspaper Maariv says Israelis need not apologize for the memorial. "The Jewish state, which rose from the ashes of destruction and killing, is allowed to make sure that official guests see and understand through Yad Vashem, Israel's sensitivity to its citizens' security," it said in an editorial.

But another daily, Davar, sided with Mr. Beilin. "Israel in 1995," it wrote, "can be sure of itself and the justness of its case even without force-feeding its visitors."

For its part, Yad Vashem stood above the fray. "Visiting this institution," it said in a brief statement, "is a privilege and not an obligation."

This visit to Massada is crucial in teaching people that Jews are the ones with the historical and legal rights to the Land. A few quotes from the Bible would have also demonstrated the real truth that no Christian or Arab could refute, because both Christians and Arabs do respect the Divine Jewish Bible.

They are not cruel or wicked; they are merely a political entity consisting of people who happen to have been born Jewish by accident. This situation can be best understood by comparing it to, perhaps, a situation in America. Suppose a congressman is elected and this congressman happens to have been born Jewish. Does that accident of birth alter the responsibilities of office? After all, as an American citizen, he was elected to Congress to represent the best interests of the United States and the situation does not change because he was born a Jew (or an Indian or a Catholic). The United States does not hate Jews or the State of Israel. America is really indifferent and rightfully so — because decisions in Washington are based primarily on what essentially benefits Americans. If American interests will be advanced through an Arab alliance, then we would expect congressional activity to pursue that goal — even if it hurts Jews and/or Israel or Icelanders or any other people. America must care for itself first and then if there is no conflict, they could also accommodate Israel. This is the way it should be for Americans: America should care about itself *first*. We may not like to recognize this position, but we are only guests and a very small minority who cannot expect blind obedience to our every demand. And based on their current analysis and perceptions, America feels that it is in their best interest to placate the Arabs.

That Israeli government was not a wicked or cruel government. That Israeli government appears to operate as the proxy government for America. Remember, all the rumors that were flying during the time of the most recent Israeli elections? Everybody remembers how two United States Presidents entered Israeli politics by supporting Rabin (against Shamir) and Peres (against Netanyahu). The Rabin government was not a Jewish government; the Rabin government appeared as an extension of an American government on Mid-East soil. It's like an annex. This Israeli government is just *not affected* when Jews are scarred or maimed or murdered — just like an American government is simply not affected when Israeli Jews are scarred or maimed or murdered. It is almost a total incorporation of the identity of another group.[14]

---

14. The unconscious motivates us to do strange things. For example, consider the concept of 'identifying with the aggressor'. In all instances of hostage/kidnap for an extended period of time, the victim eventually identifies with his cruel captor and, when released, is able to support these criminal activities and philosophies no matter how repugnant, distorted, or false they would have been judged by the very victim before experiencing this terrifying, life-threatening incident. Remember Patty Hearst who, after being held captive for a period of months, became an active member of the very terrorist gang that held her captive?

This 'exile' government operates like the extension of a foreign government (from another part of the world). To those Israeli politicians, Jews of Israel are not any more special than any other citizen of the country.[15] That Israeli government had no special connection to the people or to the Land.[16] Never before in the history of modern Israel have captured Jewish soldiers been allowed to languish in Arab captivity for so many years — that Israeli government did not even attempt to negotiate for their release (while thousands of Arab criminals and murderers were being released from Israeli prisons *unconditionally*). How easy it would be to trade imprisoned Arab murderers for these captured Jews. How easy it could have been to demand that Ron Arad, an Iranian captive for twelve years, be exchanged for the 170 hostages on the hijacked Iranian airliner that landed in Israel in September 1995. But that Israeli Government was just plainly indifferent to the plight of Jews — all Jews. And that is why they can offer to parcel off Jewish real estate to Arabs and that is why they can allow Arab murderers to roam freely throughout the Land. As a matter of fact, the decisions of that Government are exactly the decisions we would expect the American government to make, if America were actually ruling Israel today from afar.

The Zohar captures this entire spirit by referring to the Peres-Israeli ruling power as *Erev Rav* — opportunists and minimal Jews with no special identification as Jews. The *Erev Rav* are people who have no unique relationship with Jews. They are ready to sacrifice Jews and undermine Judaism and threaten its continuity — behaving just like Egyptians might (or some Western power).

The *Erev Rav* has always changed sides 'at the drop of a hat', at the first sign of tension. They are frightened people who have no real commitment to Torah, to Jews, or to the Land. The *Erev Rav* is the group that brought the Moslem and Christian countries together — Yishmael and Esav, the two arch enemies that could never unite — except through the very persistent efforts of Rabin and Peres, the leaders of the *Erev Rav*. The two arch enemies are united by the *Erev Rav* to create a world-wide federation whose purpose is to dismantle the little country called Israel as predicted in *TaNaCh*[17] — even including the designated names of the members. As we saw earlier, Oral-Torah explains that this alliance was formed as a direct result of the efforts

---

15. See T'hilim 106:35 — ויתערבו בגוים וילמדו מעשיהם — Hashem tells us about the period when Jews will imitate the thinking and behavior of non-Jews — even in the area of how to treat other Jews.

16. Also see Shamir's column in Jewish Press, January 20, 1995, page 4.

17. T'hilim 83

of the *Erev Rav*, the actual catalyst that bonded the Yishmaelites and non-Moslems together in their quest for the Land. And so, indeed:

ובני ישמעאל זמינין בההוא זמנא לאתערא עם כל עמין דעלמא למיתי על ירושלים

ויזדווגון כלהון עממיא על ברתיה דיעקב לאדחייא לה מעלמא ועל ההוא זמנא כתיב ועת צרה היא ליעקב וממנה יושע

"The Arabs will fire the entire world to arise against Jerusalem." [18]

The Hebrew language is a most unique method of communication. The letters are used to make words; these very same letters are also used for numbers. In the English language, words have *literate equivalents* like 'caring' and 'concern'. But because the Hebrew letters are also numerals, the Hebrew language also has *numerical equivalents (g'matrya)* — when letters of two different words share the identical arithmetic sum. It is interesting to note that the arithmetic sum of 'Armelus' is 347. It is also interesting to note that a *numerical equivalent* for the *Erev Rav* leader, **'Armelus'**, is **'Peres + 7'** — numerically, both Hebrew phrases add up to 347. The numeral 7, whether it appears in the unit's column (as 7) or in the ten's column (as 70) — they're both the same numeral. [19] **Armelus** refers to **Peres** + 7 [or **70**] nations. Even though Rabin had dominated the spotlight, it should be noted that the real architect of this entire fiasco is Peres. So maintains Shamir in his autobiography, [20] and in his weekly newspaper column. [21] So maintains Peres in his recent book. [22] So maintains the Jerusalem Post [23] and so decided the Nobel Peace Prize Committee by also recognizing him (and not just Rabin). So **Armelus** is **Peres** as affirmed by the Nobel Committee. **Armelus** is **Peres supplemented by the 70 nations [of the world] who arise against the Jews of Israel.** But it gets 'better' yet.

After the Israelites left Egypt, they were chased by the Egyptian Army who unilaterally abrogated their agreement which had just been negotiated with Moses. The 'ink from the signatures had not even dried yet'. The Egyptian-

---

18. Zohar I, 25a and 119a; Pirkei D'Rebbi Eliezer 28

19. The zero in the number '70' is just a 'place-holder'. We call this מספר קטן.

20. Wherein he states how he very harshly reprimanded Peres several times for his approaching the international community in order to solicit their involvement in Arab-Israel affairs. Shamir maintained that the world will find this a golden opportunity to pressure Israel to give away their Land. Ironically, it was actually Shamir, as Prime Minister, who really started this whole PLO Fiasco by organizing its forerunner, the Madrid Conference.

21. Jewish Press, March 3, 1995, page 4

22. "The New Middle East"

23. International Edition, week ending December 18, 1993: "Peres is the person who makes the peace process happen," says Raphaella Bilski Ben-Hur, a political science professor at the Hebrew University who has worked with Peres and Rabin. "He is not only the engine. He is the steering wheel."

Israelite Principles of Peace and Disengagement were only seven days old and are already about to be violated by our 'partners in peace'.[24] The Torah describes the impending and inevitable clash of forces; the Egyptians are closing in on the Israelites. Carefully note the exact words:[25]

> *"The Egyptians chased after them and Pharaoh's horses and chariots overtook them, and [also] the riders and soldiers, as the Israelites were encamped by the sea."*

At first blush, this verse is difficult to understand. The Torah says that "horses and chariots overtook" the Israelites. But horses do no capturing. The independent clause should have been the "soldiers and riders" because they are the fighters and it is the soldiers who attack and overtake. The sentence should have read: 'The Egyptian soldiers overtook the Israelites'. Yet, the main focus of the Torah is upon chariots and horses — chariots and horses, the tools for the army. Tools are controlled [by people] and tools do no damage and tools do not capture Israelites or anybody — unless these tools of the enemy are **people who are being used as tools!!!!**

So I searched the verse for encoded words and names; I was searching for the identity of the tools that bring the Jews close to tragedy and destruction, G-d forbid.

Do you believe it? The word **'Peres'** is encoded in that very sentence and is spelled, in the text, with equidistant spacing of two letters between each letter from his name. Indeed, Peres is the tool for the enemy of the Jews. The name 'Peres' is **spelled backwards,** because that is how Hashem indicates the period of time when this event will occur. Events of the early period of Diaspora are spelled in the regular fashion (i.e. frontward) while names and events that occur at the end of the Jewish exile are *usually* spelled

---

24. I guess, not much changes.
25. Sh'mos 14:9

backwards in order to indicate that the particular person will be at the **back-end of the Diaspora**. Indeed, Peres is the tool that will appear on the scene at the end of the exile-period in order to help the enemy with their plans to kill Jews and/or expropriate the Land.

The Chairman of the United States Senate Committee on Foreign Relations, Jesse Helms, writes: "... I mistrust Arafat profoundly ... I will never completely understand how the leaders of Israel reached the decision to enter into negotiations with Yasser Arafat ..."[27]

Peres is the tool for the Arabs, because he is, indeed, the real architect for this entire sell-out of the Land. This Land was always destined to return to its original Jewish owners. And once the Jews were returning and after winning three wars so miraculously and so gloriously, Peres, **the vehicle for the Arabs,** figured a way for the thrice-defeated Arab enemy to finally attain its military objective in a *pieceful* fashion. After a history of fifty years of military failures and of an inability to strip the Jews of their territorial possessions through these wars, the Arabs are now on the path that will help them accomplish their goals of Land conquest — in a peaceful and piecemeal fashion, Heaven forbid. **Peres, the tool for the Arabs, has been able to figure out a way to help the Arabs dismantle ALL of the Land** — Peres, the vehicle of the Arabs, is able to overtake the Israelis. Unbelievable??!!

---

27. Letter to Alice Novick, dated March 12, 1996

CHAPTER
XVII

The Peres Plan

I am so incensed and alarmed because after reading Peres' new book,[1] I began to see how he was attempting to develop his ridiculous position of giving away the Land of Israel to Arabs and how he was attempting to rationalize this extreme belief. Peres makes many points in his book that are so illogical. As a matter of fact, many of these points are purposive and willful distortions and fabrications. This type of dishonesty is inexcusable. His dishonesty and extremist attitudes and approaches have enraged me to the extent that I feel compelled to expand upon what was initially to be a footnote in this *sefer*, in order to help the reader gain a deeper understanding of the current events in the Middle East.

Some of these matters require the allotment of extensive space in order to refute them with proper historical documentation. Therefore, only several easier points will be reviewed at this time.

---

1.   "The New Middle East"

The basic question is: For 100 years, Political Zionism has espoused the restoration of Israel to Jews. How can it be that Peres, a disciple of Political Zionism, now advocates a position which is in direct opposition to the main platform of his political movement?

In discussing Middle East history since World War I, Peres fails to mention several very crucial facts:

1) When the Ottoman Empire in the Middle East was conquered by the British and French during World War I, the victors divided up the huge territory into their own protectorates according to the provisions of the Sykes-Picot Agreement. Essentially, France and Britain took the area of what was then called Syria. France took control of the area now known as Lebanon, Southern Turkey, Southwest Armenia, and Northwest Iraq. Britain gained control of Palestine and the rest of the Arabian Peninsula.

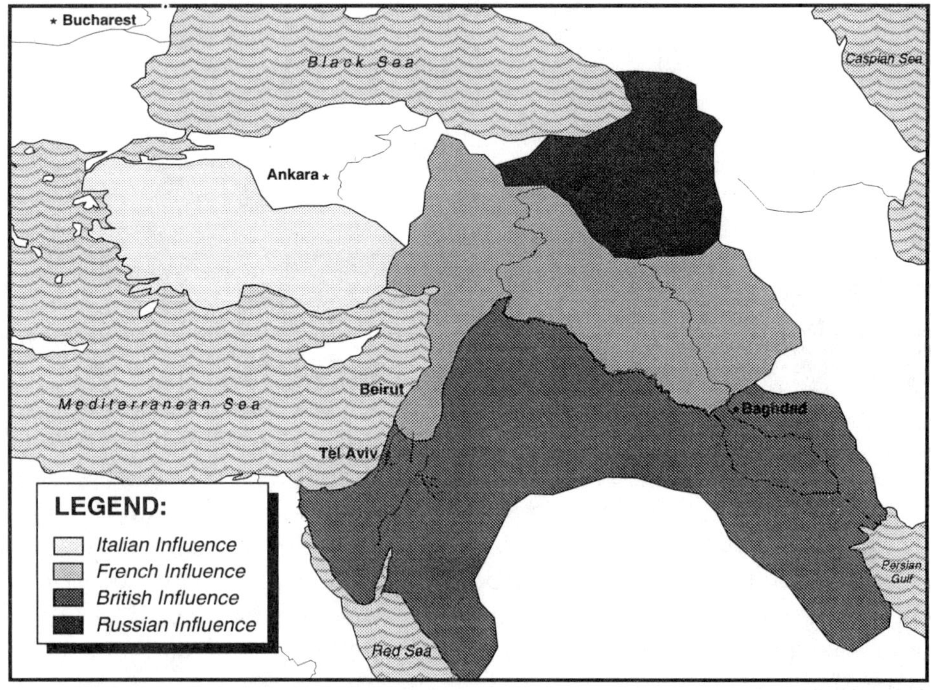

Eventually they would actually carve up the entire Middle East from Africa to India so that ultimately there would be 21 countries for Arabs — with the area that we once knew as Palestine to be for Jews. (Some time later, however, the world would renege on this agreement TWO TIMES with each successive reneging creating a smaller and smaller territory for Jews.)

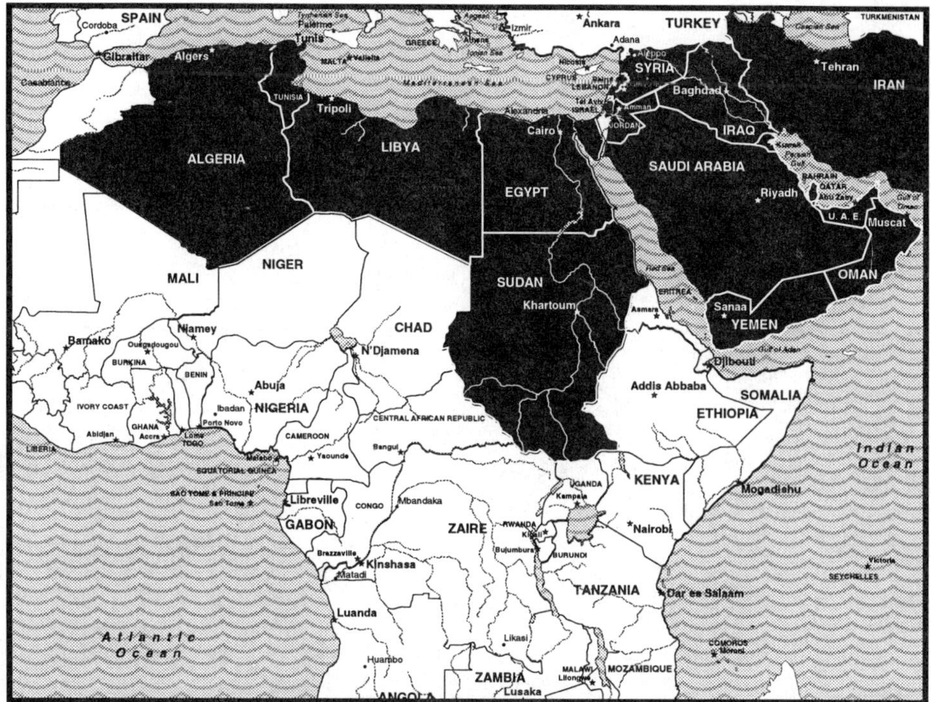

2)   Emir Feisal, son of the Sherif of Mecca and soon to become King of Iraq, represented the Arab interests in the subdivision of the British Protectorate into what would eventually be called Palestine for Jews and Syria, The Arab State. Feisal stated clearly and unequivocally that the Arabs have absolutely no affiliation with the remaining land that was called Palestine. (Despite this declaration, however, the world would soon sub-divide Palestine — with 80% of Palestine for Arabs and only 20% remaining for Jews, subdivisions of Palestine that are now-called Israel and Jordan.)

Nor did Feisal, the Arab representative, ask for Jerusalem or even mention its name in any of the official Arab documents of that day — so really, how important could Jerusalem be for the Arabs?! The truth is that **Jerusalem was never special for Arabs!!** As a matter of fact, Feisal was delighted to accept the area of Syria (as it was then called) and agreed that this area would be reserved for Arabs; the remainder, **Palestine in its entirety should be the homeland for Jews.** This territory also consisted of Jerusalem, Judea, Samaria and what is now-called Jordan. That is what was negotiated with the British in the aftermath of World War I between Arabs and Jews who were represented by Feisal and Weizmann, respectively.

As a matter of fact, Feisal writes to Felix Frankfurter "... and there is room in Syria for us both (i.e. Arabs and Jews)". Feisal also agreed with Weizmann "... all such measures shall be adopted as will afford the fullest guarantees for carrying into effect the British Government's [Balfour] Declaration of the 2d of November, 1917."[2]

Feisal continued: "... all necessary measures shall be taken to encourage and stimulate immigration of Jews into Palestine on a large scale basis and as quickly as possible to settle immigrants upon the land..."[3]

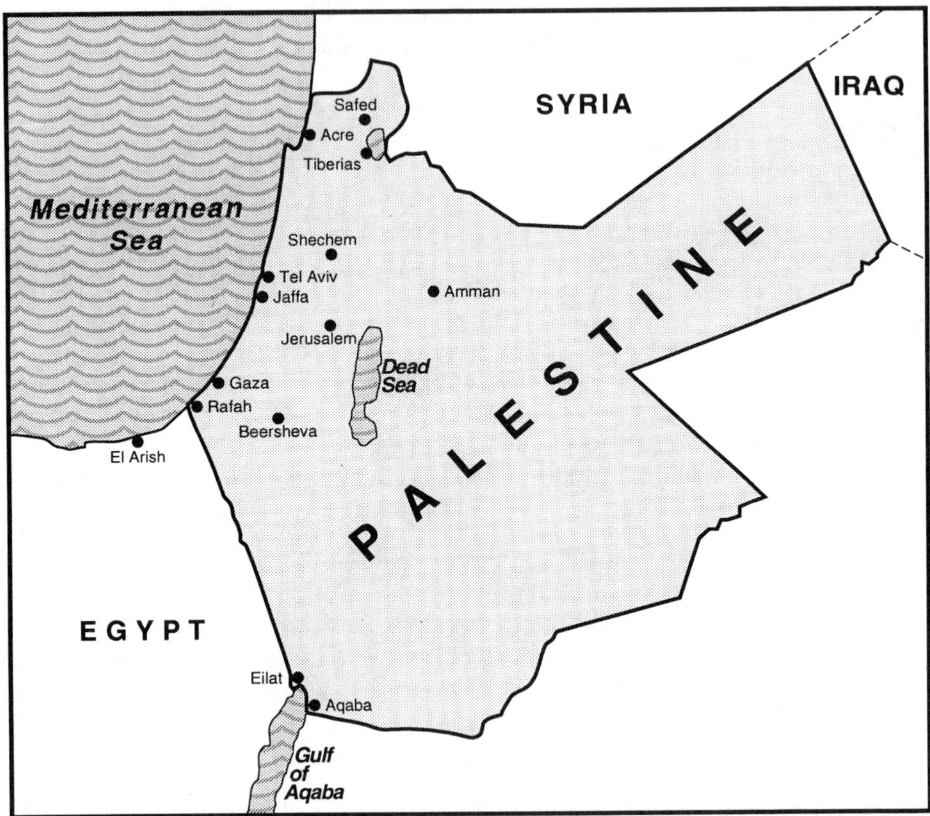

3) Peres failed to mention that in approving this negotiated agreement executed under British auspices, the League of Nations granted the Jews **both sides of the Jordan River** and mandated Britain to fulfill this order by encouraging Jews to emigrate to Israel and by assisting the Jews in

2. Agreement Between Emir Feisal and Chaim Weizmann, January 3, 1919 — Article III
3. Ibid. Article IV

developing the capabilities to govern themselves. Peres failed to mention how, in violation of their charge, Britain tried to undermine this mandate by setting up circumstances to prevent the Jews from ever achieving possession of their homeland including the attempted manipulation of Lawrence of Arabia in order to create the first of several major Arab myths.[4] Peres also failed to emphasize how the world, through the UN, changed their mind — on this occasion taking away 80% of Palestine from the Jews and creating **another Arab country** — this one to be called Transjordanian Palestine.

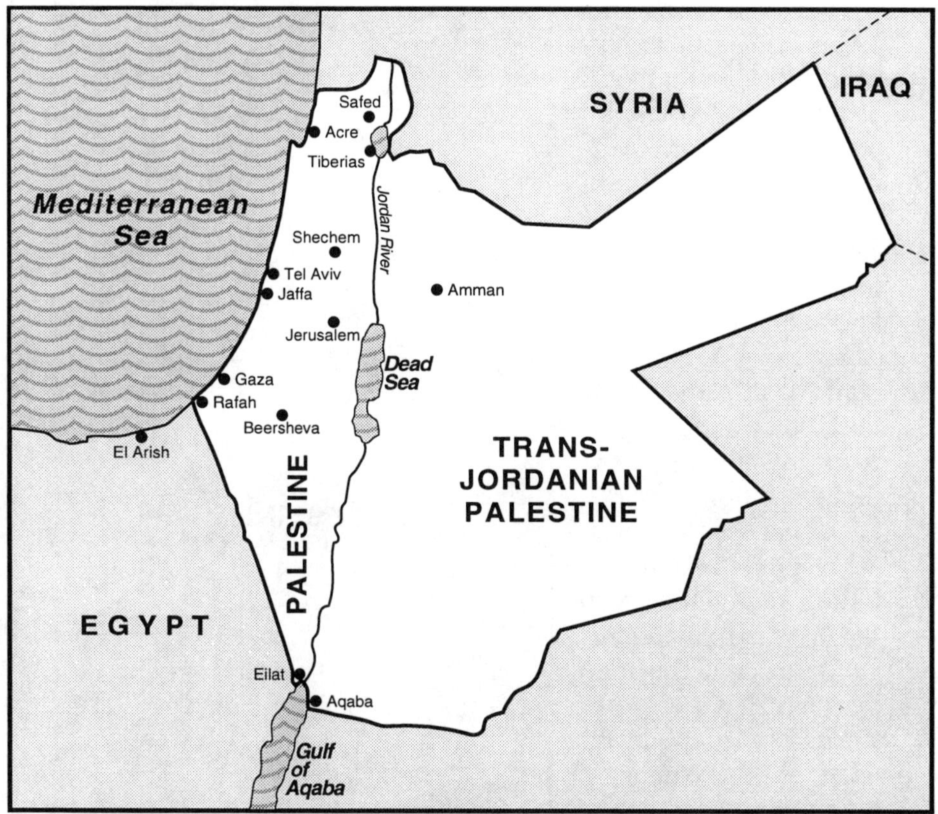

So after 1947, less than 10% remained of what was the original Syrian/ Palestinian Protectorate — that 10% was now referred to as Palestine and would be reserved for The Jewish State. From the remaining 90% were created Syria, Lebanon, Iraq, Kuwait, Saudi Arabia, and Arab-Palestine.

---

4.   See Katz, S. "Battleground: Fact and Fantasy in Palestine", Bantam Books, 1973

4) Peres does talk about the tiny Palestine that developed after one more change to the UN Partition Plan and he maintains that this is *essentially* the territory that Jews should possess. He states that the West Bank (i.e. Judea and Samaria) as well as Gaza and most of post-1948 Israel should be Arab territory. It is important to note that in the UN Partition Plan, **Jerusalem was not to be sovereign Jewish territory** — and neither Judea and Samaria nor the Golan Heights. Even this plan has been totally rejected by all Arab governments for all these years, beginning in 1947. I think we need to look at the map of Israel that was formulated by the UN in 1947, the map that Peres validates and the map that he wishes to return to — *Hashem Y'rachem*. Indeed, may Hashem be merciful and protect us from further anguish and bloodshed.

From the adjacent map, you will notice that Israel really consists of three small and **not-connected** counties. By the way, did you ever see such

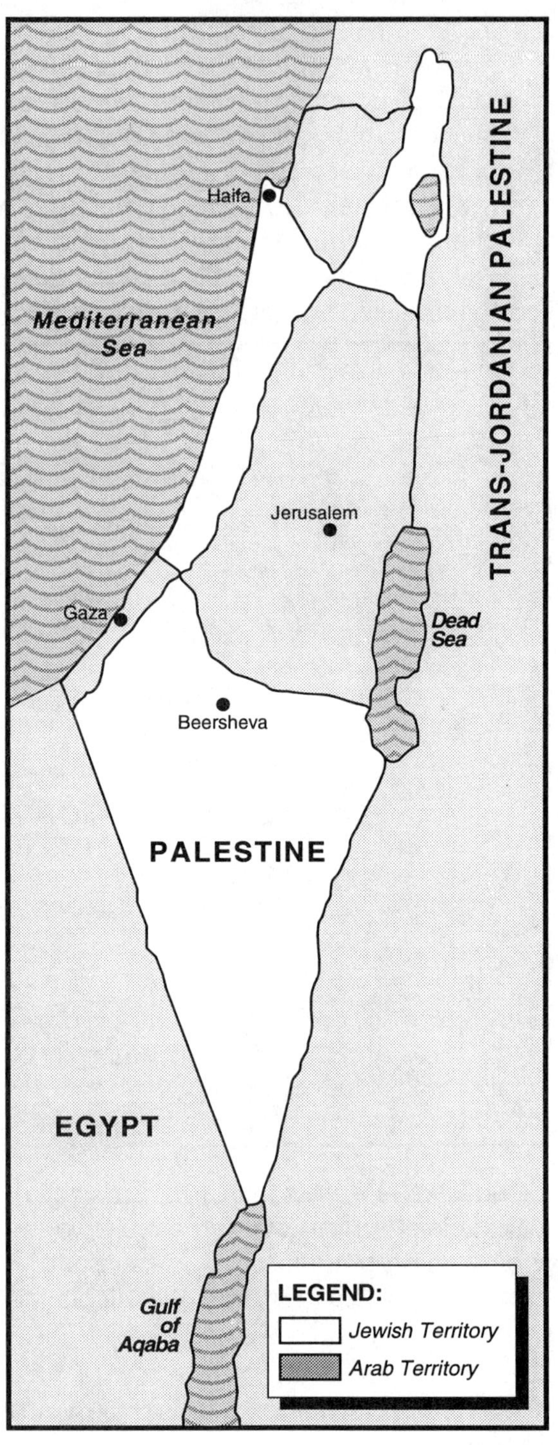

a configuration of a country anywhere in the world?! Do you have any idea how secure these three distinct counties will be? How many Arab soldiers would it take to keep the three parts of Israel separated from each other?! Well, that is precisely what occurred. In 1948, the Arabs did isolate each county from the other two and **actually did strangle the Land** with a very effective blockade for a very long time. Many Jewish lives were lost, as a result. Peres does not discuss these factors — obviously, he would not dare show the map either.

The part that disturbed me the most, however, was when he stated that "the Palestinian people have existed [in Israel] **from time immemorial**".[5] I know those last three words because they are the title of one of the most important books that have ever been written about the ownership of Israel and about the true Mid-East events during the early part of this century. Peres does credit Joan Peters for writing "From Time Immemorial: The Origins of the Arab-Jewish Conflict Over Palestine". And he describes the book as being "in full agreement with the Palestinian point of view in the matter of [Arab] historical rights to the land". Peres maintains that Joan Peters' book supports the position that the entire Land of Israel belongs to Arabs and that the Jews stole the Land from the Arabs.

My friends, let me tell you a little about how this book by Ms. Peters came to be written. Ms. Peters went to the Middle East because, like everyone else, she already knew that Arabs were the rightful owners of the Land. She went to the Middle East in order to find the documentation to support her pre-judged position that Jews had no business at all being in the Middle East. After many months of researching hundreds of documents and interviewing dozens of witnesses, she wrote her book. And the point that follows now is the most crucial to everything that we have been talking about.

Ms. Peters discovered that she was prejudiced and that **all evidence proves that the Arabs are trying to perpetrate a hoax and that the British were integral to this hoax of 'Palestinian rights'.** She entitled the book by the original name — the name that she chose when she believed that the Land belonged to Arabs — and not Jews. She entitled the book "From Time Immemorial" because that is how long the Jews own the Land, that is how far back their ownership rights go. If you have not read this book, you must buy it because this book will be used over-and-over again by your entire family as the classic reference manual on this subject — the historical basis behind the crisis in the Middle East. This masterpiece abounds with proofs and every point is well-documented.

---

5.   Op. cit. Peres, pages 165 and 210

For Peres to substantiate his bizarre position by quoting Joan Peters is but one flagrant example of how he is distorting facts and lying in every imaginable way — to the point of purposely distorting research conclusions in order to suit his policy. Indeed, our period is noted by the absence of honesty and by the willful and conscious distortions of truth.

What Treaties Are Permitted?

Not long ago, our family went to a very large convention sponsored by an international orthodox organization. There were classes from 6:30 in the morning until 11 in the evening. It was really great. The giants of the Torah world spoke and gave lectures. What a wonderful experience it was for the three generations in our family. Everyone enjoyed and learned. The program was varied so as to accommodate everyone's interests and backgrounds. It was so great that I was even willing to sacrifice some of my sleep on Friday night in order to attend a discussion that was to be lead by two prominent orthodox Israeli figures. I was so excited that, together with my daughter Rivka, I sat in the front of this large auditorium. We didn't want to miss one word — especially since it was Shabbos and there could be no microphones. The first to speak was a well-educated Jew whom I had admired since my youth; I had met him many times — he was a genius, as I remembered him from 30 years earlier. I was excited that he was chosen to address us on Friday night on the topic of the Israeli-PLO negotiations which, at that time, were already underway. I looked forward to chatting with him privately after such a long absence.

I expected to hear the insights of someone who had been living as an Israeli in the inner circle of Israeli politics for decades. His presentation opened with the citing of much background information after which he began to speak in glowing terms about the 'Peace Treaty' with the PLO. I figured that soon he would provide us with some Torah insights. After all, he is orthodox and brilliant, as I remembered him from his youth. But as the time passed, I began finding it difficult to concentrate. It was Friday night after all; maybe I really was tired. But I noticed that I was also becoming jittery. No, I realized, I wasn't tired; it wasn't the jitters, either. My heart was beating faster. I was becoming annoyed. My breathing became more labored. I was becoming angry and frustrated. Here was an orthodox Israeli politician who was spending too much time lauding Rabin and Peres and emphasizing how important it is for Arabs to have a *twenty-third homeland.* Now I was real angry — it's bad enough to lose Shabbos sleep, but now to be subjected to Jewish ignorance clothed in sophisticated language? I looked around. It appeared that everyone was quiet and calm. Was it that they were beginning to believe that he was correct in his assessment or were they awaiting the next Israeli speaker? A few minutes more passed and I noticed that I was becoming very angry. He had not quoted one Jewish source yet. He had not made mention of any Torah concepts. He had not attempted to discuss whether it was permissible to give away **any** Land. I could not take it any longer. Generally, my daughter Rivka acts as my super ego and she usually tells me to 'behave myself' in public. After we each expressed our disbelief in what we were hearing from this speaker, I took my clue; she wasn't telling me to sit quietly. I stood up and shouted, "What about the *mitzvah* of לא תכרת ברית[1] and לא תחנם?[2] What about the Talmud Bavli and Y'rushalmi?[3] What about the different *G'moras* in Avodah Zarah, Eruvin, and Sanhedrin?!"[4] I didn't ask him about the reminder of the *Chazon Ish*[5] that giving away Land

---

1. Sh'mos 23:32 and 34:12-15; D'varim 7:2; Yehoshua 2:2; Yeshayahu 28:15. Herein, Hashem repeatedly forbids Jews from entering into treaties with the immoral non-Jews who are living in the Land and who have an established history of criminal activity. This is to prevent security problems as well as limiting their sphere of influence. These are all in addition to the law forbidding setting up situations that might eventually threaten the lives of Jews.

2. D'varim 7:2; especially Rambam, Sefer HaMitzvos, Prohibition 51; Tosfos in Avodah Zarah 20a; Rambam, Hilchos Avodah Zarah 10:10-13 — here it's even forbidden when there's no possible risk to the security of Jews, where Jews feel a non-military type of pressure; certainly, giving away Land is all the more so forbidden if the security of Jews may be threatened by allowing the enemy to "breathe down our necks".

3. Talmud Moed Katan 2:4 and Sotah 8:10; Y'rushalmi: T'rumah 5 and beginning of Ma'aser Sheni

4. Talmud Avodah Zarah 20a; Eruvin 45a; and Sanhedrin 16b

5. Sh'viis Chapter 24

is no less forbidden than eating *treif* or meat and milk that were cooked together. You know what his answer was? He said that he would discuss these issues privately — after the formal program was concluded. Privately? Like these are insignificant Jewish laws that don't merit public consideration? It was obvious; he had already decided on an issue without the use of *Halachah*. He ignored every Torah source; he had to, because all Torah sources contradict his thesis and prove that he doesn't know what he's talking about — not from a Torah point of view, not from a political point of view, not from a sociological or historical point of view, not from any point of view. These opinions were actually *his* opinions — but *definitely not Torah views.* He said that he would deal privately with the Torah principles of *Halachah* after the formal program was concluded. He didn't! Of course, he didn't because he couldn't. No one can argue with Hashem and Torah Laws. How could you save this for 'after the program'? These are crucial laws that he chose to ignore. It is only with the input of the Written and Oral-Torah that a position becomes a Jewish position.

What amazed me most about this presentation was the fact that here was an orthodox leader ostensibly speaking as an orthodox leader who actually spoke exactly like all my non-orthodox and non-Jewish acquaintances. They don't quote Torah principles — nor did he. They speak glowingly of "peace in our time" as Chamberlain did after making 'peace' with Hitler in 1939 — and so did he speak fervently of "peace in our time".[6] They don't ever mention the historical or Biblical connection that Jews have to the Land — neither did he. I began to wonder: 'How is he different from the average non-Jew in the world?' The only difference I could generate was that he obviously observed *mitzvot* but, at best, it was obvious that he was not really understanding Torah. Certainly, he was unable (or unwilling) to assimilate Torah and apply it to daily living. (He also heckled and interrupted the next speaker — a disrespectful characteristic that no Jew should ever display.) He probably had never learned how to incorporate Torah principles into daily living.

It was clear to me that he was analyzing situations and drawing conclusions without utilizing any Torah principles in his analysis. OH YEAH, HE DID MENTION *PIKUACH NEFESH* MANY TIMES THAT EVENING. He did mention how it was important to prevent bloodshed. It was magnanimous of him to introduce one Torah concept. He mentioned this Torah concept,

---

6.   This is the same Chamberlain who also proclaimed that after the mountains of the border were given to Hitler: "...under the Munich Agreement...the new Czechoslovakia will find a greater security than she ever enjoyed in the past."

but he was unable to apply it properly.[7] He did not mention that prior to his speech, more than 150 Jews were murdered by Arabs who are desperate for peace — so desperate for peace that **they are willing to murder every Jew that they meet in order to achieve peace.**

He described these murdered Jews as the 'price for peace'. Did you ever hear anything as ridiculous as this?! I, for one, would rather have all Jews alive and describe them as "the price for conflict". Jews are murdered by murderers and the criminal is ignored and the victim becomes the price we have to pay for peace?! I ask, 'Would this speaker sacrifice his own family members as the "price for peace"? I think not, so let's not persist in this gross perversion that **murdered Jews are the "price for peace".**

It seemed to me that he was not thinking like an orthodox person. Before beginning his analysis, the orthodox Jew always studies Written and Oral-Torah in order to ascertain the proper *Halachah,* the appropriate response. This approach also helps us analyze the situation because 'History repeats itself'. When we study Torah, we invariably discover a historical prototype and a recommended course of action. After all, that is the purpose of authentic Judaism. Judaism is not limited to the laws of Kashrus or Shabbos or Kaddish. It is also the laws of interpersonal relationships, of real-estate responsibilities, of business ethics, of nationhood, of government decisions, of treaties, and of specific measures for protecting Jewish lives.

How disappointed I was to hear the non-Torah reasoning of a presumed Torah person. What a 'let down'. Why was this happening? How could a Torah person ignore *mitzvot* in the Torah and ignore very single Jewish source on this subject?

It seems to me that the problem is that most Jews don't realize that principles of Torah apply to *every* situation. Judaism is not a religion that can be compartmentalized into a prayer-service once or twice or thrice a day and then 'Do what you want boys'. Judaism is *Halachah;* **Judaism is a *way of life* that affects everything that we do** — as individuals, as a community, and as a nation. To be a conscientious, serious, and committed Jew means that we always *first* ask what is the Torah's approach to a certain situation; then we act. The orthodox person never decides in a vacuum without consider- ing Torah principles. Improperly educated Jews and those who haven't really assimilated their Torah learning properly reason as follows: 'If I'm aware of Torah principles that agree with my *predetermined* position, then I'll quote them; if they contradict my predetermined position, then I will just ignore Torah principles and, instead, talk about global values and the general beauty of

---

7.   See next chapter for an explanation about the saving of lives.

Judaism without making any reference to the fact that I am not speaking from a foundation of Torah principles'. We do not decide in a vacuum; **we do not decide without studying Written and Oral-Torah.** At least, honest and learned Jews don't analyze and then decide with no regard for Torah. First we study the sources, then we learn what the approach of Judaism is in this particular situation — this is Torah Judaism. It is precisely this issue which serves to differentiate between a Jewish philosopher and a philosophy of Judaism. Spinoza was a Jewish-born philosopher who developed a philosophy of life that was totally unrelated to Judaism because he did not utilize Torah principles. In this respect, Spinoza was a **Jewish philosopher**[8] — only because he was accidentally born a Jew. On the other hand, because Rambam utilized Torah principles, his is a **philosophy of Judaism.**

This speaker's position was hogwash. After learning the sources, it should become clear to us as to what the Torah approach is towards the Arabs, towards the PLO, to terrorist-murderers, and to the Land of Israel. Let's take a careful look.

When the Israelites enter Israel, Joshua offers the inhabitants three options — the same three choices that are required of us at all times when we are in the Land:[9]

1) The Canaanites can live peacefully with the Israelites if the Canaanites will **recognize the legitimacy and authority of the Israelites.** The Land is not a democratic country; Israel is a Jewish community and everything possible must be done to ensure that the quality of life will be maintained with all its beauty. As such, not only must the non-Jews **pledge allegiance to the government** of Israelites, they must also abide by the **Seven Noachide Laws** of Basic Morality which include prohibitions against theft, immorality, asocial behavior, and murder. Sounds pretty reasonable? In order to maintain a healthy society, we insist that all people commit themselves to a pattern of constructive and respectful behavior; all residents of Israel must be law-abiding.

2) If the non-Jewish inhabitants feel that the demands are beyond their capabilities and that they're **unable to behave in a civilized fashion** — they are asked to **leave the country.**

3) If the non-Jews feel that they **cannot accept the basic principles of humanity and decency** and if they **chose not to leave** the country, then it became the obligation of the Jewish people to **forcibly deport** these non-Jews who cannot even promise to stop their murdering.

---

8. Even though he was a heretic.
9. See: Y'rushalmi Sh'viis 6; Tosfos in Talmud Gittin 46a; and Vayikra Rabah 16.

As the Torah states very clearly and explicitly[10]

> *'If you do not evict these [uncivilized and violent] people from the Land, then they will become great troublemakers and disturb you constantly and prevent you from achieving the relaxed and beautiful life that can be yours.'*

Written and Oral-Torah take it a step further by stating that we are forbidden to make peace treaties with some of the nations that are found in the Land. There can never be any form of alliance with any entity that:

a)   will not recognize **Jewish sovereignty** over the Land of Israel

b)   will not **pledge allegiance** to the Jewish government in the Land of Israel

c)   will not behave with **respect** for human life

d)   will not **forbid killing** and murdering

e)   will not accept upon themselves a code of behavior that is **decent** and respectful of everyone — no matter their religious or national background.

How could any orthodox person not be aware of this directive? People who are bent on destruction and murder are not permitted to live in Israel! Why would we want our children and friends to be m-------, Heaven forbid, (I can't even say the word). Every elementary school youngster is aware of the Seven Noachide Laws of Basic Morality. As a matter of fact, there are many non-Jewish groups throughout the world who are leaving the Church[11] and are adopting these Seven Noachide Laws as the foundation for their way of life. They even call themselves by various names — but the names have a common denominator: somewhere in the title is the word "Noachide". Non-Jews are excited to study Torah concepts as it applies to their living moral and ethical lives. As a matter of fact, thousands just gathered in Texas for an international conference and thousands more are studying. In fact, I just received a phone call from a Protestant minister who wants to study the Noachide Laws in order to teach them to others.

If all this is not enough, I found a very, very interesting Code.

In the passage dealing with the prohibition against entering into any formal treaty with the other inhabitants of the Land[12] we find the year התשנ״ה (5755) encoded six times in the same passage.[13] For a code to appear six times in the same passage indicates that it must be something important or alarming.

---

10. Sh'mos 34:12-15

11. Because of all the distortions and perversions

12. Sh'mos 34:15

13. I'm only showing three of the Codes because the presence of all six would create visual clutter.

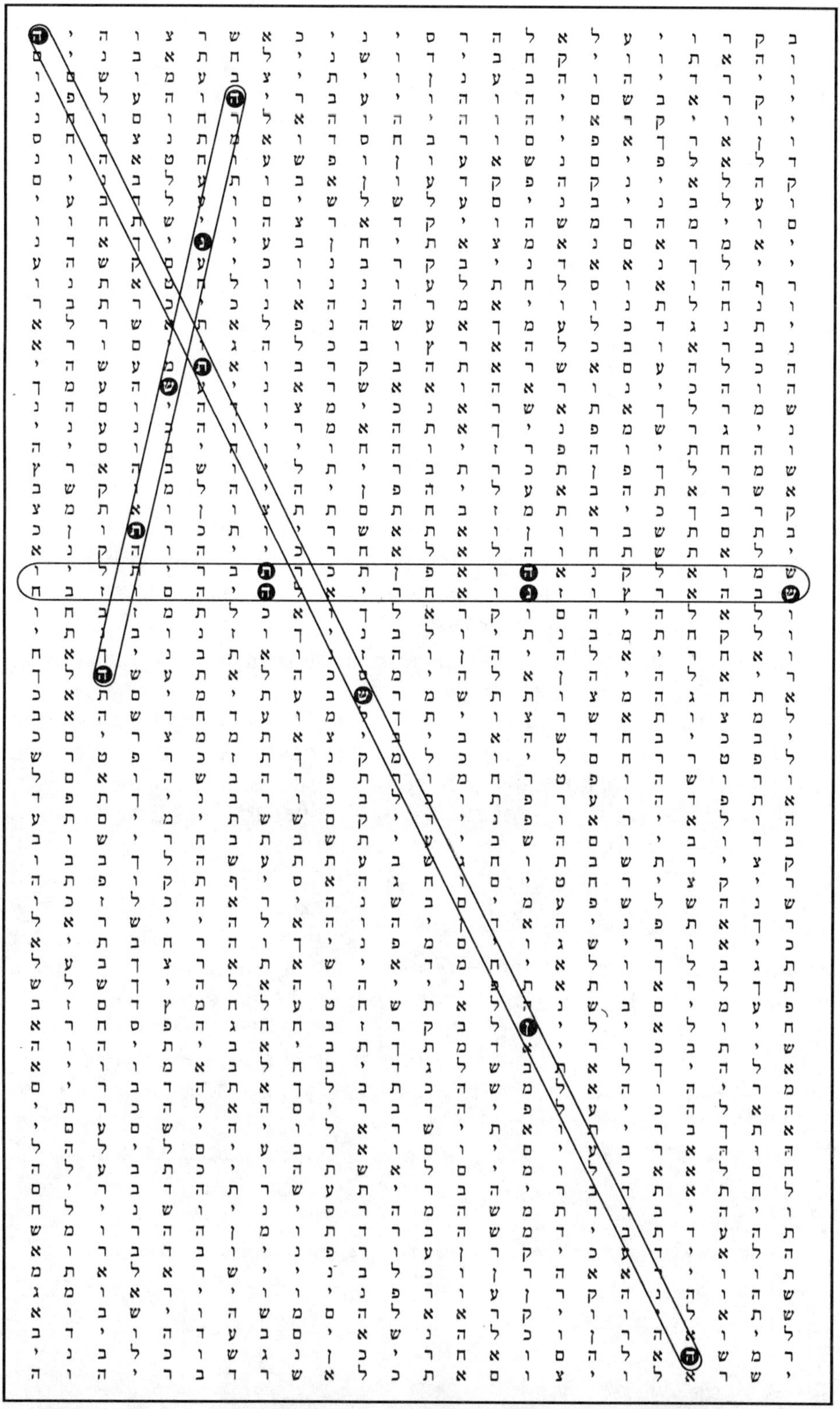

In this very passage we are told not to enter into a treaty with the other inhabitants — not at any time, including the PLO negotiating in the years of 1994/95. It is so fascinating to discover encoded messages — that were unavailable to most Jews for all time. But *Chazal* already said[14] that

וכד יהא קריב ליומי משיחא אפילו רביי דעלמא זמינין לאשכחא טמירין דחכמתא ולמנדע ביה קיצין וחושבנין

> *"even youngsters [with a computer [15]] will have access to information that was beyond the grasp of almost all the Jewish adults from previous generations."*

So far, there have only been two periods in our history when we were independent and when treaties could have been written with the other inhabitants of the Land:

❖ First **in the time of Joshua** — and he followed the Torah and did not allow murderous and uncivilized entities to live in the Land

❖ The second time, **in our days,** when Peres and Rabin, in their 'infinite wisdom' discarded all logic and became obsessively involved with giving away as much of the Land as is possible — and, adding insult to injury — **to murderers.**

The first instance with Joshua showed commitment to Torah, concern for the safety of Jews, logical planning for the future development of a civilization that could blossom without any weeds or entities that could uproot the saplings. On the other hand, the second time that the Jews are confronted with non-Jewish inhabitants living in the Land — this time the response from the political leaders is self-destructive and perverted. To allow Arabs to protect Jews instead of having Jews protect other Jews — this is tantamount to replanting the *Galus* of Poland in the *g'ulah* of the Land, of substituting Polish Diaspora for Israeli freedom. In Europe, we experienced first-hand how non-Jews really protect Jews!! For Peres to say that the area called **'Greater Jerusalem'** is only a political term and is not based on reality — this is ridiculous — unless Peres was already prepared to give Jerusalem to the Arabs. Can you imagine any greater insolence[16] — Hashem, in 1967, presented us with most of the Land at a tremendous cost in Jewish lives and we turn around and give it all away?!! This is tantamount to rejecting all the good that Hashem has accomplished for us in our day — like 'a slap in the face'. וימאסו בארץ חמדה – *Jews detest the Land [and are repulsed by owning it.]*[17]

---

14. Zohar I, 118a

15. Several software programs on Codes are being marketed for less than $100.

16. Talmud Sotah 49b

17. T'hilim 106:24

150

I never imagined that Jews could stoop so low. I pray that Jews will not stoop lower. We all pray that this absurdity stop before more damage is done. In question is the continued existence of a Jewish country. More importantly, the lives of Jews are in extreme jeopardy. Perhaps Netanyahu will help.

To begin with, the Torah forbids giving away any land.[18] There are never any conditions. This is an **absolute law** that can never be violated — not even when Jews are frightened. Think about it: Is Peres tempted to give Israeli land to Costa Rica or Greenland? When else would a government feel pressure to give away territory if not when they feel threatened? If the government feels secure and if Jews have a healthy self-concept, then giving away territory is totally out-of-character. This is probably the most profound, yet largely unnoticed, factor involved in the Peres-PLO discussions. Why was Peres negotiating with the PLO — an entity that had already posted a sign: 'Going out of business'?! After Desert Storm, there was no more funding for the PLO. Left alone, they would have disappeared in a few months — had Peres only ignored them.

Peres was negotiating with the PLO because Peres feels weak or Peres feels that the PLO are seriously 'hurting' us. In other words, Peres has an enormous inferiority complex that causes him to fear this very tiny flea. Peres and company are afraid of the PLO. With Hashem's help we defeated many very numerous and powerful Arab countries and now a little puny non-entity is bringing Jews to their knees. The political leaders of Israel feel weak — and this is after demonstrating immense strength during all the Arab wars. **Now, they are being 'cut down' by a non-entity** — by persons who are **not even a nation.** But it is there; it is all there.

In the Book of Daniel[19] there is a prediction of

> *'a contemptible person, upon whom has not been conferred the majesty of a country [because he doesn't represent any nation]. He shall arrive on the scene during a period of relative ease and will attempt to wrest the Kingdom of Israel through fabrications ... and those who reject Judaism will try to be overly patronizing by trying to ingratiate themselves with this fraudulent person while those who understand Judaism will show strength and prevail ... and some of the wise will also stumble [in not understanding how to resolve this issue of this contemptible person who represents a non-nation and who attempts to gain control over the Land].'*

18. *"Lo Sechanaym"* (D'varim 7:2); Talmud Y'vamos 10 and Avodah Zarah 32 wherein it's emphasized that even if Jews don't make treaties with these evil people, these evil people are forbidden to live in the Land. But this issue is not today's priority.
19. Chapter 11:21-35

Hashem says that if we do not accept Torah principles of Life and if we do not view our lives from a Torah point of view, then our judgment will fail us and we will imagine that we are being menacingly threatened by a 'foe' which, in reality is nothing but a non-entity, a non-nation. And so Hashem tells us that, at the end of the Diaspora, we will cower in fear in the face of a **"non-nation"**[20] — הם קנאוני בלא אל ... ואני אקניאם בלא עם

Hashem says that,

> *'Right before Moshiach arrives, we will be confronted*[21] *by a* ***non-nation*** *claiming legal rights [to our land] just as we attributed ownership of our destiny to non-Divine factors.'*

This sentence describes the relationship very clearly. Hashem says: 'Just as you refuse to recognize all the miracles that I have performed on your behalf — in reestablishing the Land and in protecting you in all the Arab wars (including **no loss of life from 39 scud missiles**) — just as you attribute your very existence to coincidental factors and just as you claim that these factors (i.e. non-gods) control your destiny, so I will treat you in the same fashion. If you attribute the rightful ownership of My world to non-gods (by saying 'Jews are smarter or stronger or that Arabs are illiterate or stupid and that's why Jews were victorious in the Arab wars) — if you attribute the ownership of the world to non-divine factors, if you remove Me from My domain, then I will create a situation where you will be confronted with the very same issue: the rightful ownership of your domain.[22]

This Principle of Jewish History is expressed very clearly[23]

ואם תלכו עמי קרי ... ויספתי עליכם מכה שבע כחטאתיכם

> *"If you interpret events as a series of coincidents, then I will increase your troubles seven-fold."*

Rambam[24] emphasizes this point: "Not giving Hashem due recognition or denying Hashem's direct guidance of world affairs is a very cruel stance because it increases the number of troubles confronting us." Violations of

---

20. D'varim 32:21

21. קנא is a concept and concepts are never easily translated nor can they ever be translated literally. קנא means to speak-out for what is *right*, to expect and demand what is legally due. As such, קנאי means someone who stands up for what is *just and legal*. Similarly, א-ל קנא does NOT mean a jealous god; rather it refers to Hashem who *demands what is right and just* (from His subjects). In our particular context, then, אקניאם means that Hashem will create a situation where we will be confronted by a non-nation over issues of legalities. For further elucidation, see Reb Shimshon Raphael Hirsch on B'reishis 37:11. A full treatment of this subject matter will be found in my next *sefer*, with Hashem's help.

23. Vayikra 26:21

24. Hilchos Ta'anis 1:2-3

the Oslo agreements come only from the Arabs, for example, yet the world blames the Israeli Jews and demands more and more territory from Jews. As long as we do nothing to change our view of current events, the situation will worsen and the solution will become more elusive.

Hashem will make the non-Torah observing community so **weak, in their own eyes,** that they will be humbled by an insignificant and puny **non-nation.** Such a small group will frighten the entire Jewish population of the Land. In all of Jewish history was there ever a time when a non-nation attempted to wrest the Land from Jews?! Can you imagine anything more degrading? Even intelligent people will fail to discover a solution to this confrontation. It does not have to be, for the Torah states very clearly and emphatically:[25] ***"When you enter the Land, don't be afraid of the enemy"***.

And then you say 'it's all here': *Chazal*[26] already described this period as the time שיהיו שפלים לאחר שהיו חזקים as the time when

> *'Jews in the Land will be debased and cheapened and devalued after a time when they were in their full glory and were immensely powerful and mighty [during the various Arab-Israeli wars].'*

They will discard their earned glory — all the while justifying the process with their subjective thinking. Without Torah as a measuring stick, there are no real and absolute values; anything is possible. What was wrong yesterday could now be declared as appropriate. Torah consists of absolute and un-changing values and principles. Without Torah values, anything is permitted. The sale of the entire Land of Israel is permitted — even allowing Jews to be murdered as the 'price for peace', as the price Jews have to pay for giving someone else a present. People can discard even their hard-earned glory when they have no Torah approach to life. Whosoever has no Torah principles can justify trading his earned glory for even the most elusive and vague uncertainty. The mind does play tricks if we have no way of measuring our overall functioning; we can even exchange glory for immediate ruination — even attempting to justify the exchange by describing all the 'benefits' that will accrue to us as a result of this transaction. The really sad part is that Peres does truly believe that this exchange will benefit Jews.[27] But the Torah is very specific and emphatic:

> *We are not permitted to give away Israeli territory — never, under no circumstances!!*

---

25. D'varim 7:17
26. Talmud Sanhedrin 98a
27. See his book, "The New Middle East" for his plans and dreams (and fantasies) in this matter.

Finally, we are not even permitted to allow them to live in the Land lest they destroy us — physically and spiritually. What more can the Torah do!! Hashem has told us — many times!! There are already reminders in the Written Torah, in the Prophets, and in the Oral-Torah! But if people choose to ignore them ...

As a matter of fact, Hashem has promised just the opposite **and delivered according to that schedule** and yet, we have the **chutzpah** to reject the gift. Hashem said[28]

> *"Regarding all those bad inhabitants who are tampering with the inheritance that I have reserved for My people Israel, I will rip them away from the Land and replace them [in these very vacated places] with Jews who will then be returned to their entitlement."*

Because this concept is so important, *Chazal* emphasize and amplify this principle[29]

תא חזי מאי כתיב יראה כל זכורך וכתיב בתריה כי אוריש גוים מפניך
דהקב"ה עוקר דיורין [דעכו"ם] מאתרייהו ואתיב דיורין [ישראל] לאתרייהו

> *"Hashem will uproot an ENTIRE population from their place and replace them with Jews in that very same area."*

There is nothing more to say. Hashem promised to remove the Arabs and replace them with Jews in that very same area. And so it was! Hashem said it all and Jews have 'spit in Hashem's face'. Nothing can be said. Indeed, it is very depressing and the present situation in Israel is extremely frightening.

Getting back to our Friday night Israeli speaker with whom we opened this chapter — how is it that Torah values are not relevant to a seemingly orthodox person? This is a question that I am going to ignore; I just wanted to mention now that this unfortunate condition exists and that Jewish people should strive to increase their Torah learning and incorporate these teachings into *all* aspects of their lives. May we all walk proudly as intelligent orthodox people whose lives are based on the learning of Torah and that we be able to apply these Torah principles to all of life. I know that you, too, pray so hard to Hashem that the killing of Jews stop, that peace shall reign throughout the world, and that our spokesman appear soon — the one who is to teach all people the true art of living together peacefully.

---

28. Yirmiyahu 12:14-15
29. Zohar II,124a and see Chapter 14 above.

CHAPTER
XIX

Security Threats to a Nation

Some people maintain that if we do not give away the Land, the PLO will kill us and that if we give away territory to them, they will stop hurting us and killing us. Since many well-intentioned Jews claim that there is an element of *pikuach nefesh* in the current Israeli situation, I thought to discuss the matter briefly — to treat the subject in a thorough fashion would require about three or four chapters. The entire area of saving a life has two different sets of laws, because there are two different situations — the *pikuach nefesh* for the individual and the *pikuach nefesh* for the nation. There are very distinct and different parameters for each.

True, there is a *mitzvah* to maintain ownership of the Land. Yes, on an individual level, it is generally well-known that in order to preserve Jewish life, *mitzvot* are suspended. We ignore Torah statutes when a Jewish life is in jeopardy. However, in truth, there are four situations where another principle supersedes the *preservation of life*, where *pikuach nefesh* does not apply and where the Jew must fight or sacrifice his life. Even when coerced or pressured, a Jew is never allowed to murder another, commit incest or adultery, nor may he 'convert'[1] — **not even to save a life!** Lastly, if anti-Semitism is the basis, then there is absolutely no practice that a Jew is permitted to violate — not even a minor custom.

However, many people claim that there is an element of *pikuach nefesh* involved in the present Israeli-Arab situation — I did want to say that there does exist a concept of *pikuach nefesh* on the national level — but nothing like they think. The parameters of **national** *pikuach nefesh* operate within very different parameters than *pikuach nefesh* **for the individual**. Without learning the Torah sources, people mistakenly apply some of the principles of *pikuach nefesh* for the individual to the situation confronting a nation. The word '*pikuach nefesh*' may be utilized in each of the two cases but the operating laws are very, very different.

Consider for a moment — on the national level — the issue of a defensive war. The enemy is about to attack and the question is: Should we fight back? Perhaps **we should immediately surrender** because in every military confrontation **lives will be lost.** So continuing with this logic:

> *in order to prevent individual casualties in a national war and by applying the principle of* pikuach nefesh *for the individual, we should save the lives of individuals and not defend ourselves — no matter the consequence. We should similarly decree that Jews should not enter the war. Jews would never fight any war because there is a good chance that lives of individuals will be lost in any national combat situation. So, following this logic, utilizing the principles of* pikuach nefesh *for the individual but applying them for the nation,* **Jews would not ever fight any national war** *— never, not even to protect themselves from an invasion and not even to prevent the human destruction that inevitably accompanies attacks against Jews. Instead, they should surrender and do* pikuach nefesh *(in their way of thinking), and 'save' lives. (See Minchas Chinuch Mitzvah 425).*

But of course, even on an intuitive level, this reasoning is obviously fallacious, because it is clear that national *pikuach nefesh* has different parameters than *pikuach nefesh* for individuals. Indeed, sometimes the lives of individuals are sacrificed in order to preserve the nation. As a matter of fact, we know from *TaNaCh* that **pikuach nefesh for individuals must be suspended** in order to maintain the physical and/or religious continuity of the nation. That is why there are several types of wars that we are permitted or obligated to wage.

---

1. Or worship in the manner of other religions.

As a matter of fact, the truth about **national *pikuach nefesh*** is just the opposite — as summarized by Shulchan Aruch.[2] After discussing all the various cases that are presented in Written and Oral-Torah[3] and while discussing the **security situation of the border towns,** Shulchan Aruch summarizes the points very succinctly:

ומשם תהא הארץ נוחה ליכבש לפניהם

This is the law. This Torah position is true in every instance and applies in every age. **National *pikuach nefesh* dictates that we NEVER give away cities that are near the borders** — not even to save the lives of individuals and not even when we think that it will prevent a war. As a matter of fact, the Oral-Torah emphasizes just the opposite — we make it worse. By giving away the cities that are near the border, **we jeopardize the entire country.** And so it was in the time of the Temple that we were conquered by the enemy after we abandoned the settlements on the border. We make the entire country vulnerable because

> *"with the border towns in the hands of the non-Jews, it becomes very easy for these non-Jews to then conquer the entire Land from right in front of our noses."*

As a matter of fact, the Oral-Torah states that Jews must chase away the enemy even if only **straw** is demanded from the residents of a border town. Even on Shabbos, Jews must mobilize to fight and chase them — even if the non-Jews only act like petty extortionists.

The Oral-Torah and the *halachah* as cited in Shulchan Aruch go one step further:

> *Even if there's only a REMOTE DOUBT* (ספק ספיקא) *that Jewish lives will be threatened, that nation must be routed — even if it requires a militant response.*

This is what national *pikuach nefesh* involves. No concessions are permitted whenever border towns are threatened — especially when the Arabs admit publicly that they are not demanding stubble. The Arabs have proclaimed many times that they are coming for Jaffa, Golan, Lod, Ramle — and Jerusalem.

> *To give away cities and towns near the border is to commit national suicide!! So states the Talmud and so is the **Halachah**. And so it has happened in the past. We pray for the future!! Please, Hashem, not again!!*

---

2. Laws of Shabbos, Chapter 329
3. Talmud Eruvin 45a; Rambam, Laws of Shabbos 2:23

There are two different types of *pikuach nefesh* with each type having unique and dissimilar principles — and not to be confused one with the other. Indeed, the words are the same — they are both called *pikuach nefesh* — but the principles of each differ one from the other as night differs from day. Certainly, there is a *mitzvah* of *pikuach nefesh for the individual* but its laws are very different from the laws that apply for national *pikuach nefesh*.

The above discussion is merely an introduction to the theory. On a pragmatic level, however, the current Israeli-Arab situation becomes much less abstract. Some people maintain that if we do not give away the Land, the PLO will kill us and that if we give away territory to them, they will stop hurting us and killing us.[4] It is also interesting to see non-Arabs acting as the spokesman for the PLO but **the PLO themselves have never promised to behave in a civilized fashion.** On the contrary!! The PLO Charter, which most people have never read, continues to call for the establishment of an Arab State in *all* of Palestine. Arafat has stated publicly that the PLO Charter will *never* be changed, just as the Jews will never alter the Torah. This PLO document remains valid.[5] This document has never been revoked! The May 1996 decision was only to create a committee to 'study' the document. It is more than two years since the infamous handshakes in Oslo and Washington and the PLO covenants continue to call for the annihilation of all Israeli Jews — as did Arafat in his recent video-taped speeches to the Arabs in May, June, and September of 1995 when he called publicly for the destruction of Israel. At a January 5, 1996 rally in front of thousands of Arabs (and again during the first week of August 1996), Arafat eulogized Yahiya Ayyash, "The Engineer", and hailed him a martyr for bombing 350 Jews during a 15 month period of 'activity'. In addition, just three weeks earlier, Arafat stated publicly before an Arab audience: "First we will kill the Saturday people. Then we will kill the Sunday people." For some people, the Oslo Agreement may sound like a method for attaining *pikuach nefesh*, but the PLO Charter and the constant barrage of Arafat speeches sound like the **cries of war** to me.

Arafat's speeches and plans are already described:[6]

"אני שלום וכי אדבר המה למלחמה"

"I yearn for peace but when I speak [of my plans in this direction], they are [speaking and planning] for war."

---

4. It is ironic that the Jewish giant who has survived against all odds because of Hashem is now cowering before a grasshopper.
5. See the Appendix for excerpts from this vile document.
6. T'hilim 120:7

To claim that surrendering to the PLO will enhance Jewish life in the Land ignores reality and bespeaks the shouts of the uninformed. Above all, this position denies the principles of Torah because:

1) The Torah already specifies the prerequisite conditions necessary for non-Jews to reside in the Land — no treaties: just pledging allegiance to the Jewish government, swearing off murder, and adopting the Seven Basic Noachide Laws of Morality.

2) At border towns, the Torah forbids 'buying peace' with 'straw' money — let alone giving away even a small piece of a border town, let alone giving away the actual cities.

3) The PLO are not interested in a piece of land — they want the entire country and will settle for nothing less. They continue to restate this position publicly and the PLO Covenant does also.

CHAPTER
XX

Religions Distorted the Truth:
For a Purpose

hen I first learned the *G'mora*[1] that truth would be hidden in the period before Moshiach, I could not understand how that could be possible. How can any normal person deny what is true? I did not understand this *Chazal*. How could rational people ignore the truth when it stares them in the face? As has been my practice whenever I come across a passage whose meaning escapes me, I just place it on the side with the hope that some time later I will be fortunate enough to achieve a higher level of understanding. After some time passed, I realized that the past 150 years have seen a real intensification and proliferation of falsehoods — especially as it relates to the Jewish people and the Torah. First came the Bible critics followed by Darwin's Theory of Evolution. Then came people who "reformed" Judaism and who began to discard the truths of Torah, one after the other. This trend continued as the Catholic Church intensified their teaching that the Jews were guilty of deicide, that they were no longer the Chosen People, and that they were actually an

---

1. Talmud Sotah 49a

accursed people. The Nazis took this position one step further and said that
if the Jews are accursed, then they can be murdered — since Jews are
sub-human and killing them is no different from killing rodents.[2]

If we still haven't experienced enough dishonesty, here comes the *coup
de grâce:* the Arabs now claim that the Land belongs to them and that Jews
have no rights to the Land. It struck me that, indeed, truth is hidden; how
easy it must be for the average person to accept what the masses believe as
truth; how difficult it must be to find honest and objective answers; how
difficult it must be to 'buck the system' and do original research in order to
ascertain the real facts and then maintain that conclusion even if it is a
minority position — even in the face of an overwhelming majority. After all,
we would all like to have our viewpoints validated by others.

But it appears that the common denominator in all these various
movements is their intent to mislead people. It used to be, until forty years
ago, that people knew that there was the proper Jewish way and that was
orthodoxy. True, certain Jews were not observant, but those people knew what
was right — just that they chose not to observe certain *mitzvot.* Similarly, the
entire world knew this when they described us as "orthodox" which literally
means that we possess the "authentic" or "true doctrine" — in contradistinction
to those movements that have falsified or vilified normative Judaism. It used
to be that no Rabbi was available to perform interfaith marriages. Incidence
of intermarriage was also low. Today, matters are very different: a Jewish
person who might hesitate to marry without the blessing of a Rabbi — such
a person can now select a Reform clergyman who says: 'It's a great idea you
have, Miss Jew, to marry a non-Jew. It's such a great idea that I'll be there to
officiate at this marriage between a Jew and a non-Jew.'

If Reform clergymen would not officiate at interfaith marriages, the young
Jewish person would learn the truth: Judaism does not permit interfaith unions.
Many Jews would not even have an 'innocent' first date with a non-Jew;
after all, what rabbi would sanction such a marriage?! Jews would not marry
non-Jews if they could not have their guilt[3] assuaged by the official presence
of a Jewish-born clergyman who distorts the truth by encouraging
intermarriage.

Indeed, this is but one example; it is just so difficult for the unsophisticated
person to find the truth in a world that is so perverted. Think of the images
and role models and values coming from Hollywood or from the television.

---

2. Please never use the phrase that "The Nazis **exterminated** Jews" because it implies subtle
    acceptance of this sub-human categorization of Jews. The truth is that rodents and
    termites are exterminated. The truth is that Nazis **murdered** Jews!!

3. Or the guilt of parents, as is usually the case.

Think of how many people are negatively influenced by such distortions and perversions. How many marriages dissolve because the frequent movie-goer feels that the glamour that is depicted in the movie is lacking in his or her marriage. Some of my patients would inevitably say, "Something's missing in my marriage." After interviewing the couple, I often could not see what was missing. Invariably, the response to my probing questions would elicit something to the effect that the 'glamour' is missing. "Well, was life ever 'glamorous' — like when you were first married? What glamour?" But if you see it often on TV or in the movies, it must be true — so think the masses.

The Theory of Evolution, Bible Criticism, reforming of Judaism — all these topics require complete chapters in order to disprove the notion that the world evolved by accident, or that a monkey typed the Torah, or that a group of people wrote *TaNaCh* over a period of hundreds of years. But isn't one of the purposes of the Evolutionists to deny the existence of G-d? Is not one of their purposes to discredit the Torah? Isn't it interesting that, with the spread of this theory, there was a concurrent growth of the movement called Reform Judaism. That's because these two movements share at least one thing in common: they try to distort the truth; they reject the truth that Hashem created the world and gave us two Torahs — the one that was given to us in written form (i.e. The Bible or Pentateuch or *Chumash)* and the accompanying oral explanations that were first committed to writing centuries later (e.g. Talmud, Sifri, Zohar).[4]

However, for our purposes, the movement that requires elucidation is the Church and its theology and philosophy. The biggest threats to their very existence are presently unfolding and threatening to create havoc and destroy the entire Church by eating away at the very foundation of their religion.

The entire theology of the Church is based on **their** premise that they are the 'new' Jews and have replaced the Israelites and, as proof, they have historically maintained that the Jews have been permanently ejected from the Holy Land and have permanently lost all their rights to the Land. They continue by stating that there is no stronger proof that the Jews are accursed and rejected than the Jews' having no homeland. Furthermore, they maintain that because Jews are wanderers — there is no greater proof as to the validity of the Church's religion; they contend that the Church has supplanted the accursed and homeless Jews.

But *TaNaCh* records many prophecies of the Jews returning to the Land and the Church knows that all Biblical prophecies will eventually be realized.

---

4.   See Chapter 1 for a more complete discussion.

So to deal with these prophecies which indicate that the Jews will return to Israel before Moshiach, the Church then countered, during the Middle Ages, by stating that all the promises regarding Zion and the return to Jerusalem — all these Biblical promises refer to Christians, the 'new' Jews, but not to the 'old' Jews who are 'rejected and accursed'. The 'new' Jews, they claimed would be the ones to eventually own the Land. The Church, therefore, maintains to this day that *TaNaCh* prophecies refer to Christians as eventually possessing the Land. You see, **even the Church always knew that the prophecies would be realized someday.** That is why it was so important for the Crusaders to conquer the Land for the Church in order to publicly demonstrate that Christians control the Land (and not the 'old' Jews or other infidels). Of course, the Church was largely unsuccessful except for a few brief moments.

"The 'old[5] Jews' will never be in control of the Land again", they maintained. The proof that Jews are rejected, they say, is found in the wandering status of the Jews and the fact that Jews will never again be independent in the Land — such has been the Vatican's position for more than 1000 years.

This is why the Church promotes giving the Land to Arabs — give it to anybody, but not to Jews. Once the Jews acquired a country of their own in the Land, then the Church was faced with a major problem because they had been teaching all along that the Jews were accursed and would never be independent again and that the Jews have been supplanted by Christians. This is one of those miracles that, again, is not really noticed. In 1947, except for Greece and the Moslem countries, virtually all the members of the UN voted for the creation of the State of Israel. Most of the UN is Christian and despite the traditional Church teachings that Jews must wander without a homeland, these Christian countries voted for Jewish ownership of the Land. This includes the South and Central American countries which are even 'officially' Catholic — many of which were also pro-Nazi, as demonstrated by their providing refuge for the escaping Nazis in the post-war years.

Don't you see the hidden miracle? The Church says there can never be a homeland for Jews in Israel and, yet, by their 1947 vote in the UN, almost all the Christian countries upheld that very Land as a Homeland for Jews. The Christian member-States themselves have destroyed their very own foundation for their own distorted religion.

---

5. That's why we must never refer to *TaNaCh* as the 'Old' Testament — it is the *TaNaCh* or the Jewish or Hebrew Bible. To refer to *TaNaCh* as the 'old' and the Christian Bible as the 'new' is tantamount to our agreeing with them that our Bible has been supplanted and replaced by theirs.

The greatest challenge that the Church has ever faced is dealing with the State of Israel. The mere existence of the State of Israel is living proof that the entire premise of the Church is false and, by extension, that all their teachings are, similarly, being challenged. To 'add fuel to the fire' and aggravate their self-inflicted wounds, they now have to say the word "Israel" which obviously causes them untold pain. So, to save face after Jewish Israel became a reality, the Church began to advocate the internationalization of Jerusalem — anything, but not Jewish ownership of Jerusalem. You can well understand why they have always insisted that Jerusalem not be in Jewish hands and why they would love to see the Land controlled by anyone else — any group, as long as it's not the Jews.[6]

---

6. I'm indebted to the Rav, the Gaon Reb Yosef Dov Soloveitchick *zal* for opening my eyes. This is only one of six unnatural events surrounding the creation of the State of Israel. See his article *"Kol Dodi Dofek"* — "My Beloved is Knocking" (i.e. Hashem is intervening to create the State of Israel). This magnificent and brilliant essay, in English translation, appears in "Theological and Halakhic Reflections on The Holocaust".

CHAPTER
XXI

Jericho —
Inextricably Linked to Israel

he *M'chilta states*[1] that when the Jews return to Israel after their long exile, they will suffer some initial 'upsets' but, ultimately, the aggression against Jews will stop in ***"Emek Yericho"***. The parceling off of Jewish real estate will stop here, *at* Jericho or *because* of Jericho. We will come back to this point, but first we have to understand what happened at Jericho when there was that *first confrontation* there, during the time of Joshua, right after the exodus from Egypt.

The Israelites were returning to the Land after a long absence of several hundred years. They left the Land during the days of Joseph and were now returning to the Land under Joshua's leadership, after the death of Moses. The Israelites, reentering the Land after a long absence, encounter many challenges to their legal rights to the Land. The Canaanites claim the Land is theirs. How do you resolve the situation of claims and counterclaims?! Wars do not ever prove the truth of a claim; they only tell us who is stronger; at best and on a very subtle level, wars could instruct us that Hashem wanted

---

1. Section on Amalek, Chapter 2

something to occur at that point. But wars do not prove the veracity of a claim to land ownership.

The first task the returning Israelites faced was to establish the credibility of their claim to the Land. The very place that was to be the focus of attention was Jericho. As *Chazal* state:[2]

יריחו נגרה של ארץ ישראל — "Jericho holds the key to all of Israel"

How do you prove the legitimacy of your claim to the Land?! Let's take a look at the first time that the Jews confronted this issue during the time of Joshua. The Israelites march around the city walls for an entire week and on the last of the seven days the Israelites walk around seven times while sounding the *shofar* in unison. But what is a *shofar* if not an instrument of prayer — an unprocessed instrument of prayer in its natural state. That is why in the *Shofros* prayer in the *Musaf* of Rosh Hashanah, we utilize the same language as we do when we pray thrice daily that:

כי אתה שומע תפילת עמך ישראל ברחמים

*Hashem "should **listen** to our prayers **with kindness**".*

Similarly, after the Rosh Hashanah *Shofros* service, we pray that

כי אתה שומע קול תרועת עמך ישראל ברחמים

*Hashem "should **listen** to the cries of the shofar **with kindness**".*

The *shofar* is an instrument of prayer — so I learned from my Rebbi, the Gaon Reb Yosef Dov Soloveitchik *zal*. That is why the words that we use for the *Shofar* Service are exactly the same words we utilize when we ask Hashem to accept our Daily Prayers. It was this method of natural prayer that came from the depths of the Jewish soul; it was the vehicle of natural prayer that the Israelites utilized in Jericho and it was this method and the Divine response that the non-Jewish inhabitants witnessed. After seven days of encircling the city and after sounding the *shofar* on the seventh day, it became obvious that the Jews do truly possess the exclusive and legitimate rights to the country. Hashem provided the visible proof. With no military intervention whatsoever, the city literally fell apart. The very ground testified to the legitimacy of the Israelite claims — the earth shook, the walls fell, the entire city fell apart without even the lifting of one Israelite weapon. Here was the required proof to substantiate the Israelite claims to the Land. Indeed, Jericho is a special city. **Jericho was the place where the Israelites demonstrated their 'document' of ownership of the entire Land** to all the inhabitants of the entire Land of Israel and to the whole world.

---

2. Bamidbar Rabah 15:12; see also Midrash Tanchuma, B'haaloscha 10.

- ❖ Not only was Jericho the first city that was confronted by the Israelites at the time of Joshua,

- ❖ Not only is Jericho the entrance to Israel,

- ❖ Not only does it hold the physical key to the Land, but

- ❖ True to the prototypes of history, Jericho is in the limelight again — in our day.

Jericho also appears to be the focal point for the seventy nations of the world in their fight with the Jews — in our day.

But Jericho holds the keys for entry into Israel in another way. On the eastern border of Israel are five passes through the mountains that connect Jordan and Syria to Israel on Israel's eastern border. These are the *only* roads that connect Israel to Jordan and Syria. Most people are unaware of the extent of the total impassibility through these borders on Israel's east. Most people do not realize that the **eastern Israeli border is totally and naturally impenetrable** — while Hashem supports our efforts and while we maintain complete ownership of the mountains and their passes. The only way that an army can invade Israel on the eastern border is on five narrow roads that are carved out of the Judean Mountains. Parallel to these five mountain roads is impassable terrain. These are five very narrow and circuitous roads and it is impossible to traverse the jagged rocks and mountains which envelop these narrow roads. **Only through these five mountain roads can a person enter Israel from the east.**

It is very important to note that, during Biblical times, every non-African invasion of Israel was never from the east. When Jews control the Judean and Samarian Mountains, the enemy will have no other choice but to invade from the north; the Judean mountains are virtually impenetrable. A sampling should suffice to illustrate this fact.[3]

"The enemy shall come from the North..."

"The violent enemy 'storm' shall come from the North..."

"The non-Jew shall arise against you from the North..."

"The smoke of destruction will come from the North..."

"The evil invasion will occur from the North..."

To appreciate this fantastic natural and topographical feature consider: with virtually one strategically placed boulder, one Jew can stop an entire invading army that is attempting to invade through this mountain range. As a matter of fact, it was during the Yom Kippur War that **several dozen**

---

3.   Yirmiyahu 6:22; Yechezkel 1:4; Yirmiyahu 50:3; Yeshayahu 14:31; Yirmiyahu 1:14 .

tankists[4] **stopped an invading Syrian Army which included more than 1000 tanks and thousands of soldiers** — and that was on just one of these five mountain passes.[5]   Of course, we can fathom the strategical significance of these five roads through the mountains! Dear readers: two dozen Israelis with tanks stopped an entire invading army!! The Judean and Samarian Mountain Range, including the Golan Heights, are not just names. They protect Israel in such a dramatic fashion. Indeed, **the entity that controls these five roads controls the traffic and the peace in the region.** Coming from the East — once through the mountains and finally beyond the very territory of Judea and Samaria — the terrain is relatively flat. Once into Israel, these five mountainous roads branch out into dozens of different roads going in dozens of different directions — a situation not easily defended.

During the urban riots of the 1960's, my parents *zal* lived in Bayonne, a small New Jersey community that was adjacent to Jersey City with its rioting blacks. Essentially, my parents lived only 1.5 miles from the border, beyond which lay the rampant and savage violence of Jersey City. You can well understand why we were very concerned for Father's and Mother's safety.

There are only three streets that link these two communities. The rioting mobs did attempt to invade Bayonne, but they were stopped at the border by the Bayonne Police. My friends, there are only three streets that link these two communities. Bayonne was unaffected by the horrific terror because the police controlled the passes. Relatively few policemen were able to protect an entire city from an invasion of hundreds of armed rioters. Had the rioters been successful in entering through the border, they would have had free access to any number of different routes — an alarming situation that could then no longer be contained.

Certainly, Jericho controls the entrance into Israel. On a topographical level, in the Jericho region, **only mountainous roads allow entry into Israel.** Please keep in mind that **two of the only five entry points into Israel go through the Jericho area.** Beyond these mountains to the West — these two roads branch out into an uncontrollable number of **tributaries.**[6] Indeed, as

---

4. Although there was an inventory of 100 tanks, only several dozen tankists were present during the Syrian invasion attempt. Whenever an Israeli tank would be rendered inoperable, the Israeli tankist would quickly emerge in order to then man an operating tank. The facts are: **approximately 25 tankists stopped the entire Syrian Army!**

5. Unfortunately, the other road into Israel was unmanned and served as the ultimate route for the Syrian invasion.

6. The Golan area has two mountain passes and Sh'chem controls the fifth road. Why do you think the Arabs insist on owning the entire Golan, Jericho, and the entire Judea and Samaria?!

Chazal state[7] יריחו נגרה של ארץ ישראל, אם נכבשה יריחו מיד כל הארץ נכבשת

"*Jericho holds the key to all of Israel. If Jericho is lost, then the entire country will be conquered.*"

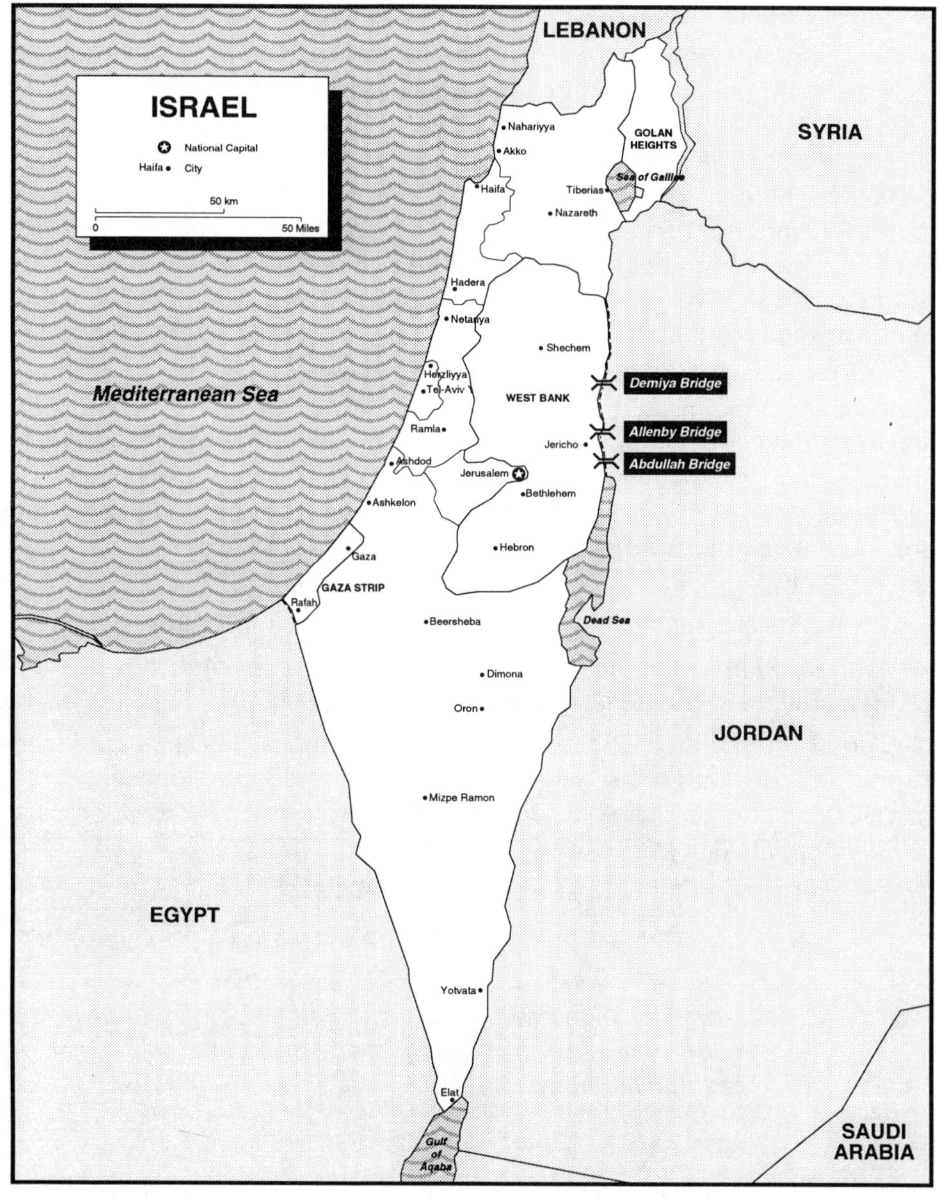

---

7. Bamidbar Rabah, ibid.

But there is another level[8] to the principle of Jericho's being the doorway into Israel. It was in Jericho that certain axioms were publicized and, in this regard, all of Israel is dependent upon Jericho. The message at the time of Joshua was very clear to the entire world: **The Land belongs to Jews because Hashem said so!!**

Even the earth gave itself over to the Jews in Joshua's time; the earth quaked and the walls fell. The Jericho earth rose to testify that the entire country belongs to us — because Hashem so decreed. On this level and in this regard, **Jericho is *definitely* the key to Israel.** Is it any wonder that **Jerusalem reentered our hands on that very day in 1967 when we gained control of Jericho?!** Indeed, Jericho is the key to Israel. In our opening statement to the world about ownership of Jericho — in that obvious public statement lies the very foundation for everything else about the relationship of the Jew to the entire Land.

The message, in our day, is also very clear. Unfortunately, Peres and Rabin had already announced to the entire world: "Jericho is for sale". However, Jericho is the key to Israel. If Jericho is for sale, then so is Judea. If Jericho is for sale, then so is Tel Aviv. If Jericho is for sale, then so is Jerusalem. If Jericho is for sale, then so is the entire country. Indeed, **Jericho holds the key for the entire country on two levels:**

❖ Two of the *only* five roads into Israel are in the Jericho region — and all the roads are treacherous and mountainous and impenetrable.

❖ The world listens to our statement about ownership of Jericho and then generalizes this statement to *all* of the Land of Israel.

The interdependence of Jericho and Jerusalem is very powerful and dramatic. That is precisely why both Jericho and Jerusalem reentered Jewish hands on the very same day of the Six Day War in 1967; the corollary is frightening and horrendous.

One very important note of consolation — *Chazal*[9] tell us

ולמדנו שעתידין גוג וכל המונו לעלות ולנפול בבקעת יריחו

'That the world that is against Jews — that these very same seventy nations will fall as a result of Jericho. Ultimately, the world will FAIL in their efforts to divest the Jews of their rightful property.'

---

8. Talmud Tamid 30b and Ravid's commentary . There are other connections between Jericho and the Land but they involve Kabbalah, much beyond the scope of this *sefer*.

9. M'chilta, ibid.; see also the Sifri on D'varim 34 (paragraph 32) — *"Gog nofail b'Yericho"*

CHAPTER
XXII

Israel's Statehood:
Why in the 20th Century?

he process that the Jews must now go through in our day is no different than the process the Israelites went through after their stay in Egypt some 3300 years ago. In addition to the servitude, the Israelites suffered millions of deaths in Egypt.[1] In the period before the servitude, the Israelites had already begun to discard their family traditions; they were no longer following in the footsteps of their parents and instead were adopting the values, morality, and behavior of Egypt. **"הללו עובדי עבודה זרה והללו עובדי עבודה זרה"** What's incredible is that, as *Chazal* point out, there was virtually[2] little difference between the Egyptians and the Israelites of that time. Each group was not monotheistic, as a matter of fact.

The first step in the independence of the Israelites was on a *physical level*. The Jews were freed by Hashem. The physical redemption came about when

---

1. M'chilta on Sh'mos 13:18

2. There were then really only four differences between the Egyptians and the Israelites, two of which were that the Israelites maintained Hebrew names and Hebrew language (Vayikra Rabah 32:5).

Hashem said that the Israelites had suffered enough. The Egyptian bondage, oppression, and holocaust was to end because Hashem had determined that the time had come to end it. So Hashem terminated the *Galus* on that first Pesach — more than 3300 years ago. But the spiritual 'slavery', the mental attitude — the values and practices of the Israelites were still not the values and practices for a Torah people. These changes take longer to effect and these changes have to take place in an atmosphere of free-will; these mental and spiritual developments can only occur when people wish to improve themselves. We make the necessary changes when we are ready and not before. Hashem does not ever interfere with our morality or our value system.[3] Ethical and moral life operates on the basis of free-will; were Hashem to 'force' us to become observant, then Hashem would essentially be transforming us into *mechanical robots* who would have *no free-will* and who would similarly not be held responsible for any of our actions. What then is the purpose for the world if people have no choices, if people have no decisions to make, or if people have no free-will?! So the Israelites experienced growth in this area — but the developments were based on their own self-analysis, observations, and study. The Ten Plagues, for example, were as much for the Israelites as for the Egyptians; both groups needed to witness them. But the conclusions were theirs; they could have rationalized the miracles as a series of 'natural' occurrences. Their growth was self-propelled; their development evolved because *they chose on their own* to conduct their lives on a higher level and to adopt the traditional Israelite-family values — the values that are now called Torah values — but which they initially rejected because they perceived them as antiquated and 'out of synch' with the 'modern times' in that Egypt of 3300 years ago.

Since those oppressive and cruel days, world history has seen much discrimination against Jews, many expulsions from many countries, countless pogroms, and finally another holocaust — not in Egypt, but this time in Europe. The Jews of pre-war Europe, for example, were assimilating. Their outlook, their values, and their behavior were very much the behavior and values of their host countries.[4] Observance of Judaism became very weakened. Indeed, here was another instance of "הללו עובדי עבודה זרה והללו עובדי עבודה זרה". The Jews were becoming more and more like their European hosts. Then the Nazi oppression began — a holocaust that, in its barbarism, rivaled that first Egyptian holocaust during which as many as 80% of the Egyptian Jews had perished.[5]

---

3.   "הכל בידי שמים חוץ מיראת שמים"; see also Moreh N'vuchim III, 32

4.   "ויתערבו בגויים וילמדו מעשיהם" (T'hilim 106:35)

5.   M'chilta ibid.

But, today, for the first time in 2000 years, Jews are physically free in the Land of Israel — this empirical fact demonstrates clearly that we have been physically redeemed. Jews did not conquer any oppressor as powerful as England or Russia or Germany or all the Arab countries; Hashem did. Additionally, Hashem does not make Jews observant; Jews do. Jews in the State of Israel have achieved complete freedom from foreign domination. Jews in Israel now have the ability to govern themselves in accordance with their own doctrine and they should have instituted their own traditional Jewish laws. We can see, however, that we are still in the stage of *shibud hanefesh* (assimilation and identification with other cultures) because the State of Israel is not a country that is governed by Torah principles. As a matter of fact, the laws in Israel are Ottoman and British which, incidentally, do discriminate against Jews. The laws in Israel are definitely not Jewish laws. There is not even a document of detailed principles. What country does not write a comprehensive constitution?! While Jews are physically free in Israel, many national laws are a vestige from earlier foreign governments that controlled the Land.

Unfortunately, the majority of Jews in most countries of the world are not consciously guided by the Torah. On an individual level, the majority of Jews are *not intentionally observant*. Many are ashamed of their Jewish birth. One thing we're certain of: **Hashem is not going to force Jews to be proud of their Jewishness nor will Hashem force people to become fully observant.** Hashem did not do it for the Israelites who left Egypt and Hashem did not do it for the intermarried Jews at the time of Ezra, when Jews began to rebuild Israel. We can be certain that Hashem will not force Jews to become observant today either. Hashem has never interfered with our spiritual development. Hashem only intervenes to protect us physically as it says[6]

וירא כי אין איש וישתומם כי אין מפגיע ותושע לו זרעו

"And when Hashem will notice that there are no worthy people and when He is astonished that there are no intercessors, then Hashem will extend His arm in order to save the Jews ..."

When the threats to annihilate Jews becomes imminent and great and there is no one to protect the Jews, then Hashem intervenes. That is precisely what happened in Egypt and that is precisely what Hashem says will happen right before Moshiach arrives. When there is no one to protect the Jews, Hashem will extend His arm in order to save the Jews.

The question then is: How do alienated or poorly educated Jews develop an appreciation for something they never understood or were

---

6. Yeshayahu 59:16. See also the discussion in Chapter 11

never even properly introduced to? They don't even know that Judaism is a unique and special and beautiful way of life. Furthermore, how do self-hating Jews become proud of their heritage. In general, how will these type of Jews adopt Jewish values? How will Jews become observant and proud on a voluntary basis?

After thousands of years, segments of society are still behaving like a bunch of vicious animals — both as individuals as well as on a national and international level. Germany, the epitome of culture and progress in all areas, produced the greatest human destruction the world has ever seen. **More than 50 million people died on both sides during those Nazi years.** Even America with its huge resources and great expanses of vacant land refused entry to the fleeing Jews during the 30's and 40's — even to those who literally docked at these shores after escaping the Holocaust. No better was Britain. Britain, with all its elegant finishing schools that teach proper etiquette — Britain sent thousands of Jews to the gas chambers. Britain waited at the shores of the then-called Palestine in order to intercept the escaping Jews. The Jews who had miraculously escaped from Nazi Europe were intercepted by the British and returned to the Nazis for immediate murder. The British could have issued Palestinian passports to the Six Million Jews when the Nazis requested it.

Hashem cries out[7]

ואל תעמד על הפרק להכרית את פליטיו ואל תסגר שרידיו ביום צרה

> *"You should not have stood at the crossways to cut off those who escaped. Nor should you have delivered up those who survived the day of trouble."*

Does the United Nations advance the cause for peace as was promulgated as its purpose at its inception?! Any onlooker is able to note the sheer and total moral bankruptcy of today's nations of the world!!

Even today, the great role-models of the world, the member-states of the United Nations, prey upon each other very cunningly, trying to grab whatever advantage they can over the other, trying to grab just as the animals of the jungle stealthily stalk their unsuspecting victim and then attack — all under the guise of legitimacy and morality.[8] And what do these nations accomplish in the way of world peace? Well, they do take time from their busy schedule of jungle activities in order to tame 'imperialistic' Israel. Indeed, many

---

7. Ovadyah 1:14

8. See Vayikra Rabah 13:5 where the nations of the West are described in these very terms — nations who will attempt to cloak their aggressive actions under the guise of establishing justice.

UN nations would like to destroy Israel. It is totally fascinating to see how the entire world cringes in fear of tiny Israel with its five million Jews. Israel comprises 0.09% of the world population of 5.7 billion people and only 00.014% of the earth's mass — *less than 1/70 of 1%.* Israel, this minuscule dot on the map of the world is viewed as if it is threatening the entire world.

Yet, in the face of all these persistent false accusations and despite constant discrimination, mistreatment, rejection and abandonment, the State of Israel is still groveling in its attempts to imitate those very same non-Jews of the world in so many different ways. The politicians of the State of Israel are trying so hard to emulate their role-models — the very nations that would devour Jews, if Hashem would not protect us.

*Let's take a look at what's happening with America — **the role model for so many Jews and Israelis.***

XXIII

Moral Bankruptcy in the West

Did you know that it is illegal to ship a pregnant crustacean from Massachusetts to another state? The law was enacted to protect the fetus by preventing a possible miscarriage as a result of the possible strains in being shipped over great distances. It was felt that a long trip might be too strenuous for a pregnant lobster or crab and might cause the crustacean to suffer a miscarriage. This law is most incongruous, to say the least, because the very state that allows women to purposely abort their own fetus — this same locality attempts to prevent spontaneous abortions in crustaceans. Sounds strange.

Lately, we have been inundated by acts of aggression against abortion clinic workers and, in some cases, even murders. It seems that many people feel that abortions are tantamount to murder — a position which happens to be the Torah position.[1] But in order to stop the killing of a fetus, some of these

---

1. To be more precise, according to *halachah*, abortions are acts of murder — only that abortions are not punishable by an 'earthly' court in the physical world of humans. In any event, abortions are not to be considered unless the mother's life is threatened by the birth process and/or by the actual pregnancy.

'civilized' and 'enlightened' people have recently begun to murder the workers at the clinics. Does this sound logical to you? This is somewhat comparable to an extremist who murders the Prime Minister because Rabin was creating a dangerous situation by helping create a "Palestine State". Certainly, Rabin was doing wrong by compromising the security of the Israelis. Ironically, the assasin committed the very same crime for which he criticized Rabin.

Additionally, there is now a specially enacted law that says that it is illegal to harass an abortion clinic employee. What about postal workers and what about the 'normal' citizens — do we have any legal protection?!

Recently I heard that a New York legislator was proposing a law that would punish the youth who deface property with graffiti; these teenagers would be paddled with a long wooden board. Ridiculous, you say, but it does highlight the extent of the total frustration that people are experiencing. Similarly, the decades-long capital punishment debate is a reflection of society's feelings of total helplessness in the face of so much crime. People are frustrated and angry and confused — they just do not know how to stop the monstrous levels of criminal activity. What is this society coming to?

I remember when I was completing my graduate studies in psychology, I was interviewed for a position as a psychologist in a mental health clinic. During the interview, I was asked to explain how I would deal with a patient who threatens to commit suicide. I described the details of how I would make immediate arrangements to have the patient hospitalized. They asked me the same question a second time. I thought some more, perhaps I left out some crucial information in my response. So I elaborated nicely on my first answer. When they asked me the same question for a third time, I just knew I was in big trouble. Either I didn't understand the question — which means I'm stupid and now they know and so I don't get the job. Possibly I understood the question, but they couldn't understand my response — which means I'm inarticulate and so I don't get the job. Perhaps, I understood the question but gave the wrong answer — which means I'm unqualified and so I don't get the job. I selected a fourth possibility as my working hypothesis: 'We were all intelligent'. So I confronted them by saying, "You've asked me the same question three times and the content of my response has been consistent. Obviously you would like a different answer. Please tell me the answer you want to hear." They then went into a long monologue on how all people have the right to decide how to live their lives and how we, as psychologists, have no right to meddle in their affairs and how we have to permit the patients to commit suicide. You could 'throw up' from this type of liberalism and phony patient-advocacy. If we have no right to 'meddle', then why are we trying to help patients in their weekly psychotherapy sessions? Leave them alone altogether.

They had no idea of how important human life is and how their amazing profession could lift the veil of depression from the sick, how they could help depressed people become more optimistic. I explained to them that I could not be a part of their **distorted and perverted world.** Thanking them for the experience and practice I gained in being interviewed, I went to search for other employment.

Could you believe a society that maintains that a person may not murder another, but permits murder of one's self?! To teach people that suicide is an appropriate response to discomfort or pain is probably the most ridiculous of the ridiculous.

It is classified statutory rape when a teenaged girl has sex with a male — even if she consents. The person who has sex with a school-aged child commits a crime and is faced with the prospect of a long prison term. The law states that it is a crime for school-aged girls to have consenting sex. But for years now, schools have been distributing condoms so school-aged children can have 'safe sex' while they're still minors. Ridiculous! The law says that it is forbidden to engage in sex with a youngster under the age of 18 and the schools push these very same minors, now armed with condoms, to engage in sexual activity. Schools thereby appear to encourage students to engage in criminal activity. Schools encourage little children to engage in sex. What a perversion! What *chutzpah!*

Americans live in a democracy where everyone is supposed to have equal rights. It seems that many years ago, there was discrimination in America. The Irish could not get certain jobs in Boston in the late 1800's, blacks were enslaved in the South, and Jews could not get into medical school and were refused employment by banks and many other corporations. Women suffered, too. Now, Americans finally understand: it is wrong to discriminate against any person or group of people. Yet, recent laws permit discrimination against certain people; Americans are encouraged to discriminate against 'regular' people if, by that act of discrimination, they are now helping a person who belongs to an ethnic group that experienced discrimination 100 years ago. One may discriminate against an innocent person — if that person is a member of one group; one may not discriminate against another equally innocent person — if this person is a member of a second group. Does this sound logical? Society justifies these practices by calling them "affirmative action". I guess "All people are created equal, but some are created more equal."[2] What is this society coming to by promoting discrimination? And the public goes along like sheep. To legislate laws

---

2.   See Orwell's "Animal Farm".

promoting discrimination and to attempt to justify it and for the populace to accept it[3] — this is a perversion! This is truly ***chutzpah!***

Some years ago, a farmer began to suffer at the hands of a thief who was stealing his animals during the wee hours of the morning. The thefts persisted. Several times each month, he would discover that another animal had been stolen. No one *can* continually suffer such losses. No one *should* suffer in this manner. So this farmer rigged a shotgun to the barn door in a way that someone, opening the door at night, would trigger a blast from the shotgun. The blast would, no doubt, scare off the robber. It was hoped that the stealing would thus stop; no more losses! Inevitably, one evening while the farmer was sleeping he was awakened by the blast of his shotgun. Armed with a rifle, he approached the barn to investigate and sure enough, he found the culprit —wounded in the leg by the blast. The police and ambulance responded and the thief was arrested and eventually convicted. Shortly thereafter, the farmer was sued by the thief on the grounds that the farmer had used *excessive force* in protecting his property. What **chutzpah!**[4] Well, if you think that was *chutzpah* — the court agreed with the thief and ruled that the farmer had indeed used **excessive force.** Ridiculous, you say, but the court awarded the thief so large a sum, there was just no way the struggling farmer could ever be in a position to pay off such a sum in one payment. The farmer, as a matter of fact, was in such financial straits that he wasn't even able to make any scheduled payments of any amount whatsoever. Now, are you ready for the very ultimate in ridiculousness?? With the judgment in hand, the court awarded the thief the entire farm as full settlement of his claim. For his efforts, the thief who attempted to steal one animal at a time was now being rewarded with all the animals in 'one shot' — together with the entire farm. Yea! Justice is served again!

But the secularized government of the State of Israel is part of the same world wherein is found secular America. To illustrate how perverted and

---

3. Nazi Germany also passed laws promoting discrimination with the justification that it was protecting the downtrodden and unemployed (i.e. the native-born German) by favoring them for employment over another group (i.e. the recent immigrants). The entire German populace wholeheartedly supported these efforts. On January 18, 1996 the University of California Board of Regents voted to reaffirm their earlier decision to stop admitting students, hiring staff, and awarding contracts on the basis of race. They maintain that "racial preferences are by definition racial discrimination". Upon learning of their decision, President Clinton criticized them when he stated that "Affirmative action has been good for America".

4. It reminds me of the child who, after murdering his parents, begs the court for mercy because he's now an orphan.

bankrupt thinking is so characteristic of Peres and his henchmen, one episode that was reported in the media will suffice.

It seems that after several Israelis were murdered by Arab-planted bombs, the borders were sealed once again to prevent dangerous and murderous Arabs from entering Israel to do their atrocious work. As always, when the borders are sealed in this manner, all murders of Jews stop. Then, after a few weeks, the borders are invariably reopened and the murders resume. Then, as a reaction, the borders are resealed. After several weeks of no murders, the borders are reopened. And so the cycle has continued for months. Therefore, if you were the Israeli leader, you would conclude that:

a) The closing of borders to Arabs irritates the American President because he has never had to close his borders [to Canadians]; so why should anyone seal a border?!

b) The closing of borders to Arabs annoys Arabs by denying them equal opportunities for certain 'activities'.

c) The closing of borders to Arabs annoys Israelis by denying them a source of cheap Arab labor.

d) More scientific research is necessary in order to determine why there are no murders of Jews during these periods when the borders are sealed.

Well, Peres and his henchmen had not selected any of the above choices. As reported[5]

> *"On Tuesday, the army chief of staff, Lieut. Gen. Amnon Shahak, warned a parliamentary committee that a prolonged territorial closing could cause Mr. Arafat's self-rule government in Gaza to collapse. The restrictions may have reduced the number of attacks [against Jews] inside Israel, but they have deepened poverty and bred hatred in Gaza."*

So spoke General Shahak, Peres' expert. The General did admit that border restrictions eliminate all murders of Israeli Jews. But he maintains that:

❖ It is necessary to sacrifice Jewish lives in order to prevent poverty amongst Arabs.

❖ It is necessary to sacrifice Jewish lives in order to prevent Arabs from hating Jews.

Similarly, for Peres,

❖ It is necessary to sacrifice Jewish lives in order to allow Arafat's government to thrive.

---

5. New York Times, April 25, 1995, page 12

Did you ever hear of anything as illogical and absurd as this —

❖ That we should allow Arabs to murder Jews so that Arabs will become happier people;

❖ That if we allow Arabs to murder Jews, then the Arabs won't hate us anymore;

❖ That we should allow Arabs to murder Jews, so that Arabs won't be poor anymore;

❖ That we should allow Arabs to murder Jews to enable Arafat to have a government.

Indeed, in Peres' eyes, Jewish blood is expendable and should be sacrificed in order to satisfy Arab desires. I suppose, by extension — the more Jews that are murdered, the happier the Arabs. According to Peres and Company, **we have an obligation to make Arabs happy — whatever the cost!!**

CHAPTER
XXIV

Signposts to
20th Century Life

mphasizing various passages in *TaNaCh*, the Oral-Torah has provided us with many signposts and markers to indicate that we are approaching and entering a very special era. And so I present, with limited comments, some extraordinary events[1] that were predicted as precursors to usher in a period of immense greatness.

בעקבתא דמשיחא — "in the footsteps of Moshiach" **(i.e. right before Moshiach arrives):** [2]

❖ *Chutzpah* and insolence will increase.

❖ Wisdom of the Rabbis will be distorted; Torah scholars will be criticized, denounced, and condemned as *fanatics*; and Judaism will be denigrated.

❖ People who avoid wrongdoing will be ridiculed.

❖ The populace will describe the honest/ethical/moral person as being "nuts".

---

1.   Mostly culled from Talmud: Sotah 49, M'gilah 17, and Sanhedrin 97-98
2.   See Rashi in the Talmud, ibid.

❖ Truth will be hidden (as also indicated in *TaNaCh*).[3] Only within small groups of people will objectivity and truth be found. Most people will only have access to adulterated, polluted, and distorted information.

❖ If you see several consecutive generations making light of G-d or denying that G-d exists, then you should anticipate the footsteps of Moshiach.[4]

On the Economic Scene

❖ *Presumption* will increase and costs will be very high.

❖ *Unemployment* will also increase[5] — because of the advancing technology there will be no need to hire as many people as in the past; machines will replace working people.

❖ Nor will there be a need for animals for the purposes of transportation or work [because they, too, will be replaced by machines].

❖ There will be a system of *universal pricing*; every city and location in the world will offer the exact same goods at virtually the same price.

❖ One of the most obvious signs: as long as the Jews are not significantly represented in Eretz Yisrael, the *Land will not produce* in accordance with its magnificent potential — a potential that has been emphasized so many times in *TaNaCh*.

❖ When Jews first return to the Land, the vine will yield its fruit and wine in a bountiful manner, yet they will be *expensive*. Until 1970, it was the rule — rather than the exception — that an ordinary family, without any higher education, could sustain itself financially on the income of only a single breadwinner. Twenty years later, even college-educated families would find it extremely difficult to survive — notwithstanding the combined salaries of *both* spouses. It is fascinating because the past few decades has seen two digit percent inflation. As a matter of fact, America experienced a period, during the late 1970's, when mortgages had interest rates of 22%. But Israel, by 1985, had experienced a period when the *inflation rate exceeded 400% per year*. And this situation prevailed in the Land even though the vines yielded beautiful harvests of grapes. Even though agriculture is profitable, inflation persists and prices continue to soar today — although at a slightly slower pace than those alarming levels of the previous period.

---

3. Yeshayahu 59:15
4. Shir Ha'Shirim Rabah, Chapter 2
5. See Maharsha in the Talmud, ibid.

On the Societal Level:

❖ There is no more obvious a sign than: "Before those [Messianic] days, the [Israeli] commuter will experience no safety or security".[6] Indeed, all will be susceptible to *roadside terrorism.*

❖ The *government of Israel will be atheistic* and there will be no effective and organized protesting nor rebukes against its policies. In fact, [for a very long time] very few people will be trying to correct those objectionable, dangerous, and immoral policies of the government nor will there be a real effort to help regular citizens change their life-styles and improve themselves to the point of becoming observant Jews.

❖ [Because of.....] *residents of the Israeli border areas will face the real threat of losing their homes and becoming homeless* and they will go around and there will be *none to pity them* [or to support their cause for the security of the Country].

❖ But eventually, this worthless Israeli leadership will have no more influence and will be replaced by a true Jewish government, a government that cares about Jews and honors Judaism and respects and observes Torah values.

On a Moral Level:

❖ Throughout history, acts of sexual immorality were committed discreetly. Until our day, for example, those who engaged in acts of homosexuality did so discreetly. Now, they have 'come out of the closet' to publicly flaunt this type of perversion. And society even approves and encourages this type of deviant behavior as demonstrated through special treatment and protective legislation. Now, the Talmud states, even places where people congregate in large numbers will witness *themes of immorality* prevalent — with absolutely no one experiencing shame. Public buildings, where people gathered in large numbers, were usually reserved for constructive purposes. At this time, disgusting rappers appear in public theaters, cursing their mothers and fathers and their wives or girl friends. Now these rappers call for the murder of white people and no one complains. Now the public gathers to celebrate all expressions of aggression, vulgarity, and immorality. The 'theaters of culture' popularize much *indecent and deviant behavior.* In our generation, indeed, degeneracy is flaunted and shame and modesty are declared obsolete and derided as values of the unenlightened past. College campuses are dangerous places

---

6. Zecharyah 8:10 — "וליוצא ולבא אין שלום מן הצר"

for our children — how many come home less religious than when they arrived there? How many come home with non-observant or non-Jewish fiancees? The college campus is also a place of gross immorality especially with co-ed dormitories and the permitting of overnight visitors of the opposite sex.

❖ The younger generation will no longer respect their elders; as a matter of fact, they will *shame the elders.*

❖ Children will *debase parents* and rebel in a most disgraceful way.

❖ The elder generation will have to 'give in' to the younger generation and the *elders shall stand in fear of their children.*

❖ As a matter of fact, children will not be ashamed of their fathers' embarrassing and disgusting behaviors.

❖ Even married children will *defy their in-laws.*

❖ Family members will become *enemies with each other.*

❖ The face of this generation will be as the "face of a dog" in the sense that people will have no shame[7] and people will act like hypocrites with each other — on the surface appearing as a friend but, underneath the facade, really disliking each other.[8] In other words, the entire generation will appear to be "going to the dogs".

❖ It was true in the past that if someone did not wish to be observant or if someone became an atheist or if someone acted immorally, these individuals still treated the scholarly and their elderly with respect. Even the vicious American gangsters of the early 1900's — even those violent murderers were noted by their respect for their parents. In this generation, however, all inhibitions have been lifted. As we discuss elsewhere, the main purpose of the evolutionists and Bible critics has been to discredit Torah and its spokesmen — the teachers and rabbis. The next goal was to abolish all traditions (from parents and grandparents), then to defy parents and elders. In this way, all the values of previous generations could be easily trashed. Indeed, arrogance and defiance are, unfortunately, found everywhere. Who is the respected individual today? Unfortunately, the insolent free-thinker is the one who is placed on society's pedestal — the person who is an 'independent thinker', who rejects the treasured and time-honored values of the past and replaces them with hedonism and arrogance.

---

7. See Rashi in the Talmud, ibid.
8. See Maharsha, ibid

These passages are describing a *huge* generation gap. Actually, what is being felt today is more like a rebellion than a generation gap.

❖   **We have learned that no one person can help us — no person or nation; the situation is so depressing and so very frightening. The situation is totally out-of-control now. In the context of these times and under these awful conditions, Oral-Torah emphasizes:[9]**

"ואין לנו על מי להשען אלא על אבינו שבשמים"

ONLY OUR FATHER IN HEAVEN CAN HELP US!

---

9.   Talmud Sotah 49b

CHAPTER
XXV

Why Such Decadence?

here are many groups emerging on the American scene. People are disgusted with the trend, with the popularized 'values'. The 'average' Americans have had it. More and more people are beginning to demand changes. Only they do not even know where to begin to remake this country. Interestingly, for many Jews, a dominant force in life was, historically, to identify with the culture and country where they found themselves. As a matter of fact, the Jew was determined always to be a better citizen than his host. For example, it had been common since the early 19th Century for German Jews to deny their ties to the Land of Israel. They were Germans — not German Jews nor Jewish Germans.[1] Those Jews even 'changed' a verse from *TaNaCh* to read "that from Berlin shall come forth Torah" — instead of "from Zion".[2] Indeed, the Jews would assimilate into all aspects of German life and eventually adopt the values of the host country — and gradually discard Judaism. At the turn of the

---

1. Even observant Jews were uncomfortable displaying their Judaism in public.
2. See Meshech Chochmah on Vayikra Chapter 26.

century, the intermarriage rate in Germany was 50%; the parallelism in America is too frightening to even discuss.

It is fascinating, but very painful, to see how some Jews are so ignorant of Torah Judaism, while others are ashamed of their birthright. Unfortunately, most Jews were never afforded the opportunity to study Judaism and see the beauty of a real Jewish community. The major reason that outreach-*kiruv* workers are able to help so many people become observant is because Torah Judaism is logical, consistent, practical, meaningful, and beautiful. It is just that people have not been properly introduced to mature Jewish learning nor to the beauty of Jewish life. Certainly, many have attended Hebrew School; some have attended an elementary yeshiva, but how much expertise does a 13-year-old or a 17-year-old have? For that matter, how much expertise does an adult have — an adult who only has an elementary education or even a high school background? Think about it — a college graduate with a pediatric understanding of Judaism. What could such an adult know about Judaism? Certainly not an appreciation of its beauty! A few stories perhaps. A few songs. An awareness of several *mitzvot*. When adults become objective, they absorb Torah learning exactly as a sponge absorbs water. I have yet to meet an alienated or Jewishly-uneducated person who did not become proud as a Jew after learning Torah; a significant number become fully observant with a real, solid foundation; the majority increase their levels of observances.

This, however, is a unique sociological phenomenon. It used to be that if a parent was not observant, their child also remained non-observant and similarly did all subsequent generations remain non-observant. Almost **never** did we experience a situation where adults or teenagers became orthodox while their parents remained non-observant. Now things are changing dramatically. Children, as adults, are rejecting the meaningless and/or bankrupt values of their non-observant parents. The new adults are proud of their birthright. The new Jewish adults are becoming observant — some even together with their parents and siblings.

Hashem says that the Jews will have to experience the bankrupt values of the so-called great countries of the world. This will happen after the Jews realize that these countries only look good from the outside but, internally, these countries are morally bankrupt and decaying.[3] Once the Jews begin to become more objective and analytical, they too will realize that Western values are based on distortions and do not contain the blueprints for the Utopia that they were purported to achieve. It is only after more and more Jews realize that they have taken on poor role models and it is not to their advantage to

---

3. This is not to minimize their help in that they protected us and allowed us to 'blossom'.

assimilate into Western culture, that Western values are unhealthy — only then will Jews begin to search for real values and meaning in life.

The passages from the previous chapter are describing a *huge* generation gap. Actually, what is being felt today is more like a rebellion than a generation gap. But, on one level, we should not be frightened since this is Hashem's plan. Perhaps this is the only way that a corrupt world can be changed; this change can come about solely through a complete break between the generations. Only after people are confronted with the moral bankruptcy of a world that is devoid of real values, when people will face up to their own perversions, distortions, *chutzpah*, and ridiculousness — then the necessary changes can be made.

The period of Moshiach will involve the greatest revolution the world has ever experienced, even greater than the fast-paced technological advancements of the past thirty years. But human behavior can never change without tremendous pressure. It cannot change unless people are able to detect the bankruptcy of their thinking and the destructiveness of their behavior. We see this all the time — especially in marriage counseling: the aggressive spouse does not alter behavior until there is recognition of that destructiveness. We call this *"cheshbon ha'nefesh"* or *"hakaras ha'chayt"* (i.e. self-analysis or recognition of shortcomings and/or failures). Similarly, a bankrupt society must be able to recognize and experience its own failures and face up to it responsibly before it can change and improve. This is the human way — the 'natural' way!!

As a matter of fact, many Jews are *now* searching for principles that show respect for others, that protect the rights of all people without sacrificing the rights of another, that promote a truly civil society, that create a thriving and beautiful society on all levels. Many Jews are now becoming observant because they realize how meaningless their lives are without Torah values; at last they understand the extent of the bankruptcy of Western civilization. It is only after we experience the מדבר העמים — the moral bankruptcy of the countries and their animalistic behavior — only then does the prophet cry out [4]

קול קורא במדבר פנו דרך ה'

"A voice cries out from society's desert. Clear a path for Hashem."

In other words, the objective confronting of the effects of living in a **desert** together with people who have bankrupt values, amidst a world that acts immorally and unethically and that often acts like a vicious animal — these

---

4. Yeshayahu 40:3 (Isn't the definition of the term *midbar* a 'barren wasteland', a place that's *devoid of a civilization?!*)

experiences will engender a period of **pursuing and following Hashem —**
of becoming observant. This concept is found in many places in *TaNaCh*.

"כי ימים רבים ישבו בני ישראל אין מלך ואין שר...
אחר ישבו בני ישראל ובקשו את ה' אלקיהם... באחרית הימים"

*"The Israelites will sit many days without an effective leader...
Afterward shall the Israelites... seek Hashem right before the
Era of Moshiach".* [5]

"הנה ימים באים נאם אדנ-י י-ה-ו-ה ושלחתי רעב בארץ
לא רעב ללחם ולא צמא למים כי אם לשמע את דברי ה'"

*"Behold there will be days, says Hashem, when I will bring
hunger to the world — not a hunger for bread and not a thirst
for water — but only to hear [truth as propounded by]
the Divine teachings..."*

5. Hoshaya 3:4-5
6. Amos 8:11

XXVI

The Prediction of Three Arab Wars:
So Who is Saddam Hussein?

We spoke about the troubles that Arabs would make for the Jews who return to live in Israel. Now, we will take a look at how the Arabs will try to stop the Jews from reclaiming the Land. We learned[1] that Avraham's elder son was named Yishmael because this very name describes a time when the Arabs will inflict extreme suffering upon the Jews in the Land, when the Arabs will try to destroy the Jewish people who will be living in Israel באחרית הימים, in the period right before Moshiach. This passage can only be referring to our generation **because this century has been the only time that Arab countries have ever tried to destroy all the Jews of Israel.** It must be that this passage is referring to the events of our day. After all, the same passage states very clearly that **the Arabs will be the cause of three wars** — not four wars or two — but specifically three wars. Now, you are probably counting the military conflagrations that have enveloped Israel since its rebirth in 1947. Well, yes, there was the War of Independence, the Six Day War, and the Yom Kippur War.

---

1.   Pirkei D'Rebbi Eliezer, Chapter 30

That's great! The Written and Oral-Torah state unequivocally that there would only be three wars.

But you are probably wondering: "So what about the Sinai Campaign of 1956 or the incursions into Lebanon or other battles?" This passage says that there would be three wars involving not just one Arab entity or country but the **B'nai Yishmael as a united Arab front.** The military action against Egypt in 1956 was just that — a war involving only *one* Arab country that was attempting to strangle tiny Israel. The Sinai Campaign did not involve several Arab countries that had assembled to kill Jews. Similarly, the Desert Storm War with Iraq does not meet the qualifications as an Arab war against Jews. It was the work of *one* madman who rained terror upon the defenseless Jews — so physically defenseless that even the Patriot Missile system proved to be totally ineffective. We can only remind ourselves of the prophecy[2] which describes the period right before Moshiach as a time when Jews will be overwhelmed by intense feelings of helplessness, of complete impotency. Can you picture any situation where all you can do is watch as giant scud missiles destroy your country and there is no way to protect yourself or your family?! You do not know whether they carry biological or chemical death with them. Perhaps, the missiles are only the kind that blow people up (you know: the 'normal' kind). We defend ourselves very differently based on the unique characteristics of each type of armament transported by the missile. You don't know whether to enter the underground bomb shelter. Perhaps it's nerve gas and we should enter the above-ground sealed room. But if we go to the sealed room and it's a conventional bomb, we'll be killed — Heaven forbid. And if we go the bomb shelter and it turns out to be a chemical or biological weapon ... So what do we do?

On top of it all, while the Patriot Missiles generally protected American soldiers in Saudi Arabia, these very same Patriot Missiles failed miserably in their attempts to destroy the scuds that were aimed at Israel. As a matter of fact, the 39 scuds actually by-passed the Patriot Missiles. Can you imagine: the system operates effectively in one country and the very same system fails miserably in Israel! No one had any idea what to do, where to go, or how to defend against guaranteed death. Can you imagine anything more frightening than an entire country totally preoccupied with fear and totally paralyzed and rendered completely powerless?! It certainly appears to be one of the characteristics mentioned as being typical of the period before Moshiach — when we are unable to extricate ourselves from terrible threats and when we can turn to no other country for effective protection. So what did we do?

---

2. Talmud Sotah 49b

I'll never, ever forget that dark night in January. I'll always remember walking with my wife when a friend stopped her car to ask us if we had heard the terrible news. "Iraq just bombed Israel", she hysterically screamed out. In total disbelief and overwhelmed with fear, we raced back home. We each grabbed a Book of T'hilim and ran into different rooms to listen to different radio and television news briefings — all the while praying with all our might that Hashem would protect the Jews of Israel. We prayed for hours and so did thousands of other Jews throughout the world — and Hashem listened and made miracles that are now being compared to the Ten Plagues of Egypt. Iraqi scuds plow into a US Army location and scores of soldiers are killed. Thirty-nine missiles destroy 15,000 apartments in Israel — each with a different story. But everyone of the tens of thousands of residents were protected. That's no coincidence!! **Thank G-d, not one Jew was killed.**

As an aside, a vice-mayor in one of the northern cities that was badly damaged by scuds described how, after one such attack, he went to the site in order to survey the extent of the destruction. While walking around at the bomb site, he noticed how an elderly man was speaking incoherently. He wanted to help this man. He listened closely but couldn't understand him at all. Maybe he was traumatized — he was speaking so quickly. The vice-mayor asked him to slow down and speak slowly and clearly. There must be a serious problem to warrant this elderly man to be frantically scrounging through the debris. Maybe — Heaven forbid — maybe a person is trapped, or worse. Said the vice-mayor, "Speak slowly so I'll be able to understand you better. Is anybody missing? Is anybody buried in the debris? Is anybody dead? Are you hurt?" The elderly man shook his head in the negative to each question. "So what are you doing? So what's the problem?" The elderly man then points into his open mouth to show a mouth with no teeth.

My friends, a giant bomb lands in a neighborhood and wrecks hundreds of apartments and what's the worst that happened? A man's dentures were lost in the debris!! Thank G-d, it's much better to laugh over dentures than to cry for dead Jews. It's much better to thank G-d for protection! Can you imagine a greater miracle? Thirty-nine scud missiles and no effective humanly designed defense system. But, you know, we have something far superior. **We have the best defense system in existence!**

A scud hits the main gas line of Gush Dan. A direct hit! Do you know what this means? Every home is connected to every other home by means of the gas line. When the gas line suffers a direct hit from a Scud in one spot and then explodes into a raging fire, every house that's connected to this line will also be engulfed by a ghastly inferno. Well, a scud missile hit the gas line and there was no chain reaction!!! Why? Because Hashem protects in a natural manner. Can you believe it — shortly before that scud scored the direct hit, a malfunction was detected in the gas line. The first step obviously is to shut-off the gas and drain out all the gas. Can you believe it — that scud hit this gas line. But there was no gas in the line. There was no person or people to help the Jews — only our Father in Heaven.

Can you imagine a greater miracle? Thirty-nine scud missiles and no effective humanly designed defense system. But, you know, we have something better. We have the best defense system in existence! We turned to Hashem and prayed. Thirty-nine scud missiles landed in Israel and thousands of homes were destroyed. Hashem answered our prayers: a miracle greater than most — **not one Israeli was killed by any of these 39 bombings.** So it certainly showed our total dependency upon Hashem, one of the signs of the times:

"ואין לנו על מי להשען אלא על אבינו שבשמים"

"We will have no one to rely upon, except for our Father in Heaven."

But this still was not an Arab war against Jews. As a matter of fact, Egypt and Syria joined the coalition to fight against Iraq. While this was an attack upon Israel by one Arab country, it wasn't an Arab war; it was merely the work of one Arab dictator. But one of the signs of the time was evident for all to see: a feeling of complete impotency with no earthly hope whatsoever. Hashem must protect us. Hashem does protect us in a glorious fashion. **So, we have hopefully passed the prediction of three Arab wars against Jews.**

But if the Iraqi Desert Storm War was not one of the three Arab Wars, what was its purpose?!

In the Spring of 1990 while using the traditional method to win an Arab consensus in his favor, Saddam threatened to burn half the State of Israel with chemical weapons. He then organized a summit meeting of the Arab League for May 28th which he entitled as "The Summit of Pan-Arab Security" and which was to deal with the threat posed by the mass immigration of Soviet Jews to Israel. In the name of confronting Israel and the West, he intended to use the Summit to legitimize his arms build-up and to act as the natural protector of the Arab nation. The PLO delegates to that meeting maintained that Iraq must achieve military parity with Israel. "For the sake of peace", they maintained, "Iraq should be allowed to acquire the atomic bomb."

Saddam Hussein felt intense pressure because he feared that Israel, with U.S. backing, was preparing to carry out a pre-emptive strike — this time against his missile plants — just as they had earlier bombed the Osirak reactor in 1981 and just as they had destroyed the reactor core in France in 1979 just three days before it was to be shipped to Iraq.[3] He saw the reluctance of the Gulf States to support him — he saw this as part of a conspiracy against Iraq that was being spearheaded by Kuwait. It was Kuwait, after all, that was increasing oil production; it was Kuwait that was attempting to manipulate the oil market as a way of keeping prices down and thus starving Iraq. The Iraq that was now nearly bankrupt after its protracted war with Iran — this same Iraq would now be unable to pay its debts or service its loans or rebuild its shattered economy if the price of oil would drop below $22 a barrel. Kuwait's actions would cause the price to dip way beyond this point — to probably $18 a barrel.

The restoration of Kuwait to the motherland (i.e. Iraq) — as it was until the early 20th Century — was only the first step towards 'the liberation of Jerusalem'. On August 12th, Saddam disclosed the terms for ending the aggression against Kuwait by linking the Kuwaiti issue to the Palestinian problem. The solution involves "all issues of occupation ... in the entire region ... [including] the immediate and unconditional withdrawal of Israel from the occupied Arab territories in Palestine, Syria, and Lebanon ..." Only after all these problems were settled in chronological order would there be any resolution to the situation in Kuwait. As a matter of fact, in a speech to the U.N. on September 24th, President Francois Mitterand linked the occupation of Kuwait with the Arab-Israel conflict. And so did President Bush one week later by stating that the Iraqi assertiveness would pave the way "for all the states and peoples of the region to settle the conflict that divides Arabs from Israel".

Can you believe this: **Saddam invades Kuwait and the world calls for Israel to withdraw!** Saddam saw himself as the **Liberator of Jerusalem,** as the Arab leader who would give the Israeli-Arabs their own homeland in Israel. And so the Arabs saw him in the same light as noted in a remarkable transcript of a July 9th telephone conversation between King Fahd and the Emir of Qatar, Sheik Khalifah al-Thani. The King began by saying:

> *"We have had enough. Israel threatens Iraq and now Iraq threatens Israel. Now we're back to the same old story of Nasser before 1967."*

Because of all the many disputes between all the various Arab countries, Saddam saw himself as the new leader of the Arab world. He realized that the only way to attain that position would be to 'take on' Israel — the one uniting factor in Arab politics. And, so, Israel took his threats seriously and

---

3. Do you see Hashem's hand? Can you imagine where we would be if Israel would not have ignored the world's criticism and not insulated itself against the world's wrath in order to complete these two missions?! If Iraq had an operating nuclear reactor in 1990...

began holding gas drills after issuing free gas masks to the entire population in October 1990 — three months before the threats were actualized.

But Saddam Hussein was more frightened by Israel than Israel was by Baghdad. He knew that Israel had nuclear warheads and he rightfully understood that they would not hesitate to use them. What Saddam was trying to do was to use the threat of Israel to unite the Arabs under his leadership. He also harped on the links between America and Zionism and talked constantly of an alleged conspiracy between Israel and America to carve up the Arab nation. He announced to the Arab leaders that he was under attack by a Superpower-Zionist conspiracy bent on preventing the emergence of Arab power. Later, during Desert Storm, he maintained that Israel repainted their planes to look like American planes and that Israeli flyers were dressing up as American servicemen. And so, of course, the PLO supported Iraq during this fiasco — even though their major financial support came via Kuwait (which they, of course, lost after this fiasco).[4]

Later, President Bush insisted that Saddam must not gain anything by his seizure of Kuwait. So even Saddam's increasingly desperate attempts to link the Palestinian Question to his invasion of Kuwait would not be allowed.

The real sin was not the invasion of Kuwait as such, but Iraq's refusal to reduce its army to the point where it would not be able to threaten Israel's security as operationalized by the Center for International and Strategic Studies.

We did notice that the dominant aspects were the impotency of Israel and our complete dependency upon Hashem. Not many people, however, have analyzed Saddam's real intentions. Here is a man who is 'hurting bad', he is being attacked unmercifully by coalition forces, and — if this is not enough — in the midst of losing so badly, he opens another military front by attacking the Jews of Israel. This unusual military tactic only makes sense if we realize that Saddam's real imperialistic intentions and military objectives did not include stopping with the invasion of Kuwait. **Kuwait was not his real military objective.** Invading Kuwait was the means to achieve economic survival but his actual military objective was **the total destruction of Israel.**[5]

---

4. Isn't it fascinating to note how the PLO was now financially bankrupt as a result of this caper. With no more funding, they would have become extinct in just a few more years. It is very painful to note who revived them and brought them back to life just in the nick of time. And who was the one who armed them so they could use *our* weapons against *us?*

5. The following books are representative of a bibliography that shed light on this modern-day dictator: "Saddam Hussein: A Political Biography" by E. Karsh and I Rautsi; "Beyond the Storm" by P. Bennis and M. Moushabeck; "Instant Empire: Saddam Hussein's Ambition for Iraq" by S. Henderson; "The Gulf War Assessed" by J. Pimlott and S. Badsey; "The Outlaw State: Saddam Hussein's Quest for Power and the Gulf Crises" by E. Sciolino; "Saddam's War: The Origins of the Kuwait Conflict and the International Response" by J. Bulloch and H. Morris.

To achieve this military objective, besides other supplies, Saddam needed much fuel for his planes and motorized equipment. For such a huge military operation and for one that would take place hundreds of miles from his territory, a great deal of oil had to be secured. The invasion of Kuwait was also supposed to provide his army with the much needed oil necessary to destroy Israel. So it was not true to say that in the middle of being beaten down by the United States and her coalition forces — that in the midst of a war, he opened up another front. It should be understood that his *primary* objective was to unite the Arabs behind him where the military objective would be the destruction of the Jews of Israel. And he might have succeeded except for several factors — two unlikely partners: Hashem and atheistic Russia. It is indeed fascinating to study history with the benefit of both Written and Oral-Torah. Because it is only through Torah that we can understand what truly is happening in the world.

To understand Saddam Hussein's behavior, we must first note that **Nevuchadnetzar was the first person to cause us to go into *Galus*.** This Babylonian King murdered many Jews and he forced us to be exiled from our Land about 2500 years ago. But he never received his 'due' for these terrible crimes committed against humanity. The Oral-Torah[6] says that before Moshiach comes,

"זמין קב"ה לאחייי... נבוכדנצר... וזמין קב"ה לאפרעא מנייהו באתגלייא"

> *"Hashem will bring Nevuchadnetzar **back to life**... and this time Hashem will pay him back [to be humiliated] **in public.**"*

Before the time of Moshiach, Nevuchadnetzar will once again attempt to destroy the Jews. This time, however, Hashem will repay him 'in spades'; this time when Nevuchadnetzar attempts to destroy the Jews of Israel, he will be publicly humiliated — **everyone** will witness his humiliation. The entire Desert Storm Fiasco doesn't make sense without Torah. Obvious clues and pieces of information go unnoticed without Torah.

It should be noted that **Saddam Hussein is infatuated and obsessed with Nevuchadnetzar** — which is illogical from start to finish. After all, Nevuchadnetzar was a pagan and why is a contemporary Arab leader identifying with a non-Moslem, with a pagan?! With several famous (or infamous) historical Arab figures to choose from, there is no logical basis whatsoever for any Arab to exalt a non-Moslem pagan as a role model — especially at a time when non-Moslems are repulsive to Arabs and especially in a part of the world where Arabs kill for less. According to the Koran, as a matter of fact, Nevuchadnetzar is an accursed individual because he is non-Moslem

---

6. Zohar II, 58b; P'sikta, Chapter 36

and a pagan. When Saddam dreams of creating a pan-Arab empire consisting of so many varied elements, it would be expected — on a logical level — that Saddam would have selected an Arab role-model.

Several source books[7] helped me understand this fiasco and I would like to share their findings in order to paint a picture of Saddam, who is described as a madman, but who will be seen very shortly in a totally different light. This entire episode would appear illogical if we were ignorant of Written and Oral-Torah. I remember reading in the newspaper from time to time that Saddam was attempting to rebuild the magnificent Hanging Gardens of Babylon. Millions of bricks were being used — tens of thousands were already inscribed with the same message that compared Saddam Hussein to Nevuchadnetzar. The bricks carried the inscription that

> *"The Babylon of Nevuchadnetzar was rebuilt in the era of the leader, President Saddam Hussein".*

As a matter of fact, once during an official nighttime celebration, foreign diplomats were asked to cast their eyes upwards into the black desert sky. There, above them, hung twin portraits of Saddam and Nevuchadnetzar etched against the lights by laser beams. Saddam's features were rendered unusually sharp in order to resemble more closely the ancient carved images of Nevuchadnetzar. But it was not until I read several books about Saddam Hussein that this entire matter became very clear.

Saddam has been consumed by dreams of glory and identifies with Nevuchadnetzar in an obsessive-compulsive fashion. Saddam believes that there can be only *one* supreme national Arab leader — and he is the one. He is driven by what he perceives as his mission to lead the Arab world. Saddam identifies completely with Nevuchadnetzar. What makes Nevuchadnetzar so appealing to Saddam is not merely his regional prominence, but also his victorious campaigns in southern Israel where he destroyed the Kingdom of Judea including the Holy Temple and the entire city of Jerusalem. Saddam has admitted this desire on many occasions — to follow in the footsteps of Nevuchadnetzar, the great Babylonian king. And so he is often quoted:

> *"And what is important for me about Nebuchadnezzar is the link between the Arabs' ability and the liberation of Palestine ... Nebuchadnezzar was the one who brought the bound Jewish slaves from Palestine ... I like to remind the Arabs of their historical responsibilities."*

The Zohar says[8] that there will be a reincarnation of Nevuchadnetzar in the generation preceding Moshiach. And so, Saddam and the Desert Storm War

---

7. See footnote 5
8. Ibid. footnote 6

have nothing to do with an Arab confederation attacking the Jews of Israel. This was not an Arab war against the Jews. Even the enemies of the Israeli Jews, like Syria and Egypt, joined America in the efforts to stop Iraq. So it has nothing to do with Arabs against Jews. Nor does it have anything to do with the Iraqi people fighting against Jews, because the most amazing feature about this war/fiasco was the fact that almost all the Iraqi soldiers were not interested in fighting. They couldn't care less — Israel or not, Kuwait today or not. The Iraqi soldiers didn't even entertain any major plans to attack American forces nor did they attempt to defend themselves against American forces. They just were not interested in fighting, because **this was a private and personal campaign of Saddam Hussein, the Nevuchadnetzar of the 20th Century.**

The Zohar indicates:

> *"Hashem will bring Nevuchadnetzar back to life...and this time Hashem will pay him back [to be humiliated] in public.*

Nevuchadnetzar started the entire *Galus* condition (during the Babylonian Era); therefore, **Nevuchadnetzar has to herald the end of this Diaspora condition.** The *Galus* ending will be wondrous — with everyone seeing miracles and the humiliation of Nevuchadnetzar/Saddam Hussein. Where else and at what other period in the annals of history was an entire war televised for the entire world to witness?! This is the first time that a war was televised in its entirety, and all the world witnessed the total humiliation of Nevuchadnetzar/Hussein — the events unfolding exactly as the Zohar described. Nevuchadnetzar initiated the *Galus* cycle, so he has to conclude it by attempting to destroy the Jews but, on this second occasion, he will not succeed at all; this time he will only be publicly humiliated.

It is amazing — you will agree in another moment that it is REALLY MIRACULOUS how the events unfolded:

(1) The Jews of Israel were **attacked by "Nevuchadnetzar"** for a second time — but they were not killed.

(2) "Nevuchadnetzar" was defeated and **publicly humiliated,** this time by a coalition of forces who are definitely not pro-Israel.

(3) The **Jews of Israel did not even have to protect themselves** from an enemy that was bent on its destruction.

It is also interesting to note that when the Torah describes the cities of refuge that shield a Jew from potential killers[9] — in those very verses where the *Land's unique protectiveness* is described — coded into these

---

9. D'varim 19:1-13

verses about עָרֵי מִקְלָט is the name of a potential murderer who is thwarted from fulfilling his destructive objectives. Here, **the Land itself protects all its inhabitants from Saddam Hussein.**

ו נ ש ל ה ב ר ז ל מ ן ה ה ע ו מ צ א
י נ ו ס א ח ה ת ה ע ר י ס ה ה א ל ה
ה ד ה א ר ה י ר ה צ ר ח כ י ח ס ל ב
ב ה ה ד ד ה ו ה כ ה ו נ פ ש ו ל ו א
א ש נ א ו א ל ו מ ת מ ו ל ש ל ש ו ה
ך ל א מ ש ל ש ע ר י ס ת ב ד י ל ל ל
ה א ל ה י ך ד א ת ג ב ל ד כ א ש ר נ ש

What is more amazing is that had this invasion of Israel been initiated but a year or two earlier, it probably would have been successful. Two years earlier, there was a powerful supporter of Iraq; two years earlier there was a nation that supplied Iraq with all its military needs; two years earlier, Iraq was being supported by Russia — the very same Russia that self-disintegrated only one year before this fiasco. But two years earlier, Iraq was bogged down with their protracted and stalemated war with Iran. Can you imagine what could have happened had that war with Iran ended earlier? Had Russia still existed with all its power, Russia would have intimidated America — as was done in Afghanistan, in Hungary, in Czechoslovakia, and constantly before the world in the U.N. The only reason that America was able to muster the forces of so many countries in order to stop Iraq was because Iraq no longer had its personal protector — Russia the superpower was dead. Can you imagine what could have happened had Hussein begun his military incursion but two years earlier?! This, too, is mindboggling because America was never able to assert itself; America was never able to stand up to Russia. The closest we ever got was once when Kennedy stood up to a Russian vassal (during the Cuban Missile Crisis). But Russia itself? America had always felt powerless to stand up to Russia. But two years earlier, Iraq was too involved in its prolonged war with Iran. Wow! What a difference two years make in the life of the Jews of Israel!!

Summarizing the Iraqi connection: In order to legitimize his arms build-up and, in the name of confronting Israel and the West, Nevuchadnetzar/ Saddam Hussein organized a summit meeting of The Arab League. Until this point in time, he would periodically shout-out threats against Israel. But in 1990, on May 28th, he began to threaten the ENTIRE WEST. On Purim later that year, which corresponded to February 28th, the war ended and he was, indeed, publically humiliated — but not until this Nevuchadnetzar had intimidated the ENTIRE world for EXACTLY nine months — just as the Oral-Torah states[10]

"אין בן דוד בא עד שתפשוט מלכות ארם בכל העולם ט' חדשים"

"Before Moshiach arrives, the Kingdom of Iraq[11] will menace the world for nine months."

Granted that Nevuchadnetzar initiated the entire concept of exile from Israel and granted that Nevuchadnetzar had to be publicly humiliated for this horrible precedent and for his slaughter of Jews some 2500 years ago. But there is one more aspect that sheds light on the ultimate significance of the Desert Storm Fiasco and it, no doubt, is related to the year of its occurrence.

The year 5750 (1990) is the beginning of a new era; it parallels the end of the sixth Cosmic hour of the first Friday of Creation and the beginning of the seventh Cosmic hour.[12] **The Cosmic *sunset* after that first Thursday parallels the year 5000 with that first Friday's *sunrise* being equivalent to the human year of 5500 and with that Friday's *noon* being equivalent to the year 5750.** The Desert Storm Fiasco in the year 5750 occurred ¾ **into the Sixth Millennium. The year 5750 parallels noon of that sixth day of Creation because noon is ¾ into the day which begins at the previous sunset.** The previous era of 41⅔ years, beginning in 5708(1947) ended in glory in 5750(1990), with 39 scuds and a war/fiasco that introduced a new era with a real Big Bang. Now, everyone was to see the miracles; now everyone was to learn that Hashem protects Jews. Finally, everyone should begin to understand that the Israeli Jews did not win any of their wars because they were smarter or better trained or better in any other worldly way than their Arab attackers. The Israeli Jews were victorious because Hashem has been protecting them all these years.

We are now in the period of time when the true nature of everything will be discovered. This is now the period when people will become more objective in analyzing facts, issues, and events — those facts and issues which, until now, have eluded proper analysis, those facts which have been distorted, the facts which have been ignored, the miracles that have not been noticed.

---

10. Talmud Yoma 10a
11. Biblical Aram includes The Fertile Crescent and Mesopotamia — parts of modern-day Iraq.
12. See Chapter 13 regarding how time is divided into units of 41⅔ years.

I remember hearing of a story of a gentleman who gave a Jewish-born clergyman a Bible that had most of its pages torn out. The reform clergyman asked in amazement, "Why are you giving me a mutilated Bible? What would you like me to do with it? How did it become so torn?"

The man responded: "Each time that you spoke in public, I listened carefully. When you said that Jews no longer have to observe kosher food laws, I tore that page out, since you said that it didn't apply to us. When you said that laws of intermarriages no longer applied to Jews, I tore out that page, too. Then when you told us that conversions were no longer necessary nor religious divorces, I tore out those pages, too. *T'filin*, interest-free loans, Shabbos, *mikvah*... And so I continued tearing-out pages as you continued 'teaching' us. You finally told us that it was no longer necessary to observe any biblical practices. There's nothing left. Only the title page remains. I have no further need for this book."

Several years ago, I received a phone call from the president of a Metropolitan New York synagogue. They were looking for a Rabbi and I had been recommended to him by a mutual acquaintance. After discussing the matter with my wife who possesses בינה יתירה — *insight* that is more common in women[13] — I went to be interviewed by the congregation. Many questions were posed, but I could not believe their low level of Jewish education and observance — and this is within the confines of New York City. I accepted the challenge and immediately went to Rabbi Chaim Segal, whose reputation in outreach is legendary. Boy, was I disappointed with the outcome. I made a special effort to free myself up for several hours so I could learn many techniques from the master. It was a fast day. The Rabbi was busying himself with synagogue matters. We had a formal appointment and here I am sitting quietly while he keeps answering phones and speaking to various congregants who require his services. It's getting real late now; in half an hour we will be praying *Minchah,* the Afternoon Service. I had freed up hours for this meeting and in the end I would be lucky to talk to him for just minutes. Finally, we spoke. Actually, only he spoke. "You must emphasize Torah", he repeated many times. "Torah, Torah, Torah." The meeting was over; it was time for Afternoon and Evening Services. I just couldn't believe it. I came to learn the techniques to raise a Jew's level of observance and Rabbi Segal tells me "You must emphasize Torah. Torah, Torah, Torah." Well, we prayed and, needless to say, I returned home, a very disappointed person; I didn't learn any magical techniques.

Sure I had been a synagogue rabbi before, but never with a congregation that had such a low opinion of themselves as Jews and never with a

____

13. Talmud Nidah 45b

congregation with such an insufficient level of Jewish identity and Jewish education, in addition to minimal levels of *Mitzvot* observances. As a matter of fact, once we had a community-wide observance in honor of Israel. Three hundred people attended including local and State politicians. We made an appeal for Israel and collected a 'whopping' $200 for the Jewish National Fund — and, mind you, this was from 300 people. The people didn't even understand the importance of caring for another Jew or for saving another's life.

So, I began teaching different classes every night. We learned the weekly Torah portion one night and on another evening we learned Jewish history. There were classes in *Mitzvot*. We even began a program to teach people how to read Hebrew. What I saw amazed me — people were becoming less hostile to Judaism and Jewish observances. Slowly, for the first time in their lives, people began to feel a sense of pride in being Jewish. The distortions that had been presented to them by Jewish-born clergymen were now being slowly discarded. You see, they were accustomed to reading articles and hearing speeches from people who were ashamed of their Judaism. The people saw the texts; they realized at last that those other clergymen had either lied to them or were ignorant. The study groups began to grow; we were now attracting dozens of people every evening — each on a different level, each with a different set of baggage that they carried into class. But they all shared one thing — they had not realized how thirsty they were to learn or how starved. Rabbi Segal was right — we must emphasize Torah, Torah, and more Torah.

I could not believe what was happening. One day when I saw Rabbi Binyamin Kaminetsky, I said to him: "I don't understand. I haven't yet spoken to the group about Shabbos and already a few people asked to study the laws of Shabbos so they could begin to properly observe Shabbos." Reb Binyamin responded by telling me a story of a man who had to ingest a medication twice a day because of an illness. At the end of the week and feeling much better, he asked the doctor: "Which pill made me better?"

And so it was and so it continues. People are not observant — not out of conviction. As young adults, they were just never afforded the opportunity to study Judaism. Sometimes, it is because poorly-educated people have biased their minds with untruths or distortions. Once the real facts are explained, the Jewishly uneducated become educated, proud, committed, and observant.

This is the period when the world will learn many types of truth. Jews will become educated in Torah — and really appreciate and like it. The world will see the fabrications of the Arabs. The Church will have to become more honest in their teachings, stop picking on the Jews, and desist from teaching that the Jews are an accursed people. The media will have to cease employing double standards — one for everybody, but a very harsh level for Jews. The media will finally end their bias against Jews and against Israel. The truth will become accessible for those who are serious and for those who wish to be objective. Thus, people will no longer be biased in their thinking.

This is the quest for truth that is so beautifully described by the prophets:[14]

"הנה ימים באים נאם אדנ-י י-ה-ו-ה ושלחתי רעב בארץ
לא רעב ללחם ולא צמא למים כי אם לשמע את דברי ה' "

"Behold there will be days, says Hashem, when I will bring hunger to the world — not a hunger for bread and not a thirst for water — but only to hear [truth as propounded by] the Divine teachings..."

There is also **a secondary lesson to be gained from Saddam Hussein's fiasco.** Besides Saddam's role as Nevuchadnetzar, this Desert Storm fiasco demonstrates to the entire world that anti-Semitism is baseless and without real logic. The nations of the world do not care about Jews, to say the least; some nations actually hate us. Isn't it rather ironic that the coalition forces consisted of countries that have a history of warring against us. Isn't it rather paradoxical that some of our enemies were actually protecting us from other enemies. We do pray that eventually all people will learn to stop hating.

This is the period which **corresponds to the end of the sixth Cosmic hour and the beginning of the seventh Cosmic hour** when people begin to discover truth and discard the malicious, the deceptive, and the distortions; an era when people discover the true reality of the world, the names and true characteristics of everything. This is reminiscent of Adam who learned the true characteristics of the animal and vegetable kingdoms and named them in accordance with their respective characteristics.

This is the period which **corresponds to the end of the sixth Cosmic hour and the beginning of the seventh Cosmic hour** when people begin to discover truth and discard the malicious, the deceptive, and the distortions; an era when people discover the true reality of the world. We are now preparing to enter an extremely glorious period when Jews will be proud to be Jews in a world that will be filled with truth, harmony, and real peace.

---

14. Amos 8:11

CHAPTER
XXVII

1994 Stellar Collission
1994 International Collusion

בההוא זמנא ... יקום מסטר מזרח חד כוכבא מלהטא בכל גוונין.
ושבעה כוכבין אחרנין דסחרן לההוא כוכבא ויגיחון ביה קרבא
בכל סטרין תלת זמנין ביומא עד שבעין יומין וכל בני עלמא
חמאן. וההוא כוכבא יגיח בהו קרבא בטיסין דנורא מלהטין
מנצצין לכל עבר ובטש בהו עד דבלע לון בכל רמשא ורמשא.
וביומא אפיק לון ויגיחון קרבא לעיניהון דכל עלמא וכן בכל
יומא עד שבעין יומין.

he same *Chazal*[1] which discusses Moshiach, also describes a stellar phenomenon. The Zohar says that signaling the end of one era — before Moshiach arrives — there will be collisions of comets into Jupiter. This spectacle will be extremely brilliant with **seven stars** waging war against Jupiter, **three times a day for seven[2] consecutive days.** The whole world is going to witness this uniquely colorful spectacle and the planet is going to eventually absorb these seven attacking comets on the seventh day. This is a phenomenon that occurred during the week of the 9th of Av in the year 5754 (1994). It certainly was the first time that such a collision could be observed by so many people. The collisions were beyond the expectations of any scientist; people were amazed by the massive and powerful explosions. The chunks of Comet Shoemaker-Levy 9 traveled towards the planet like a string of pearls and were expected to strike Jupiter at a speed of 37 miles per second. Do you know how fast that is? Clap your hands; your right hand just moved a distance of

---

1. Zohar II,7b
2. על פי מספר קטן

one foot in one second. In the same time that it took to clap your hands, this comet traveled 37 miles — in that very same second. The speed is the equivalent of more than 133,000 miles per hour. Needless to say, at that speed and with that force — the cometary fragments carried as much energy as **100,000,000 megatons of TNT** which is **10,000 times more energy than in all the nuclear weapons on earth.** The view was majestic and magnificent: massive and tremendous explosions creating great pillars of fire that shot thousands of miles into the atmosphere. The details of this astronomical encounter are amazingly and precisely those of the prophecy described in Zohar.

Three times a day there were a multiple of seven stars or comets which 'warred' with Jupiter for one continuous week. The Zohar does not usually describe scientific phenomenon — unless it has some sort of relevance. The 'sign of the times' is captured by this Zohar. The same type of confrontation will exist on both the cosmic/galaxy level as well as on the international/people level. This Jupiter War is a reflection and counterpart of another form of war being conducted on this planet. There is a war of Yishmael, seven comets, against Jerusalem. To be specific — there is a real war against Jerusalem that is being conducted by one entity with three components — namely: Yishmael, Esav, and the *Erev Rav* — Arabs, Christians, and some Jewish leaders of Israel. It is a triumvirate of the THREE most unlikely partners. So there is a multiple of seven attacking stars to reflect the individual components of the united front. While this Zohar is obviously referring to an attack of seven stars which represents one entity, the cumulative effect of the attackers is threefold that amount. So instead of seven attacking stars that were described in Zohar, the force of attackers is **THREEFOLD** and therefore, the attacking force of stars is **THREE times the attacking force of the initial seven** that was described in this Chazal. Instead of Yishmael alone, there is triple the attacking force of seven. Therefore, **21** comets attacked Jupiter with the entire world witness to this amazing occurrence through the mediums of television and newspaper.[3] The Zohar describes this event — not because of its scientific uniqueness but because of its relevance to world events.

We will take this one step further. The *mazal* of Jupiter — interestingly enough, the *metaphysical name* for 'Jupiter' is *Tzedek* which means *honorable, virtuous, and deserving.* These comets are attacking *Tzedek,* the innocent and pure Jupiter that was trying to 'mind its own business' when attacked. Jupiter will survive this onslaught; justice will survive and the innocent will prevail in a majestic manner and become even stronger by virtue of all the

---

3. See the New York Times for the period 16-25 July 1994 for more details.

energies absorbed by the planet from the attacks. Indeed, not only was the planet unscathed by this massive stellar attack, but Jupiter the Just absorbed the threats to its very existence. So, too, thc Zohar is saying, lcgitimatc Israel will survive the onslaught from the THREE COHORTS. Innocent Israel will gloriously survive the repeated and constant attacks by the coalition of its three major besiegers — Yishmael, Esav, and Erev Rav. Not only will Israel the Just survive unscathed, but it will gain significantly from this entire episode. The innocent will prevail in a majestic manner because it will absorb energy and strength from its attackers. The spirit of the times is indeed captured by this Zohar. The same type of confrontation will exist on both the stellar level as well as on the international level.

XXVIII

Epilogue: Genuine Peace
Our Hopes and Prayers

e have seen the damage that is done when there is no true and absolute yardstick to measure values and behaviors. Without Torah there is darkness and deceit that are accepted as light and truth. But this is the best that people can do with only 'relative morality'. What is good today could very well be declared unconstitutional tomorrow and, similarly, what is wrong today with society will eventually be corrected.

While it is true that peace is a כלי מחזיק ברכה[1] one can see from the words themselves that peace is only a tool, *a vehicle that brings us to a particular goal.* Peace is *never* "the absence of war". Peace is never a goal, in-and-of-itself. Peace is a positive and constructive condition that only creates the atmosphere which allows us to attain some very necessary and critical objectives. When Israel will be able to divert money presently allocated for defense items and use that money to fund vital economic, social, and educational projects, when Israel will be able to emphasize and enhance the spiritual side of life, then it

---

1. Talmud end of Uktzin; D'varim Rabah on Shoftim, paragraph 15

can be said that true peace reigns. But peace itself is never a goal; peace is only the *means* that allow these objectives — and more — to be realized. The ultimate goal is elsewhere. Summarizing the Oral-Torah, the Rambam states[2]

"Scholars and prophets desired to live during the Messianic Age... only to be afforded an atmosphere that would be conducive for leading good Torah lives and for learning and studying — without being distracted or disturbed [by chaos or hostilities]."

Hashem says[3] אתה תקום תרחם ציון ... כי רצו עבדיך את אבניה, this time around, we must express our strong determination to hold onto Jerusalem. Jerusalem can only be rebuilt if, and when, we really demonstrate our yearning and determination — to the extent, that we crave its very stones and will not allow anyone to take it away from us. When this happens, **Hashem will reward our efforts and Jerusalem will remain ours, but only when we exhibit fortitude and persistence about our rights to the Land.** And so traditional Jews are bracing themselves for the political struggle — in order to retain Jerusalem and all the Land. May all our efforts cause our prayers to be answered and may the Eternal City with the entire Land of Israel be ours for all eternity. May our rights to the entire Land never be challenged again.

May we strive to perfect ourselves, to lead authentic Torah lives and may Hashem develop the State of Israel so that

כי מציון תצא תורה ודבר ה' מירושלים

'From Zion shall go forth the light and truth to guide everybody, everywhere.' [4]

May Hashem grant us our prayers for:

"ומלאה הארץ דעה את ה' כמים לים מכסים"

'a world that wants to benefit from Torah knowledge and values'. [5]

We pray that Hashem bless us with *real* peace so that we will be enabled to study in an undisturbed fashion and live as vibrant Torah Jews.

And finally, may we see the authentic Torah leader, the one we await so anxiously. May he arrive today — כן יהי רצון אמן ואמן!!

---

2. Hilchos M'lachim 12:4
3. T'hilim 102:14-15; see also the last paragraph of Kuzari.
4. Yeshayahu 2:3; Michah 4:2
5. Yeshayahu 11:9

APPENDIX[1]
THE PLO CHARTER AND THE PHASED PLAN EXCERPTS
(including the 1968 and 1974 revisions)

THE PLO CHARTER

ARTICLE 1

Palestine is the homeland of the Palestinian Arab people and an integral part of the great Arab homeland, and the people of Palestine is a part of the Arab Nation.

ARTICLE 2

Palestine with its boundaries that existed at the time of the British Mandate is an integral regional unit.

ARTICLE 3

The Palestinian Arab people possesses the legal right to its homeland, and when the liberation of its homeland is completed it will exercise self-determination solely according to its own will and choice.

ARTICLE 4

The Palestinian personality is an innate, persistent characteristic that does not disappear, and it is transferred from fathers to sons. **The Zionist occupation,** and the dispersal of the Palestinian Arab people as a result of the disasters which came over it, do not deprive it of its Palestinian personality and affiliation and do not nullify them.

---

1. Boldface and Italic words are added for emphasis

ARTICLE 5

The Palestinians are the Arab citizens who were living permanently in Palestine until 1947, whether they were expelled from there or remaincd. Whoever is born to a Palestinian Arab father after this date, within Palestine or outside it, is a Palestinian.

ARTICLE 6

Jews who were living permanently in Palestine until the beginning of the Zionist invasion will be considered Palestinians.

ARTICLE 7

The Palestinian affiliation and the material, spiritual and historical tie with Palestine are permanent realities. The upbringing of the Palestinian individual in an Arab and revolutionary fashion ... and preparing him for the conflict and the **armed struggle,** as well as the sacrifice of his property and his life **to restore his homeland,** until the liberation — all this is a national duty.

ARTICLE 8

The phase in which the people of Palestine is living is that of the national struggle ... for the liberation of Palestine ... On this basis, the Palestinian masses ... comprise one national front which acts to restore Palestine and **liberate it through armed struggle.**

ARTICLE 9

Armed struggle is the only way to liberate Palestine and is therefore strategy and not tactics. The Palestinian Arab people affirms its absolute resolution and abiding determination to pursue the armed struggle and to march forward toward the armed popular revolution, **to liberate its homeland and return to it ...** and to exercise its ... sovereignty over it.

ARTICLE 10

Fedayeen action forms the nucleus of the popular Palestinian war of liberation. This demands...the mobilization of all the mass and scientific capacities of the Palestinians ... to guarantee the continuation of the revolution, its advancement and **victory.**

ARTICLE 12

The Palestinian Arab people believes in Arab unity ... [and] it must preserve ... and resist any plan that tends to ... weaken it.

ARTICLE 14

The destiny of the Arab nation, indeed the very Arab existence, depends upon the destiny of the Palestinian issue...

ARTICLE 15

The liberation of Palestine, from an Arab viewpoint, is a national duty to repulse the Zionist, imperialist invasion from the great Arab homeland and **to purge the Zionist presence from Palestine ... until the liberation of its homeland.**

ARTICLE 16

The liberation of Palestine ... will prepare an atmosphere of tranquillity and peace for the Holy Land ...

ARTICLE 17

The liberation of Palestine ... will restore to the Palestinian man his dignity, glory, and freedom ...

ARTICLE 18

The liberation of Palestine ... is a **defensive act** necessitated by the requirements of self-defense. For this reason, the **people of Palestine,** desiring to befriend all peoples, looks to the support of the states which love freedom, justice, and peace in restoring the legal situation to Palestine...and enabling its people to exercise national sovereignty and national freedom.

ARTICLE 19

The partitioning of Palestine in 1947 and **the establishment of Israel is fundamentally null and void ... because it was contrary to the wish of the people of Palestine and its natural right to its homeland ...**

ARTICLE 20

The Balfour Declaration, the Mandate Document, and what has been based upon them are considered **null and void. The claim of a historical or spiritual tie between Jews and Palestine does not tally with historical realities** nor with the constituents of statehood in their true sense. Judaism, in its character as a religion of revelation, is not a nationality with an independent existence. Likewise, the **Jews are not one people** with an independent personality. They are rather **citizens of the states to which they belong.**

ARTICLE 21

The Palestinian Arab people, in expressing itself through the armed Palestinian revolution, rejects every solution that is a substitute for a **complete liberation of Palestine ...**

ARTICLE 22

Zionism is a political movement organically related to world imperialism and hostile to all movements of liberation and progress in the world. It is a racist and fanatical movement; aggressive, expansionist and colonialist in its aims; and Fascist and Nazi in its means. Israel is the tool of the Zionist movement and a human and geographical base for world imperialism... Israel is a constant threat to peace in the Middle East and the entire world ... **The liberation of Palestine will liquidate the Zionist and imperialist presence...**

ARTICLE 23

The demands of security and peace ... oblige all states ... to consider **Zionism an illegitimate movement and to prohibit its existence** and activity.

ARTICLE 24

The Palestinian Arab people believes in the principles of justice, freedom, sovereignty, self-determination, human dignity and the right of peoples to exercise them *[as long as they aren't Jews who seek these principles — NN]*.

ARTICLE 25

To realize the aims of this Covenant and its principles, the Palestine Liberation Organization will undertake its full role in **liberating Palestine.**

THE PHASED PLAN

(Approved by the PLO Council on June 8, 1974)

On the basis of the National Palestinian Covenant and the PLO's political plan as approved at the 11th session (6 -12 January 1973); and in the belief that a just and lasting peace in the region is impossible without **restoration of the FULL national rights of the Palestinian nation,** and first and foremost the right of return and self-determination on the **homeland's soil ENTIRE,**[2] and after having studied the political circumstances as they developed during the period between its previous and its present session — the Council resolves as follows:

1) Emphasis of the PLO's position with relation to Security Council Resolution 242, which overlooks the national rights of our nation and approaches the Palestinian issue as a refugee problem.

    The Council therefore rejects any action on that basis on any level of Arab and international operation, including the Geneva Conference.

2) The PLO **is fighting by every means,** and primarily by the armed struggle, to free the Palestinian land and establish a national, independent and fighting government over every part of the soil of Palestine to be freed ...

3) The PLO objects to any plan for a Palestinian entity at the price of recognition, peace, secure boundaries, surrender of national rights and deprivation of our nation's prerogative of return and of self-determination in its homeland.

4) **Any step of liberation is a link** in realizing the strategy of the PLO for the establishment of a Palestinian-democratic State, as resolved by the previous Councils **[on the entire soil of Palestine]**.

---

2. Please take note: Arabs mean what they say! When they say "entire" they mean "entire" and not one inch less. Remember the problem at Taba — even though Egypt received thousands of square miles of the Sinai, it was not the "entire" Sinai without little Taba. Remember, the few inches near the Jordan River that Jordan held-out for in 1995. The Syrian dictator says "All of Golan". Arafat says "All of Palestine". Why would anyone think they don't mean what they say or write?!

8) **AFTER** its establishment [on the soil of Palestine], the national Palestinian government will fight for the unity of the countries of confrontation, to **COMPLETE THE LIBERATION OF ALL THE PALESTINIAN LAND** and as a step in the direction of overall Arab unity.

9) The PLO fights to strengthen its solidarity with the socialist countries ... to frustrate all the Zionist reactionary and imperialist plans.

10) On the basis of this plan, the leadership of the revolution will formulate tactics that will enable these objectives to be realized.

Our Father in Heaven, please have mercy on us;
the situation is just unbearable and horrific.

Our Father in Heaven, please heed our prayers
for protection.

Our Father in Heaven, please frustrate the evil plans
of those who plan us harm.

Our Father in Heaven, please intervene
because only You can help us.

For the sake of all Jews who have been killed on the
battlefields and/or murdered in the name of 'peace',
Our Father in Heaven, please save us!

AFTERWORD

here's another concept in Jewish History that is extremely important and yet somewhat difficult to understand because it is not a concept that is familiar to Western culture. For example, if a man meets a lady whom he eventually marries, Western thinking would explain their marriage as a result of that initial chance meeting. In reality, that's not what happened. In order for the two people to get married as Hashem prescribes, they had to 'accidentally' meet. In reality the *cause* for their 'chance' meeting was the marriage which Hashem had already preordained – not that their 'chance' meeting was the *cause* and not that the *effect* was the wedding. Not because they met did they then marry each other. Rather, the *cause* is the people's need to marry each other; the *effect* was their meeting each other. The Prime Cause is Hashem.

On the national level, the Rabin-Peres government should have been in office for four years. They were elected in November 1992 and were to be in office until November 1996. For some 'unknown' reason, Peres called for new elections six months earlier – at the end of May. The results were that Binyamin Netanyahu was overwhelming elected with a majority of 60% of the Jewish vote. Theoretically, had Peres not called for early elections, he most certainly would have served for another six months and, perhaps, even been elected in November of 1996 for any number of factors. The Western mind maintains that Peres caused his own defeat by calling for early elections. He thought that he could benefit from some current trends and/or events and that this momentum would carry him to his first election victory. But, the Western mind continues, Peres miscalculated and the populace dismissed him from office after only 3½ years.

The Jewish mind knows differently. The Torah person views the same events and maintains that Peres did enough damage and had to be removed from office before the situation would became uncontrollable and irreversible. So Hashem planted in Peres' mind the notion that it was to his advantage to call for early elections. Hashem wanted the Labor government to be ousted from power and so Hashem created a 'natural' situation which Peres seized. And so Reb Saadia Gaon publicized this fact more than 1000 years ago when he stated[1] that he had been taught by his teachers who had been taught by their teachers going back to Sinai that the *Erev Rav* government that would conspire with Christians and Arabs to divest Jews of parts of the Land – that this *Erev Rav* government would be in power for 3 years [and not the usual 4 years]. This is a powerful prophecy. But more importantly, the prophecy demonstrates very clearly the principle of Divine Providence and how it works. In order to be in office for less than 4 years *(the cause-event)*, Peres called for early elections *(the effect)*. It's not that Peres called for early elections and then was defeated. Rather, the need to have him out of office caused Peres to call for elections after only 3 years in office.

Now that Binyamin Netanyahu has been elected Prime Minister by a substantial Jewish plurality, we pray that he will be able to bring the self-destructive cadence of Oslo to a screeching halt.   To solve the Israeli-Arab problem is indeed a formidable task. At this point in time, it has become an assignment for only the greatest and most brilliant.

We pray that Jewish interests will become the basis for all decisions, programs, and actions of the Netanyahu government. Indeed, we pray that with the recent increased orthodox representation in this Knesset, that authentic Torah values will begin to permeate all of Israeli society in a non-political fashion. The time is right. For the religious parties, as well as the orthodox members of other parties, to garner so many seats in Knesset means that many divergent segments of society finally united. This means that the followers of Rav Shach, Rav Ovadya Yosef, Rav Kook, Likud, and Arik Sharon

---

1.   In an essay entitled *Al Inyan HaY'shuah* — "Regarding the Redemption"

worked together with Hesder, Hasidim, Mizrachi, S'fardim, and Russian emigres. Ah! United at last!!

But the most pleasing aspect of the election results – the orthodox received many more votes than there are orthodox voters. This means that non-orthodox Jews have already begun to recognize the significance of Torah. This is the most encouraging aspect of the elections – yet the least recognized. Indeed, the majority of Israeli Jews have demonstrated that they want a Jewish State. Indeed, Israel *must* become a spiritual center for the Jews of Israel. The Israeli Jews *need* to be taught; they *want* to be taught and the time is now. Soon, with Hashem's help, the Jews of Israel will usher in a non-political Torah State – a true spiritual center for world Jewry.

In this *sefer* we have only scratched the surface. There is much more to learn and much more to discuss. But at this point in time, the most important fact to keep in mind is that we, Jews, are not floundering on a ship in the midst of storms with no captain. Truly, the Captain *will* continue to keep to His schedule, and we must remember that we have always been arriving safely at our previous destinations in accordance with the Pre-printed Itinerary. There are several more stops before our final port-of-call and, indeed, several more spectacular chapters will yet be written.

If I've accomplished my goal in writing this *sefer,* we are all completely confident that our Captain will continue to guide the ship so skillfully and that all events occur exactly as Hashem already decreed in the Written and Oral-Torah.

Indeed, there is much more good reserved for us and for the world. Let us be optimistic and not depressed by current events.

We pray "Hashem, please:
- assist our leaders to utilize objective Torah wisdom and absolute values in their various roles and assist them that they not falter or err,
- assist us to enhance our learning,
- assist us to become the best that we can,
- assist us to motivate others to lead lives that are guided by Torah, and
- assist us to become united and caring of all Jews wherever they are.

Finally, Hashem, please, soon create that special era when the entire world will be motivated to conduct themselves properly and decently with the absolute conviction that **"ה' אחד ושמו אחד"**.

תם ונשלם שבח לא-ל בורא עולם

About the Author:

A rabbi and a psychologist, Nisan Aryeh Novick has studied at Yeshiva University, Queens College, Alfred Adler Institute, and Stevens Institute of Technology and has additional degrees in Mathematics and Jewish Philosophy & History. For the past two decades, Rabbi Novick has been studying regularly with groups in Staten Island, Queens, and Manhattan.